INTRODUCTION TO
C#
USING
.NET

ISBN 0-13-041801-3

90000

C#

- Introduction to C# Using.NET
  Oberg

- Application Development Using C# and .NET
  Steifel/Oberg

VISUAL BASIC

- Introduction to Programming Visual Basic Using .NET
  Wyatt/Oberg

- Application Development Using Visual Basic and .NET
  Oberg/Wyatt

VISUAL C++

- .NET Architecture and Programming Using Visual C++
  Thorsteinson/Oberg

WEB APPLICATIONS

- Fundamentals of Web Applications Using .NET and XML
  Bell/Chang/Fang/Huang/Soong/Zhang/Zhu

PERL

- Programming PERL in the .NET Environment
  Saltzman/Oberg

THE INTEGRATED .NET SERIES FROM OBJECT INNOVATIONS

INTRODUCTION TO
C#
USING
.NET

ROBERT J. OBERG

PH PTR

Prentice Hall PTR, Upper Saddle River, NJ 07458
www.phptr.com

Library of Congress Cataloging-in-Publication Data

*A catalog record for this book
can be obtained from the Library of Congress*

Editorial/Production Supervision: *Nick Radhuber*
Acquisitions Editor: *Jill Harry*
Marketing Manager: *Dan DePasquale*
Manufacturing Buyer: *Maura Zaldivar*
Cover Design: *Anthony Gemmellaro*
Cover Design Direction: *Jerry Votta*
Interior Series Design: *Gail Cocker-Bogusz*

© 2002 by Robert J. Oberg
Published by Prentice Hall PTR
Prentice-Hall, Inc.
Upper Saddle River, NJ 07458

Prentice Hall books are widely used by corporations and government agencies for training, marketing, and resale.

The publisher offers discounts on this book when ordered in bulk quantities. For more information, contact Corporate Sales Department, phone: 800-382-3419; fax: 201-236-7141; email: corpsales@pren-hall.com
Or write Corporate Sales Department, Prentice Hall PTR, One Lake Street, Upper Saddle River, NJ 07458.

Product and company names mentioned herein are the trademarks or registered trademarks of their respective owners. The Electronic Commerce Game™ is a trademark of Object Innovations. Inc.

Printed in the United States of America

10 9 8 7 6 5 4 3 2 1

ISBN 0-13-041801-3

Pearson Education LTD.
Pearson Education Australia PTY, Limited
Pearson Education Singapore, Pte. Ltd.
Pearson Education North Asia Ltd.
Pearson Education Canada, Ltd.
Pearson Educación de Mexico, S.A. de C.V.
Pearson Education—Japan
Pearson Education Malaysia, Pte. Ltd.

CONTENTS

v

PART TWO   C# AS A LANGUAGE IN THE C FAMILY   53

▼ CHAPTER 4   Simple Data Types   57

▼ CHAPTER 5   Operators and Expressions   73

Microsoft's .NET is a revolutionary advance in programming technology that greatly simplifies application development and is a good match for the emerging paradigm of Web-based services as opposed to proprietary applications. Part of this technology is a new language, C#. This new language combines the power of C++ and the ease of development of Visual Basic™. It bears striking resemblance to Java™ and improves upon that language. C# may well become the dominant language for building applications on Microsoft® platforms.

This book is a practical introduction to programming in C# utilizing the services provided by .NET. This book emphasizes the C# language. It is part of the Prentice Hall/Object Innovations series of books on .NET technology.

This book is intended to be fully accessible to programmers who do not already have a strong background in object-oriented programming in C-like languages such as C++ or Java. It is ideal, for example, for Visual Basic or COBOL programmers who desire to learn C#. The book may also be read by more experienced programmers who desire a simple and concise introduction to C# with many example programs. It is structured so that more experienced programmers can cleanly skip the material they already know. Although designed for working professionals, the book includes enough detail, careful explanations and sample programs so that it can be useful as a college textbook.

An important thrust of this book is to teach C# programming from an object-oriented perspective. It is often difficult for programmers trained originally in a procedural language to start "thinking in objects." This book introduces object-oriented concepts early, and C# is developed in a way that leverages its object-orientation. A banking system case study is used to illustrate creating a complete system using C# and .NET. Besides supporting traditional object-oriented features such as classes, inheritance, and polymorphism, C# introduces several additional features, such as properties, indexers, delegates, events, and interfaces that make C# a compelling language for developing object-oriented and component-based systems. This book provides thorough coverage of all these features.

C# as a language is elegant and powerful. But to fully utilize its capabilities you need to have a good understanding of how it works with the .NET Framework. The book explores several important interactions between C# and the .NET Framework, and it includes an introduction to major classes for collections, files, threads, and user interface.

ORGANIZATION

The book is organized into four major parts and is structured in a manner to make it easy for you to navigate to what you most need to know. Part 1, which should be read by everyone, begins with an introduction to the .NET Framework, which is the underpinning for all applications and services in the .NET environment. Next comes a short introduction to hands-on programming using C#, so that you can start writing code on .NET right away. The third chapter introduces Visual Studio.NET, the latest incarnation of Microsoft's popular Visual Studio development environment. The new Visual Studio has many features that make application development easier and more pleasant. You will be equipped to use Visual Studio throughout the rest of the book.

Part 2 covers the C-like features of C#, which are shared by C, C++, Java, and various scripting languages. Thus, if you know any of these C-like languages, you will have a definite leg up in learning C#, and you can quickly skim this section, paying attention to the information in the sidebars. A sidebar will alert you the first time a concept new to C# is introduced. Then you will know to look for further elaborations where they occur later. If you are not familiar with C or a similar language, this section is for you. It will quickly bring you up to speed on the core topics of data types, operators, and control structures.

Part 3 is the core of the book, systematically covering the features of the C# programming language that go beyond C. The object-oriented features of C# are covered gradually and thoroughly, making this part of the book accessible to readers without OOP background. A case study is used, illustrating how the object-oriented features of C# work in combination. This case study is progressively built from Chapters 12 through 18. The C# data types, based on the .NET Common Type System, are explored in detail. We cover features new in C# such as properties and indexers. We cover practical issues of formatting and conversions, and we discuss the important topic of exceptions. We conclude this part with a study of interfaces, which provide a better level of abstraction in expressing system functionality.

Part 4 explores thoroughly the relationships between C# and the .NET Framework and introduces some important .NET services. We introduce collections, which generalize arrays, and we examine fundamental operations such as copying and comparing objects. In .NET, interfaces are provided for such basic operations, which makes for a very flexible architecture, as different classes can implement these interfaces in a manner appropriate for them. The .NET Framework provides a very flexible callback mechanism, known as delegates, which has many applications. Delegates are the foundation of events, and they are also used in starting threads. We look at directories and files, multiple thread programming, and attributes. Attributes are a powerful mechanism in .NET, enabling the programmer to accomplish tasks declaratively, with writing little or no code. You can implement your own custom attributes in C#. You can read information about custom attributes, or any other metadata, by a mechanism known as "reflection." C# permits you to code at a lower level by writing "unsafe" code, which can help you interoperate with legacy code. The book concludes with introductions to components and to Windows programming.

SAMPLE PROGRAMS

The only way to really learn a programming language is to read and write many, many programs, including some of reasonable size. This book provides many small programs that illustrate pertinent features of C# in isolation, where they are easy to understand. The programs are clearly labeled in the text, and they can all be found in the software distribution that accompanies this book. Directions for downloading the software are given below.

There is also a major case study, that is progressively developed in Chapters 12 through 18. This case study illustrates many features of C# working together in combination, as they would in a practical application. A special point is made of demonstrating the object-oriented features of C#. If you are new to OO, studying the case study is a must!

The sample programs are provided in a self-extracting file. When expanded, a directory structure is created rooted in **c:\OI\CSharp**. The sample programs are in directories **Chap1, Chap2**, etc. All the samples for a given chapter are in individual folders within the chapter directories. The names of the folders are clearly identified in the text. Each chapter that contains a step of the case study has a folder **CaseStudy** containing that step.

This book is part of the Integrated .NET Series from Object Innovations and Prentice Hall PTR series. The sample programs for other books in the series are located in their own directory underneath **c:\OI**, so all the .NET examples from all books in the series will be located in a common area as you install them.

EXERCISES

Although exercises are not provided in the book itself, a comprehensive set of exercises is available for download from our website.

WEBSITE

The website for the Integrated .NET Series from Object Innovations and Prentice Hall PTR series is:

www.objectinnovations.com/dotnet.htm

A link is provided at that website for downloading the sample programs.

ACKNOWLEDGMENTS

I am indebted to Michael Stiefel and Mike Meehan for helping this project get off the ground. They met at the PDC when Microsoft announced .NET, and that conversation put into motion what has become a substantial series of books on .NET technology, of which this volume is the first book. Mike helped me to focus, and Michael has been a great collaborator on the series as a whole, especially on the second book that we are writing together. Another early collaborator was Charlie Ferebee of Microsoft. Although Charlie had to drop out of the project for business reasons, Charlie's enthusiasm for .NET was a tremendous early boost to the project. Howard Lee Harkness reviewed the entire manuscript and provided many helpful suggestions. My wife, Marianne, has provided enormous support and encouragement for all my writing efforts. This time, above and beyond the call of duty, she went through the whole book, proofreading and checking examples. Thank you all, and the other colleagues, friends and students who have helped me over the years and who are too numerous to mention individually.

About this Series
Robert J. Oberg, Series Editor

Introduction

The Integrated .NET Book Series from Object Innovations and Prentice Hall PTR is a unique series of introductory and intermediate books on Microsoft's important .NET technology. These books are based on proven industrial-strength course development experience. The authors are expert practitioners, teachers, and writers who combine subject-matter expertise with years of experience in presenting complex programming technologies such as C++, Java™ MFC, OLE, and COM/COM+. These books *teach* in a systematic, step-by-step manner and are not merely summaries of the documentation. All the books come with a rich set of programming examples, and a thematic case study is woven through several of the books.

From the beginning, these books have been conceived as an *integrated whole*, and not as independent efforts by a diverse group of authors. The initial set of books consists of three introductory books on .NET languages and four intermediate books on the .NET Framework. Each book in the series is targeted at a specific part of the important .NET technology, as illustrated by the diagram below.

		C# Learning Pathway	VB.NET Learning Pathway		
.NET Language Introductions	Programming PERL in the .NET Environment	Introduction to C# Using .NET	Introduction to Programming Visual Basic Using .NET		
Intermediate .NET Framework Titles		Application Development Using C# and .NET	Application Development Using Visual Basic and .NET	.NET Architecture and Programming Using Visual C++	Fundamentals of Web Applications Using .NET and XML

Introductory .NET Language Books

The first set of books teaches several of the important .NET languages. These books cover each language from the ground up and have no prerequisite other than programming experience in some language. Unlike many NET language books, which are a mixture of the language and topics in the .NET Framework, these books are focused on the languages, with attention to important interactions between the language and the framework. By concentrating on the languages, these books have much more detail and many more practical examples than similar books.

The languages selected are the new language C#, the greatly changed VB.NET, and Perl.NET, the open source language ported to the .NET environment. Visual C++ .NET is covered in a targeted, intermediate book, and JScript.NET is covered in the intermediate level .NET Web-programming book.

Introduction to C# Using .NET

This book provides thorough coverage of the C# language from the ground up. It is organized with a specific section covering the parts of C# common to other C-like languages. This section can be cleanly skipped by programmers with C experience or the equivalent, making for a good reading path for a diverse group of readers. The book gives thorough attention to the object-oriented aspects of C# and thus serves as an excellent book for programmers migrating to C# from Visual Basic or COBOL. Its gradual pace and many examples make the book an excellent candidate as a college textbook for adventurous professors looking to teach C# early in the language's life-cycle.

Introduction to Programming Visual Basic Using .NET

Learn the VB.NET language from the ground up. Like the companion book on C#, this book gives thorough attention to the object-oriented aspects of VB.NET. Thus the book is excellent for VB programmers migrating to the more sophisticated VB.NET, as well as for programmers experienced in languages such as COBOL. This book would also be suitable as a college textbook.

Programming Perl in the .NET Environment

A very important part of the vision behind Microsoft® .NET is that the platform is designed from the ground up to support multiple programming languages from many sources, and not just Microsoft languages. This book, like other books in the series, is rooted in long experience in industrial teaching. It covers the Perl language from the ground up. Although oriented toward the ActiveState Perl.NET compiler, the book also provides excellent coverage of the Perl language suitable for other versions as well.

Intermediate .NET Framework Books

The second set of books is focused on topics in the .NET Framework, rather than on programming languages. Three parallel books cover the .NET Framework using the important languages C#, VB.NET, and Visual C++. The C# and VB.NET books include self-contained introductions to the languages suitable for experienced programmers, allowing them to rapidly come up to speed on these languages without having to plow through the introductory books. The fourth book covers the important topic of web programming in .NET, with substantial coverage of XML, which is so important in the .NET Framework.

The design of the series makes these intermediate books much more suitable to a wider audience than many similar books. The introductory books' focus on languages frees up the intermediate books to cover the important topics of the .NET Framework in greater depth. The series design also makes for flexible reading paths. Less experienced readers can read the introductory language books followed by the intermediate framework books, while more experienced readers can go directly to the intermediate framework books.

Application Development Using C# and .NET

This book does not require prior experience in C#. However, the reader should have experience in some object-oriented language such as C++ or Java™. The book could also be read by seasoned Visual Basic programmers who have experience working with objects and components in VB. Seasoned programmers and also a less experienced reader coming from the introductory C# book can skip the first few chapters on C# and proceed directly to a study of the Framework. The book is practical, with many examples and a major case study. The goal is to equip the reader with the knowledge necessary to begin building significant applications using the .NET Framework.

Application Development Using Visual Basic .NET

This book is for the experienced VB programmer who wishes to learn the new VB.NET version of VB quickly and then move on to learning the .NET Framework. It is also suitable for experienced enterprise programmers in other languages who wish to learn the powerful RAD-oriented Visual Basic language in its .NET incarnation and go on to building applications. Like the companion C# book, this book is very practical, with many examples, and includes the same case study implemented in VB.NET.

.NET Architecture and Programming Using Visual C++

This parallel book is for the experienced Visual C++ programmer who wishes to learn the .NET Framework to build high-performing applications. Unlike the C# and VB.NET book, there is no coverage of the C++ language itself, because C++ is too complex to cover in a brief space. This book is specifically for experienced C++ programmers. Like the companion C# and VB.NET books, this book is very practical, with many examples, and includes the same case study implemented in Visual C++.

Fundamentals of Web Applications Using .NET and XML

The final book in the series provides thorough coverage of building Web applications using .NET. Unlike other books about ASP.NET, this book gives attention to the whole process of Web application development. The book incorporates a review tutorial on classical Web programming, making the book accessible to the experienced programmer new to the Web world. The book contains significant coverage on ASP.NET, Web Forms, Web Services, SOAP, and XML.

PART ONE

INTRODUCTION TO .NET AND C#

INTRODUCTION TO
.NET AND C#

Microsoft .NET represents a sea change in how applications are developed, on the desktop, in the enterprise, on the Internet, and on new mobile devices. Part of .NET is a brand new programming language called C#, which is the subject matter of this book. In Part 1 we begin with an introduction to the .NET Framework, which is the underpinnings for applications and services in the .NET environment. Next we give a short introduction to hands-on programming using C#, so that you can start writing code on .NET right away. We conclude with an introduction to Visual Studio.NET, the latest incarnation of Microsoft's popular Visual Studio development environment. The new Visual Studio has many features that make application development easier and more pleasant. You will be equipped to use Visual Studio throughout the rest of the book.

.NET Framework

he new language C# was designed specifically to work with the .NET Framework. We will examine some of these connections throughout the book, as we learn of the powerful services that are provided to the C# programmer by the .NET Framework. In this chapter we begin by telling you just enough about the .NET Framework so that, if you so desire, you can immediately get off and running programming in C#. But if you are interested in a somewhat broader perspective, you can stay for the rest of the chapter, where we provide an orientation to the overall architecture and features of .NET. For more in-depth information about .NET you can refer to other books in Prentice Hall's Object Innovations series on .NET technology. C# programmers in particular will benefit from Application Development Using C# and .NET, *which delves into many important topics that are beyond the scope of this book.*

.NET: WHAT YOU NEED TO KNOW

A beautiful thing about .NET is that from a programmer's perspective you scarcely need to know anything about it to start writing programs for the .NET environment. You write a program in a high-level language such as C#, a compiler creates an executable (.EXE) file, and you run that EXE file. We will shortly show you how to do exactly that. Naturally, as the scope of what you want to do expands, you will need to know more, but to get started you need to know very little.

5

Even very simple programs, if they are to do something interesting, such as perform output, will require that the program employ the services of *library* code. A large library, called the .NET Framework Class Library, comes with .NET, and you can use all of the services of this library in your programs.

What is *really* happening is somewhat more elaborate. The EXE file that is created does not contain executable code, but rather code in *Intermediate Language*, or IL (sometimes called Microsoft Intermediate Language, or MSIL). In the Windows environment, this IL code is packaged up in a standard portable executable (PE) file format, so you will see the familiar EXE extension (or, if you are building a component, the DLL extension). When you run the EXE, a special runtime environment (the Common Language Runtime, or CLR) is launched, and the IL instructions are executed by the CLR. Unlike some runtimes, where the IL would be interpreted each time it is executed, the CLR comes with a just-in-time (JIT) compiler, which translates the IL to native machine code the first time it is encountered. Then, on subsequent calls, the code segment runs as native code.

Thus, in a nutshell, the process of programming in the .NET environment is:

1. Write your program in a high-level .NET language such as C#.
2. Compile your program into IL.
3. Run your IL program, which will launch the CLR to execute your IL, using its JIT to translate your program to native code as it executes.

A .NET Testbed for C# Programming

All you need to compile and run the programs in this book is the .NET Framework SDK. This SDK is available on CD or can be downloaded for free from the Microsoft .NET web site, *http://msdn.microsoft.com/net/*. Follow the installation directions for the SDK, and make sure that your computer meets the hardware requirements. (A rule of thumb for the SDK is a fast Pentium processor and at least 128M of RAM.) Part of the installation is a Windows Component Update, which will update your system, if necessary, to recent versions of programs such as Internet Explorer. The SDK will install tools such as compilers, documentation, sample programs, and the CLR.

When the SDK is installed you can navigate within it, starting from the .NET Framework SDK Overview (see Figure 1–1).

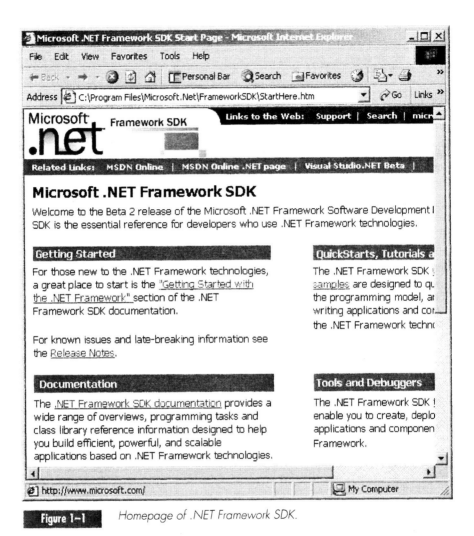

Figure 1-1   Homepage of .NET Framework SDK.

Installing the Book Software

The book software is available from the web site *http://www.object innovations.com/dotnet.htm*. Download the file **Install_CSharp.exe.** Run this self-extracting file. If you accept the suggested installation directory, the book software will be installed in the directory **OI\CSharp** on your C: drive. There are subdirectories for each chapter of the book. The directory for Chapter 1 is **Chap1.** Sample programs are in named subdirectories of the chapter directory, and we will refer to these sample programs simply by name, such as **Hello.**

Your First C# Program

Although we won't actually start to examine the structure of C# programs until the next chapter, you don't have to wait to compile and run your first C# program. Start up a command prompt and navigate to the **Hello** directory for this chapter (if you accepted the default installation, the full path to the directory is **c:\OI\CSharp\Chap1\Hello**). The source file is **Hello.cs.** To compile this program enter the following command:

```
>csc hello.cs
```

The file **Hello.exe** will be created, which you can now run.

```
>hello
Hello, World
```

Setting Environment Variables

In order to run command line tools such as the C# compiler using a simple name such as **csc** rather than a complete path, it is necessary for certain environment variables to be set. The environment variables can be set by a batch file **corvars.bat,** which can be found in the **bin** directory of the Framework SDK.

I experienced different behavior in different beta versions of the .NET Framework SDK. In one version the environment variables were set up automatically as part of the install, and in another version I had to use the **corvars.bat** file.

If you have Visual Studio.NET installed, you can ensure the environment variables are set up by starting your command prompt session from Start | Programs | Microsoft Visual Studio.NET 7.0 | Microsoft Visual Studio Tools | Microsoft Visual Studio.NET Command Prompt.

Visual Studio.NET

Although the .NET Framework SDK is all you need to compile and run C# programs, the process will be easier and more pleasant if you use the Visual Studio.NET integrated development environment (IDE). We will discuss Visual Studio.NET in Chapter 3.

Understanding .NET

If you are eager to start learning the C# programming language right away, by all means proceed directly to Chapter 2. The nice thing about a high-level programming language is that for the most part you do not need to be concerned with the platform on which the program executes (unless you are making use of services provided by the platform). You can work with the abstractions provided by the language and with functions provided by libraries.

Your appreciation of the C# programming language and its potential for creating great applications will be richer if you have a general understanding of .NET. The rest of this chapter is concerned with helping you to achieve such an understanding. We will address three broad topics:

* What Is Microsoft .NET?
* .NET Framework
* Common Language Runtime

WHAT IS MICROSOFT .NET?

In this section we will answer the high-level question "What is .NET?" In brief, .NET is Microsoft's vision of the future of applications in the Internet age. .NET provides enhanced interoperability features based upon open Internet standards. The classic Windows desktop has been plagued by robustness issues, a situation that may be greatly improved by .NET. For developers, .NET offers a new programming platform and superb tools. XML plays a fundamental role in .NET. Another feature of .NET is enterprise servers (such as SQL 2000) that expose .NET features through XML. Microsoft has announced Hailstorm as the underpinnings for many commercially available web services.

Microsoft .NET is a new platform at a higher level than the operating system. Three years in the making before public announcement, .NET is a major investment by Microsoft. .NET draws on many important ideas, including XML, the concepts underlying Java, and Microsoft's Component Object Model (COM). Microsoft .NET provides

* A robust runtime platform, the CLR
* Multiple language development
* An extensible programming model, the .NET Framework, which provides a very large class library of reusable code available from multiple languages
* A networking infrastructure built on top of Internet standards that supports a high level of communication among applications
* A new mechanism of application delivery, the web service, that supports the concept of an application as a service
* Powerful development tools

Microsoft and the Web

The World Wide Web has been a big challenge to Microsoft, which did not come on board early. But, actually, the web coexists quite well with Microsoft's traditional strength, the PC. Through a PC application, the browser, a user gains access to a whole world of information. The web relies on standards such as HTML, HTTP, and XML, which are essential for communication among diverse users on a wide variety of computer systems and devices.

The Windows PC, although complex, is quite standardized. While the Internet is based on standard protocols, there is a Tower of Babel with respect to the applications that try to build on top of it: multiple languages, databases, development environments, devices. There is an explosion of technology and a growing gap in knowledge workers who can build the needed systems using the new technologies. There is an opening for Microsoft, and the most talked about parts of .NET are indeed directed toward the Internet.

.NET provides many features to greatly enhance our ability to program web applications, but this topic is beyond the scope of this book. For more information please consult the following two books in Prentice Hall's Object Innovations .NET book series:

* *Application Development Using C# and .NET*
* *Fundamentals of Web Applications Using .NET and XML*

Windows on the Desktop

Microsoft began with the desktop. Microsoft has achieved much. The modern Windows environment has become ubiquitous. Countless applications are available, and most computer users are at least somewhat at home with Windows. There is quite a rich user interface experience, and applications can work together. But there are also significant problems.

PROBLEMS WITH WINDOWS

Maintaining a Windows PC is a chore, because applications are quite complex. They consist of many files, Registry entries, shortcuts, and so on. Different applications can share certain DLLs, and installing a new application can overwrite a DLL that an existing application depends on, possibly breaking an old application ("DLL hell"). Removing an application is complex and is often imperfectly done.

A PC can gradually become less stable, with the cure being to reformat the hard disk and start from scratch. There is tremendous economic benefit to using PCs, because standard applications are inexpensive and powerful, the hardware is cheap, and so on. But the savings are reduced by the cost of maintenance.

A ROBUST WINDOWS

.NET has many features that will create a much more robust Windows operating system. Applications no longer rely on storing extensive configuration data in the Registry. In .NET, applications are self-describing, containing *metadata* within the program executable files themselves. Different versions of an application can be deployed *side by side*.

Applications run *managed code*. Managed code is not executed directly by the operating system, but rather by the special runtime, the CLR. The CLR can perform checks for type safety, such as for array out-of-bounds and memory overwrites. The CLR performs memory management, including automatic garbage collection, resulting in sharp reduction of memory leaks and similar problems.

Languages such as C# and VB.NET (but not C++) can produce managed code that is verifiable as secure. Managed code that is not verifiable can run if the security policy allows the code to ignore the verification process.

A New Programming Platform

.NET provides a new programming platform at a higher level than the operating system. This level of abstraction has many advantages:

*   Safety and security checking can be done, providing more robust operation.
*   The higher level platform is much easier to program than at the lower level of the Win32 API or COM.
*   Potentially, the whole platform can be implemented on many different kinds of computers (as has been done with Java). A standardization effort is currently underway by the European Computer Manufacturer's Association (ECMA) to standardize C# and the supporting Common Language Infrastructure (CLI).
*   One class library is used by all the languages.
*   Languages can interoperate with each other.

We outline the features of this new platform, the *.NET Framework*, in the next section.

.NET FRAMEWORK OVERVIEW

The .NET Framework consists of the CLR, the .NET Framework Class Library, the Common Language Specification (CLS), a number of .NET languages, and Visual Studio.NET. The overall architecture of the .NET Framework is depicted in Figure 1–2.

Common Language Runtime

A runtime provides services to executing programs. Traditionally, there are different runtimes for different programming environments. Examples of runtimes include the standard C library, MFC, the Visual Basic runtime, and the Java Virtual Machine (JVM).

The runtime environment provided by .NET, the CLR, manages the execution of code and provides useful services. The services of the CLR are exposed through programming languages. The syntax for these services varies from language to language, but the underlying execution engine providing the services is the same.

Not all languages expose all the features of the CLR. The language with the best mapping to the CLR is the new language C# ("C sharp").

.NET Framework Class Library

The .NET Framework class library is huge, comprising over 2,500 classes. All this functionality is equally available to all the .NET languages. The library (see Figure 1–3) consists of four main parts:

* Base class library (includes networking, security, diagnostics, I/O, and other types of operating system services)
* Data and XML classes
* Web services and web UI
* Windows UI

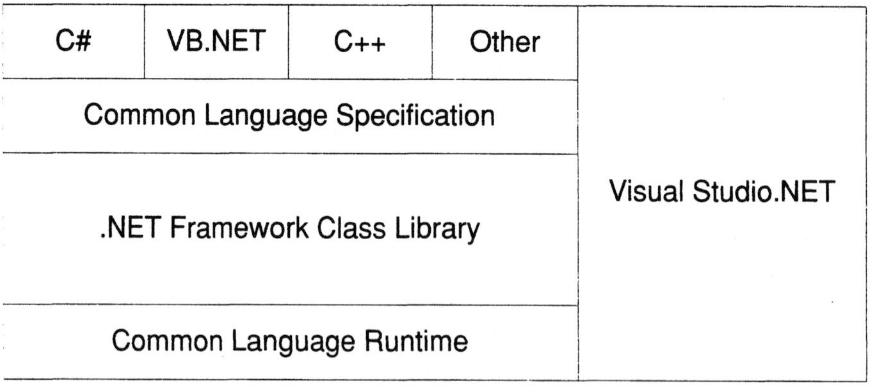

C#	VB.NET	C++	Other	Visual Studio.NET
Common Language Specification				
.NET Framework Class Library				
Common Language Runtime				

Figure 1–2   *Overall block diagram of .NET Framework.*

Common Language Specification

An important goal of the .NET Framework is to support multiple languages. But all languages are not created equal, so it is important to agree upon a common subset that all languages will support. The CLS is an agreement among language designers and class library designers about those features and usage conventions that can be relied upon.

CLS rules apply to public features that are visible outside the assembly where they are defined. (An assembly can be thought of as a logical EXE or DLL and will be discussed later in this chapter.) For example, the CLS requires that public names should not rely on case for uniqueness, because some languages are not case sensitive. The complete rules are contained in the Technical Overview of the Common Language Runtime, which is part of the .NET Framework SDK documentation.

Languages in .NET

A language is a CLS-compliant *consumer* if it can use any CLS-compliant type—that is, if it can call methods, create instances of types, and so on. (A type is basically a class in most object-oriented languages, providing an abstraction of data and behavior, grouped together.) A language is a CLS-compliant *extender* if it is a consumer and can also extend any CLS-compliant base class, implement any CLS-compliant interface, and so on.

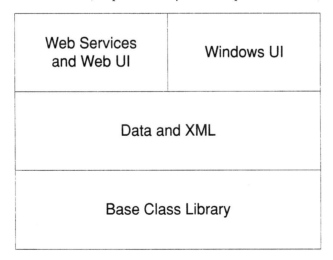

Web Services and Web UI	Windows UI
Data and XML	
Base Class Library	

Figure 1–3   *Block diagram of .NET Framework Class Library.*

Microsoft itself is providing four CLS-compliant languages. C#, Visual Basic.NET, and C++ with Managed Extensions are all extenders. JScript is a consumer.

Third parties are providing additional languages (over a dozen so far). ActiveState is implementing Perl and Python. Fujitsu is implementing COBOL. It should be noted that at present some of these languages are not .NET languages in the strict sense. For example, ActiveState provides a tool PerlNET which will create a .NET component from a Perl class. This facility enables .NET applications to call the wealth of Perl modules, but it does not make Perl into either a consumer or extender.

COMMON LANGUAGE RUNTIME

In this section we go more deeply into the structure of .NET by examining the CLR. We look at the design goals of the CLR and discuss the rationale for using managed code and a runtime. We then outline the design of the CLR, including the concepts of MSIL, metadata, and JIT compilation. We compare the CLR with the Java Virtual Machine. We then discuss the key concept in .NET of assembly, which is a logical grouping of code. We explore the central role of types in .NET and look at the Common Type System (CTS). We explain the role of managed data and garbage collection. Finally, we use the Intermediate Language Disassembler (ILDASM) tool to gain some insight into the structure of assemblies.

Design Goals of the CLR

The CLR has the following design goals:

* Simplify application development.
* Support multiple programming languages.
* Provide a safe and reliable execution environment.
* Simplify deployment and administration.
* Provide good performance and scalability.

SIMPLE APPLICATION DEVELOPMENT

With over 2,500 classes, the .NET Framework class library provides enormous functionality that the programmer can reuse and does not have to write. The object-oriented and component features of .NET enable organizations to create their own reusable code. Unlike COM, the programmer does not have to implement any plumbing code to gain the advantages of components. Automatic garbage collection greatly simplifies memory management in applications. The CLR facilitates powerful tools such as Visual Studio.NET that can provide common functionality and the same UI for multiple languages.

MULTIPLE LANGUAGES

The CLR was designed from the ground up to support multiple languages. This feature is the most significant difference between .NET and Java, which in fact share a great deal in philosophy.

The CTS makes interoperability between languages virtually seamless. The same built-in data types can be used in multiple languages. Classes defined in one language can be used in another language. A class in one language can even inherit from a class in another language. Exceptions can be thrown from one language to another.

Programmers do not have to learn a new language in order to use .NET. The same tools can work for all .NET languages. You can debug from one language into another.

SAFE EXECUTION ENVIRONMENT

With the CLR, a compiler generates MSIL instructions, not native code. It is this managed code that runs. Hence the CLR can perform runtime validations on this code before it is translated into native code. Types are verified. Subscripts are verified to be in range. Unsafe casts and uninitialized variables are prevented.

The CLR performs memory management. Managed code cannot access memory directly. No pointers are allowed. This means that your code cannot inadvertently write over memory that does not belong to it, possibly causing a crash or other bad behavior.

The CLR can enforce strong security. Evidence-based security can be based on the origin of the code as well as on the user. Good security is a safeguard against malicious code.

SIMPLER DEPLOYMENT AND ADMINISTRATION

With the CLR, the unit of deployment becomes an *assembly*, not an EXE or DLL. The assembly contains a *manifest*, which allows much more information to be stored.

An assembly is completely self-describing. No information needs to be stored in the Registry. All the information is in one place, and the code cannot get out of synch with information stored elsewhere, such as in the Registry, a type library, or a header file.

The assembly is the unit of versioning, so that multiple versions can be deployed side by side in different folders. These different versions can execute at the same time without interfering with each other.

Applications and components can be private or shared. Private components guarantee that the expected version is being run. With shared components, the CLR can use version information in the assembly to verify that the expected version is used (no more "DLL hell").

PERFORMANCE

You may like the safety and ease-of-use features of managed code, but you may be concerned about performance. It is somewhat analogous to the concerns of early assembly language programmers when high-level languages came out.

The CLR is designed with high performance in mind. JIT compilation is designed into the CLR. The first time a method is encountered, the CLR performs verifications and then compiles the method into native code (which will contain safety features, such as array bounds checking). The next time the method is encountered, the native code executes directly.

Memory management is designed for high performance. Allocation is almost instantaneous, just taking the next available storage from the managed heap. Deallocation is done by the garbage collector, which has an efficient multiple-generation algorithm.

Why Use a CLR?

Why did Microsoft create a CLR for .NET? Let's look at how far the goals just discussed could have been achieved without a CLR, focusing on the two main goals of safety and performance. Basically, there are two philosophies. The first is compile-time checking and fast native code at runtime. The second is runtime checking.

Without a CLR, we must rely on the compiler to achieve safety. This places a high burden on the compiler. Typically, there are many compilers for a system, including third-party compilers. It is not robust to trust that every compiler from every vendor will adequately perform all safety checking. Not every language has features supporting adequate safety checking. Compilation speed is slow with complex compilation. Compilers cannot conveniently optimize code based on enhanced instructions available on some platforms but not on others. What is more, many features (such as security) cannot be detected until runtime.

Design of Common Language Runtime

So we want a runtime, how do we design it? One extreme is to use an interpreter and not a compiler at all. All the work is done at runtime. We have safety and fast builds, but runtime performance is very slow. Modern systems divide the load between the front-end compiler and the back-end runtime.

INTERMEDIATE LANGUAGE

The front-end compiler does all the checking it can do and generates an intermediate language. Examples include

* P-code for Pascal
* Bytecode for Java

The runtime does further verification based on the actual runtime characteristics, including security checking.

With JIT compilation, native code can be generated when needed, and subsequently reused. Runtime performance becomes much better. The native code generated by the runtime can be more efficient, because the runtime knows the precise characteristics of the target machine.

MICROSOFT INTERMEDIATE LANGUAGE

All managed code compilers for Microsoft .NET generate MSIL. MSIL is machine-independent and can be efficiently compiled into native code.

MSIL has a wide variety of instructions:

* Standard operations such as load, store, arithmetic and logic, branch, etc.
* Calling methods on objects
* Exceptions

Before executing on a CPU, MSIL must be translated by a JIT compiler. There is a JIT compiler for each machine architecture supported. The same MSIL will run on any supported machine.

METADATA

Besides generating MSIL, a managed code compiler emits metadata. Metadata contains very complete information about the code module and all the types within it:

* Version and locale information
* All the types
* Details about each type, including name, visibility, etc.
* Details about the members of each type, such as methods, the signatures of methods, etc.

Metadata is the "glue" that binds together the executing code, the CLR, and tools such as compilers, debuggers, and browsers. On Windows, MSIL and metadata are packaged together in a standard Windows PE file. Metadata enables "Intellisense" in Visual Studio, popping up a yellow box allowing automatic statement completion. In .NET you can call from one language to another, and metadata enables types to be converted transparently. Metadata is ubiquitous in the .NET environment.

JIT COMPILATION

Before executing on the target machine, MSIL is translated by a JIT compiler to native code. Some code typically will never be executed during a program run. Hence it may be more efficient to translate MSIL as needed during execution, storing the native code for reuse.

When a type is loaded, the loader attaches a stub to each method of the type. On the first call, the stub passes control to the JIT, which translates to native code and modifies the stub to save the address of the translated native code. On subsequent calls to the method, transfer is then made directly to the native code.

As part of JIT compilation, code goes through a verification process. Type safety is verified, using both the MSIL and metadata. Security restrictions are checked.

CLR AND JVM

The main features of the CLR described so far are quite close to the JVM, but there are also some important differences. Since MSIL is packaged in a Windows PE file, you start an EXE from the shell by just running it. In Java you explicitly invoke the JVM. PE files are grouped into assemblies, and standard Windows deployment such as CAB files can be used. Java has class files and JARs.

There are multiple hosts for the CLR besides the shell, such as ASP.NET, and there is a new lightweight process model called *application domains,* which can enhance scalability. While Java uses the Java Native Interface to access native code, the CLR facilitates more flexible interoperability between managed and native code.

Most importantly, the CLR supports very complete object-oriented programming in multiple languages through a CTS. Although in principle the CLR can be implemented on many platforms, currently it runs only on different flavors of Windows. Java is implemented on a great many different platforms.

Assemblies

An assembly is a grouping of types and resources that work together as a logical unit. An assembly can be thought of as a logical DLL or EXE. An assembly consists of one or more physical files, called modules, which may be EXE or DLL files or resources (such as bitmaps). An assembly holds three kinds of information:

* MSIL implementing one or more types
* Metadata
* A manifest describing how the elements in the assembly relate to each other and to external elements

An assembly forms the boundary for

* Security
* Deployment
* Type resolution
* Versioning

Types

Types are at the heart of the programming model for the CLR. A type is basically a class in most object-oriented programming languages, providing an abstraction of data and behavior, grouped together. A type in the CLR contains

* Fields (data members)

* Methods

* Properties

* Events

There are also built-in primitive types, such as integer and floating-point numeric types and string types. In the CLR there are no functions outside of types, but all behavior is provided via methods or other members. We will discuss types under the guise of classes when we cover C#.

COMMON TYPE SYSTEM

At the heart of the CLR is the CTS. The CTS provides a wide range of types and operations that are found in many programming languages. The CTS is shared by the CLR and by compilers and other tools.

The CTS provides a framework for cross-language integration and addresses a number of issues:

* Similar, but subtly different, types (e.g., **Integer** is 16 bits in VB6 but **int** is 32 bits in C++, strings in VB6 are represented as BSTRs and in C++ as **char** pointers or a **string** class of some sort, etc.)

* Limited code reuse (e.g., you can't define a new type in one language and import it into another language)

* Inconsistent object models

Not all CTS types are available in all languages. The CLS establishes rules that *must* be followed for cross-language integration, including which types must be supported by a CLS-compliant language. Built-in types can be accessed through the **System** class in the Base Class Library (BCL) and through reserved keywords in the .NET languages.

In Chapter 4, we begin our discussion of data types with the simple data types, most of which are common to other C family programming languages. We continue the discussion of types in Chapter 9, where we introduce *reference* types such as class and interface, and we look at built-in types such as **object** and **string.** At all times, you should bear in mind that there is a mapping between types in C#, represented by keywords, and the types defined by the CTS, as implemented by the CLR.

Managed Data and Garbage Collection

Managed code is only part of the story of the CLR. A significant simplification of the programming model is provided through *managed data*. When an application domain is initialized, the CLR reserves a contiguous block of storage known as the *managed heap*. Allocation from the managed heap is extremely fast. The next available space is simply returned, in contrast to the C runtime, which must search its heap for space that is large enough.

Deallocation is not performed by the user program but by the CLR, using a process known as *garbage collection*. The CLR tracks the use of memory allocated on the managed heap. When memory is low, or in response to an explicit call from a program, the CLR "garbage collects," or frees up, all unreferenced memory, and compacts the space that is now free into a large contiguous block.

Assemblies and ILDASM

We can learn about CLR concepts such as assemblies, manifests, and MSIL through the ILDASM tool. For example, run ILDASM.EXE on the assembly **Hello.exe** in the folder **Hello.** See Figure 1–4.

```
ildasm hello.exe
```

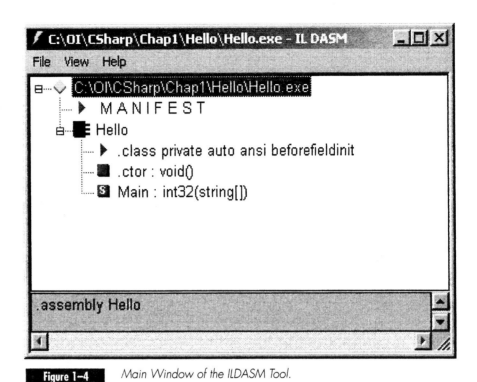

Figure 1-4   *Main Window of the ILDASM Tool.*

You can obtain a dump of intermediate language. Use the menu File | Dump. In the Save As dialog box, enter a name for the file to save.

Intermediate Language

Here is an excerpt of the MSIL code:

```
.method public hidebysig static int32
          Main(class System.String[] args) il managed
{
  .entrypoint
  // Code size        16 (0x10)
  .maxstack  1
  .locals (int32 V_0)
  IL_0000:  ldstr        "Hello, World"
  IL_0005:  call         void [mscorlib]
          System.Console::WriteLine(class System.String)
  IL_000a:  ldc.i4.0
  IL_000b:  stloc.0
  IL_000c:  br.s         IL_000e
```

```
    IL_000e:  ldloc.0
    IL_000f:  ret
} // end of method Hello::Main
```

SUMMARY

C# does not exist in isolation, but has a close connection with the underlying .NET Framework. In this introductory chapter, we began by telling you just enough about the .NET Framework so that, if you so desired, you could proceed directly to Chapter 2 and start learning C#. If you stayed for the rest of the chapter, you gained an orientation to the overall architecture and features of .NET.

Microsoft .NET is a new platform at a higher level than the operating system that provides many capabilities for building and deploying both standard applications and new web-based ones. .NET has many features that will create a much more robust Windows operating system. .NET uses managed code running on the CLR that uses the CTS.

The .NET Framework includes the CLR, the .NET Framework class library, the CLS, the .NET languages, and Visual Studio.NET. The CLR manages the execution of code and provides useful services.

The design goals of the CLR include simple application development, safety, simple deployment, support of multiple languages, and good performance. Managed code runs in a safe environment under the CLR. .NET compilers translate source code into MSIL, which is translated at runtime into native code by a JIT compiler.

An assembly is a grouping of types and resources that work together as a logical unit. Types and the CTS are the heart of the CLR. Garbage collection is used by the CLR to automatically reclaim unreferenced data. You can use the ILDASM tool to gain insight into the structure of assemblies.

In Chapter 2 we will take our first steps in C# programming.

First C# Programs

*I*n this chapter we get our feet wet programming C#. Starting with the traditional "Hello, World" program, you will learn how to build programs using the .NET Framework SDK. First, we describe the basic structure of C# programs and explain how related C# classes can be grouped into namespaces. After understanding how C#'s output works, variables and simple expressions can be used to perform simple calculations. At this point we can start to explain some of the object-oriented concepts in C#. Since input is a little more involved than output, an input wrapper class is used to simplify input in C#. Finally, we take a peek at the .NET Framework Class Library, which will be sampled later in the book.

HELLO, WORLD

Whenever learning a new programming language, a good first step is to write and run a simple program that will display a single line of text. Such a program demonstrates the basic structure of the language, including output. Here is "Hello, World" in C#. (See the **Hello** directory for this chapter.)

```
// Hello.cs

class Hello
{
    public static int Main(string[] args)
    {
        System.Console.WriteLine("Hello, World");
        return 0;
    }
}
```

Compiling and Running (Command Line)

We will see how to use Microsoft Visual Studio.NET IDE (integrated development environment) in Chapter 3. In this chapter we use the .NET Framework SDK, and you compile the program via the command line (as we saw in Chapter 1):

```
>csc Hello.cs
```

An executable file **Hello.exe** will be generated. To execute your program, type at the command line:

```
>Hello
```

The program will now execute, and you should see displayed the greeting:

```
Hello, World
```

PROGRAM STRUCTURE

```
// Hello.cs
class Hello
{
    ...
}
```

Every C# program has at least one *class*. A class is the foundation of C#'s support of object-oriented programming. A class encapsulates data (represented by variables) and behavior (represented by methods). All of the code defining the class (its variables and methods) will be contained between the curly braces. We will discuss classes in detail later.

Note the comment at the beginning of the program. A line beginning with a double slash is present only for documentation purposes and is ignored by the compiler. C# files have the extension **.cs**.

```
// Hello.cs

class Hello
{
    public static int Main(string[] args)
    {
        ...
        return 0;
    }
}
```

An alternate form of comment is to use an opening /* and a closing */.

```
/* This is a comment
   that may be continued over
   several lines */
```

There is a distinguished class, which has a method whose name must be **Main.** The method should be **public** and **static.** An **int** exit code can be returned to the operating system.

```
// Hello.cs

class Hello
{
    public static int Main(string[] args)
    {
        ...
        return 0;
    }
}
```

Use **void** if you do not return an exit code.

```
public static void Main(string[] args)
```

Command line arguments are passed as an array of strings. The runtime will call this **Main** method — it is the entry point for the program. All the code of the **Main** method will be between the curly braces.

```
// Hello.cs

class Hello
{
    public static int Main(string[] args)
    {
        System.Console.WriteLine("Hello, World");
        return 0;
    }
}
```

Every method in C# has one or more *statements*. A statement is terminated by a semicolon. A statement may be spread out over several lines. The **Console** class provides support for standard output and standard input. The method **WriteLine** displays a string, followed by a new line.

NAMESPACES

Much standard functionality in C# is provided through many classes in the .NET Framework. Related classes are grouped into *namespaces*. The fully qualified name of a class is specified by the namespace followed by a dot followed by a class name.

```
System.Console
```

A **using** statement allows a class to be referred to by its class name alone.

```
// Hello2.cs

using System;

class Hello
{
    public static int Main(string[] args)
    {
        Console.WriteLine("Hello, World");
        return 0;
    }
}
```

Note that in C# it is not necessary for the file name to be the same as the name of the class containing the **Main** method.

VARIABLES AND EXPRESSIONS

In C# you can define variables to hold data. Variables represent storage locations in memory. In C# variables are of a specific data type. Some common types are **int** for integers and **double** for floating-point numbers.

You must declare variables before you can use them. A variable declaration reserves memory space for the variable and may optionally specify an initial value.

```
int kilo = 1024;        // reserves space and assigns
                        // an initial value
int mega;               // reserves space but does
                        // not initialize
```

If an initial value is not specified, the variable must be initialized in code before it can be used.

Expressions

You can combine variables and constants (or *literals*) via operators to form expressions.

Examples of operators include the standard arithmetic operators:

```
+           addition
-           subtraction
*           multiplication
/           division
```

Here are some examples of expressions:

```
kilo * 1024
(fahrenheit - 32) * 5 / 9
3.1416 * radius * radius
```

Assignment

You can assign a value to a variable by using the = symbol. On the left-hand side is a variable. On the right-hand side is an expression. The expression is evaluated and its value is assigned to the variable on the left. Assignment is a statement and must be terminated by a semicolon.

```
mega = kilo * 1024;
celsius = (fahrenheit - 32) * 5 / 9;
area = 3.1416 * radius * radius;
```

Note that the same variable can be used on both sides of an assignment statement.

```
int item = 5;
int total = 30;
total = total + item;
```

Don't confuse the assignment statement with an equation. The expression **total + item** evaluates to 35, using the old value of **total**. This value is assigned to **total**, creating a new value.

USING C# AS A CALCULATOR

You can easily use C# to perform calculations by adding code to the **Main** method of a C# class. Declare whatever variables you need. Create expressions and assign values to your variables. Print out the answer using **Console.WriteLine.**

You can easily do labeled output, relying on two features of C#: The operator + performs concatenation for string data. There is an automatic, implicit conversion available that converts numeric data to string data when required. Hence this code

```
int total = 35;
System.Console.WriteLine("The total is " + total);
```

will produce this output:

```
The total is 35
```

Sample Program

This program will convert from Fahrenheit to Celsius. See **Convert\Step1.**

```
// Convert.cs - Step 1
//
// Program converts a hardcoded temperature in
// Fahrenheit to Celsius

using System;

class Convert
{
    public static void Main(string[] args)
    {
        int fahr = 86;
        int celsius = (fahr - 32) * 5 / 9;
        Console.WriteLine("fahrenheit = " + fahr);
        Console.WriteLine("celsius = " + celsius);
    }
{
```

INPUT/OUTPUT IN C#

We have seen how to do simple output in C# using **Console.WriteLine.** In this section we will discuss more features about output and will introduce basic input.

Output in C#

The **Console** class in the **System** namespace supports two simple methods for performing output:

* **WriteLine** writes out a string followed by a new line.
* **Write** writes out just the string without the new line.

You can write out other data types by relying on the **ToString** method of **System.Object,** which will provide a string representation of any data type. We will discuss the root class **System.Object** in Part 3, where you will also see how to override **ToString** for your own custom data type. You can use the string concatenation operator + to build up an output string.

```
int x = 24;
int y = 5;
int z = x * y;
Console.Write("Product of " + x + " and " + y);
Console.WriteLine(" is " + z);
```

The output is all on one line:

```
Product of 24 and 5 is 120
```

PLACEHOLDERS

A more convenient way to build up an output string is to use *placeholders* {0}, {1}, and so on. An equivalent way to do the output shown above is

```
Console.WriteLine("Product of {0} and {1} is {2}", x,y,z);
```

The program **OutputDemo** illustrates the output operations just discussed.

We will generally use placeholders for our output from now on. In Part 3 we will also see how placeholders can be combined with formatting characters to control output format.

Input in C#

Our first **Convert** program is not too useful because the Fahrenheit temperature is hardcoded. To convert a different temperature, you would have to edit the source file and recompile. What we really want to do is allow the user of the program at runtime to enter a value for the Fahrenheit temperature.

An easy, uniform way to do input for various data types is to read the data as a string and then convert to the desired data type. Use the **ReadLine** method of the **System.Console** class to read in a string. Use the **ToXxxx** methods of the **System.Convert** class to convert the data.

```
Console.Write("Temperature in Fahrenheit: ");
string buf = Console.ReadLine();
int fahr = Convert.ToInt32(buf);
```

Although simple console input in C# is fairly easy, we can make it even easier using object-oriented programming. We can encapsulate, or "wrap," the details of input in a class. It will be easy to use the wrapper class.

MORE ABOUT CLASSES

Although we will discuss classes in detail later, there is a little more you need to know now. A class can be thought of as a template for creating objects. An *object* is an instance of a class. A class specifies data and behavior. The data is different for each object instance.

In C# you instantiate a class by using the **new** keyword.

```
InputWrapper iw = new InputWrapper();
```

This code creates the object instance iw of the **InputWrapper** class.

USING THE INPUTWRAPPER CLASS

The **InputWrapper** class wraps interactive input for several basic data types. The supported data types are **int, double, decimal,** and **string**. Methods **getInt, getDouble, getDecimal,** and **getString** are provided to read those types from the command line. A prompt string is passed as an input parameter. The directory **InputWrapper** contains the files **InputWrapper.cs,** which implements the class and **TestInputWrapper.cs,** which tests the class.

You do not need to be familiar with the implementation of InputWrapper in order to use it. That is the beauty of "encapsulation"—complex functionality can be hidden by an easy-to-use interface. (A listing of the **InputWrapper** class is provided later in the chapter.)

Here is the code for **Convert\Step2.** We read in a temperature in Fahrenheit and convert to Celsius. The input is first done directly, and then we do it a second time using the **InputWrapper** class. The bolded code illustrates how to use the **InputWrapper** class. Instantiate an **InputWrapper** object **iw** by using **new.** Prompt for and obtain input data by calling the appropriate **getXXX** method.

```
// Convert.cs - Step 2
//
// Program converts temperature in
// Fahrenheit to Celsius
//
// Step 2 performs input, first directly and then by
// using the InputWrapper class
//
// We have changed the name of our class to ConvertTemp
// so as not to conflict with the class System.Convert

using System;

class ConvertTemp
```

```
{
    public static void Main(string[] args)
    {
        // Input is done directly
        Console.Write("Temperature in Fahrenheit: ");
        string buf = Console.ReadLine();
        int fahr = Convert.ToInt32(buf);
        int celsius = (fahr - 32) * 5 / 9;
        Console.WriteLine("fahrenheit = {0}", fahr);
        Console.WriteLine("celsius = {0}", celsius);
        // Use the InputWrapper class
        InputWrapper iw = new InputWrapper();
        fahr = iw.getInt("Temperature in Fahrenheit: ");
        celsius = (fahr - 32) * 5 / 9;
        Console.WriteLine("fahrenheit = {0}", fahr);
        Console.WriteLine("celsius = {0}", celsius);
    }
}
```

Here is the output from running the programming:

```
Temperature in Fahrenheit: 32
fahrenheit = 32
celsius = 0
Temperature in Fahrenheit: 212
fahrenheit = 212
celsius = 100
```

COMPILING MULTIPLE FILES

The program in **Convert\Step2** is our first example of the common situation of a program with multiple files (in this case, just two: **Convert.cs** and **InputWrapper.cs**). It is easy to compile multiple files at the command line.

```
>csc *.cs
```

This will compile all the files in the current directory. The file containing a class with the **Main** method will be used as the name of the generated EXE file:

```
Directory of C:\OI\CSharp\Chap2\Convert\Step2

05/17/2001  10:07a      <DIR>          .
05/17/2001  10:07a      <DIR>          ..
02/27/2001  06:09p              1,093 Convert.cs
05/17/2001  10:07a              4,096 Convert.exe
01/05/2001  12:34p                855 InputWrapper.cs
             3 File(s)          6,044 bytes
             2 Dir(s)  33,575,294,464 bytes free
```

If multiple classes contain a **Main** method, you can use the **/main** command line option to specify which class contains the **Main** method that you want to use as the entry point into the program. You can use the **/out** option to specify the name of the output file.

```
>csc /main:ConvertTemp /out:Convert.exe *.cs
```

INPUTWRAPPER CLASS IMPLEMENTATION

The **InputWrapper** class is implemented in the file **InputWrapper.cs.** We will discuss classes in detail in Part 3, but you should find the code reasonably intuitive, given what you already know about classes.

```
// InputWrapper.cs
//
// Class to wrap simple stream input
// Datatype supported:
//      int
//      double
//      decimal
//      string

using System;

class InputWrapper
{
    public int getInt(string prompt)
    {
      Console.Write(prompt);
      string buf = Console.ReadLine();
      return Convert.ToInt32(buf);
    }
    public double getDouble(string prompt)
    {
      Console.Write(prompt);
      string buf = Console.ReadLine();
      return Convert.ToDouble(buf);
    }
    public decimal getDecimal(string prompt)
    {
      Console.Write(prompt);
      string buf = Console.ReadLine();
      return Convert.ToDecimal(buf);
    }
    public string getString(string prompt)
    {
      Console.Write(prompt);
      string buf = Console.ReadLine();
      return buf;
    }
}
```

If bad input data is presented, an *exception* will be thrown. Exceptions are discussed in Chapter 16.

THE .NET FRAMEWORK CLASS LIBRARY

The .NET Framework has a very large class library (over 2,500 classes). In this chapter we have used the **Console** and **Convert** classes. To make all this functionality more manageable, the classes are partitioned into *namespaces*. The root namespace is **System,** which directly contains many useful classes, among them,

* **Console** provides access to standard input, output, and error streams for doing I/O.
* **Convert** provides conversions among base data types.
* **Math** provides mathematical constants and functions.

Underneath **System** there are other namespaces, among them,

* **System.Data** contains classes constituting the ADO.NET architecture for accessing databases.
* **System.Xml** provides standards-based support for processing XML.
* **System.Drawing** contains classes providing GDI+ graphics functionality.
* **System.Windows.Forms** provides support for creating applications with rich Windows-based interfaces.
* **System.Web** provides support for browser/server communication.

SUMMARY

In this chapter we learned the rudiments of programming in C#. Every C# application has a class with a method **Main,** which is the entry point into the application. The **System** class includes methods for doing output, such as **WriteLine**. Expressions in C# are formed from constants, variables, and operators. With the assignment statement, you can assign a value computed by an expression to a variable. Input in C# is a little more complicated than output, but you can use a wrapper class that encapsulates the required C# classes and presents a simple programming interface. The .NET Framework has a large class library that is partitioned into namespaces. In the next chapter we will learn about Visual Studio.NET, which will make our programming easier and more enjoyable.

Visual Studio.NET

lthough it is possible to program .NET using only the command line compiler, it is much easier and more enjoyable to use Visual Studio.NET. In this chapter we cover the basics of using Visual Studio to edit, compile, run, and debug programs. You will then be equipped to use Visual Studio in the rest of the book. This chapter covers the basics to get you up and running using Visual Studio. We will introduce additional features of Visual Studio later in the book as we encounter a need. This book was developed using beta software, and in the final released product you may encounter some changes to the information presented here. Also, Visual Studio is a very elaborate Windows application that is highly configurable, and you may encounter variations in the exact layout of windows, what is shown by default, and so on. As you work with Visual Studio, a good attitude is to see yourself as an explorer discovering a rich and varied new country.

OVERVIEW OF VISUAL STUDIO.NET

Open up Microsoft Visual Studio.NET 7.0 and you will see a starting window similar to what is shown in Figure 3–1.

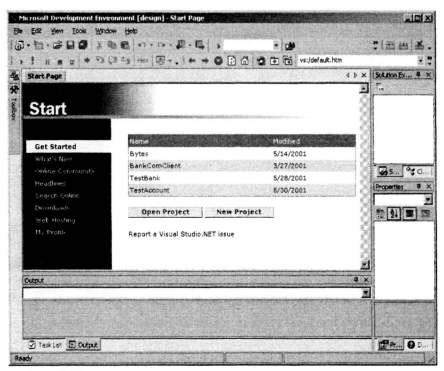

Figure 3–1   *Visual Studio.NET main window.*

What you see on default startup is the main window with an HTML page that can help you navigate among various resources, open or create projects, and change your profile information. (If you close the start page, you can get it back anytime from the menu Help | Show Start Page.) Clicking on **My Profile** will bring up a profile page on which you can change various settings. There is a standard profile for "typical" work in Visual Studio ("Visual Studio Developer" profile), and special ones for various languages. Since Visual Studio.NET is the unification of many development environments, programmers used to one particular previous environment may prefer a particular keyboard scheme, window layout, and so on. For example, if you choose the profile "Visual Basic Developer," you will get the Visual Basic 6 keyboard scheme. In this book we will use all the defaults, so go back to the profile "Visual Studio Developer" if you made any changes. See Figure 3–2.

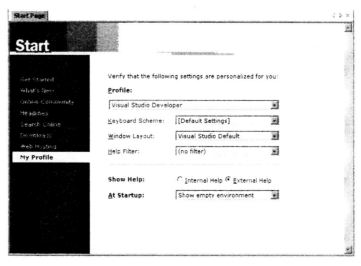

Figure 3–2   *Visual Studio.NET profile page.*

To gain an appreciation of some of the diverse features in Visual Studio.NET, open up the **Bank** console solution in this chapter (File | Open Solution..., navigate to the **Bank** directory, and open the file **Bank.sln**). You will see quite an elaborate set of windows. See Figure 3–3.

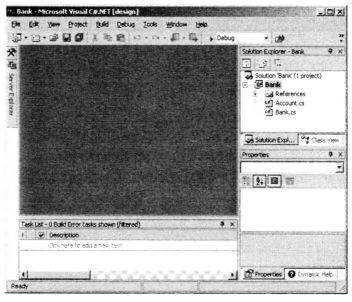

Figure 3–3   *A console project in Visual Studio.NET.*

Starting from the left are icons for the Server Explorer and the Toolbox, followed by the main window area, which currently is just a gray area. Underneath the main window is the Output Window, which shows the results of builds and so on. Continuing our tour, on the top right is the Solution Explorer, which enables you to conveniently see all the files in a "solution," which may consist of several "projects." On the bottom right is the Properties window, which lets you conveniently edit properties on forms for Windows applications. The Properties window is very similar to the Properties Window in Visual Basic.

From the Solution Explorer you can navigate to files in the projects. In turn, double-click on each of **Account.cs** and **Bank.cs,** the two source files in the **Bank** project. Text editor windows will be brought up in the main window area. Across the top of the main window are horizontal tabs to quickly select any of the open windows. Visual Studio.NET is a Multiple Document Interface (MDI) application, and you can also select the window to show from the Windows menu. Figure 3–4 shows the open source files with the horizontal tabs.

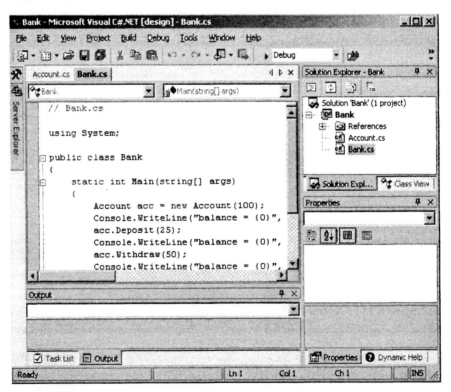

Figure 3–4   *Horizontal tabs for open source files.*

Toolbars

Visual Studio comes with many different toolbars. You can configure which toolbars you wish displayed, and you can drag toolbars to position them to where you find them most convenient. You can also customize toolbars by adding or deleting buttons that correspond to different commands.

To specify which toolbars are displayed, bring up the menu View | Toolbars. You can also right click in any empty area of a toolbar. There will be a check mark next to the toolbars which are currently displayed. By clicking on an item on this menu you can make the corresponding toolbar button appear or disappear. For your work in this book add the toolbars,

* Build
* Debug

CUSTOMIZING A TOOLBAR

We want to make sure that the "Start Without Debugging" command is available on the Debug toolbar. If it is not already on your Debug toolbar (it is a red exclamation point), you can add it by the following procedure, which can be used to add other commands to toolbars.

1. Select menu Tools | Customize... to bring up the Customize dialog.
2. Select the Commands tab.
3. In Categories, select Debug, and in Commands select Start Without Debugging. See Figure 3-5.
4. Drag the selected command onto the Debug toolbar, positioning it where you desire. Place it to the immediate right of the wedge-shaped Start ▶ button.
5. Close the Customize dialog.

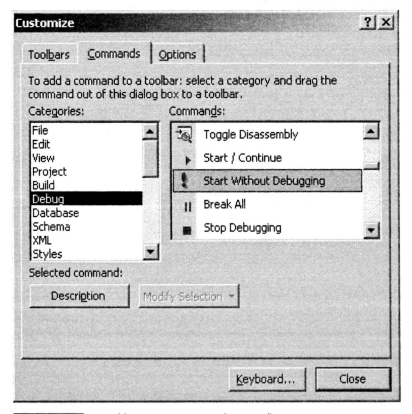

Figure 3–5   *Adding a new command to a toolbar.*

CREATING A CONSOLE APPLICATION

As our first exercise in using Visual Studio, we will create a simple console application. Our program **Bytes** will attempt to calculate how many bytes there are in a kilobyte, a megabyte, a gigabyte, and a terabyte. If you want to follow along on your PC as you read, you can use the **Demos** directory for this chapter. The first version is in **Bytes\Step1**. A final version can be found in **Bytes\Step3**.

Creating a C# Project

1. From Visual Studio main menu choose File | New | Project.... This will bring up the New Project dialog.
2. For Project Types choose "Visual C# Projects" and for Templates choose "Empty Project."
3. Click the Browse button, navigate to **Demos,** and click Open.
4. In the Name field, type **Bytes**. See Figure 3–6. Click OK.

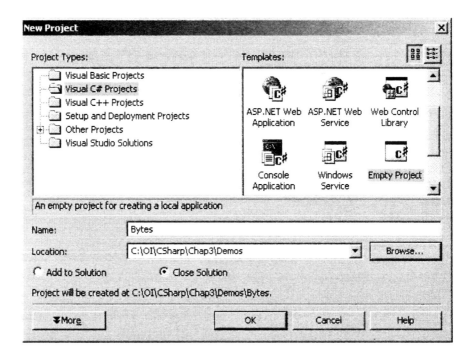

Figure 3–6   *Creating an empty C# project.*

Adding a C# File

At this point you will have an empty C# project. We are now going to add a file **Bytes.cs,** which contains the text of our program.

1. In Solution Explorer right click over **Bytes** and choose Add | Add New Item.... This will bring up the Add New Item dialog.
2. For Categories choose "Local Project Items" and for Templates choose "Code File."
3. For Name type **Bytes.cs.** See Figure 3–7. Click Open.

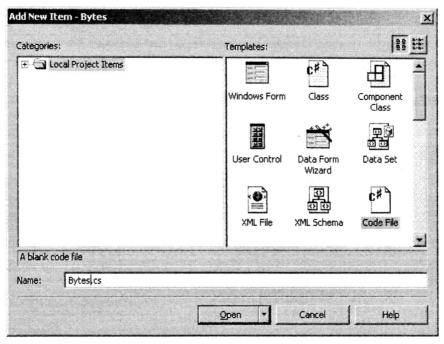

Figure 3–7 *Adding an empty C# file to a C# project.*

Using the Visual Studio Text Editor

In the Solution Explorer double-click on **Bytes.cs.** This will open up the empty file **Bytes.cs** in the Visual Studio text editor. Type in the following program, and notice things like color syntax highlighting as you type.

```
// Bytes.cs

using System;
public class Bytes
```

```
{
   public static int Main(string[] args)
   {
      int bytes = 1024;
      Console.WriteLine("kilo = {0}", bytes);
      bytes = bytes * 1024;
      Console.WriteLine("mega = {0}", bytes);
      bytes = bytes * 1024;
      Console.WriteLine("giga = {0}", bytes);
      bytes = bytes * 1024;
      Console.WriteLine("tera = {0}", bytes);
      return 0;
   }
}
```

Besides the color syntax highlighting, other features include automatic indenting and putting in a closing right curly brace to match the left curly brace you type. All in all, you should find the Visual Studio editor friendly and easy to use.

Building the Project

You can build the project by using one of the following:

- Menu Build | Build
- Toolbar ▦
- Keyboard shortcut Ctrl + Shift + B

Running the Program

You can run the program by using one of the following:

- Menu Debug | Start Without Debugging
- Toolbar ❗
- Keyboard shortcut Ctrl + F5

You will see the following output in a console window that opens up:

```
kilo = 1024
mega = 1048576
giga = 1073741824
tera = 0
Press any key to continue
```

We will investigate the reason for the strange output later. If you press any key, as indicated, the console window will close.

Running the Program in the Debugger

You can run the program in the debugger by using one of the following:
* Menu Debug | Start
* Toolbar ▶
* Keyboard shortcut F5

A console window will briefly open up and then immediately close. If you want the window to stay open, you must explicitly program for it, for example, by asking for input. You can set a breakpoint to stop execution before the program exits. We will outline features of the debugger later in the chapter.

PROJECT CONFIGURATIONS

A project *configuration* specifies build settings for a project. You can have several different configurations, and each configuration will be built in its own directory, so you can exercise the different configurations independently. Every project in a Visual Studio solution has two default configurations, **Debug** and **Release**. As the names suggest, the **Debug** configuration will build a debug version of the project, where you can do source level debugging by setting breakpoints, and so on. The **bin\Debug** directory will then contain a *program database* file with a **.pdb** extension that holds debugging and project state information.

You can choose the configuration from the main toolbar ▶ Debug ▾ .
You can also choose the configuration using the menu Build | Configuration Manager..., which will bring up the Configuration Manager dialog. From the Active Solution Configuration dropdown, choose **Release.** See Figure 3–8.

Build the project again. Now a second version of the IL language file **Bytes.exe** is created, this time in the **bin\Release** directory. There will be no **.pdb** file in this directory.

Creating a New Configuration

Sometimes it is useful to create additional configurations, which can save alternate build settings. As an example, let's create a configuration for a "checked" build. As we will discuss in Chapter 5, if you build with the **/checked** compiler switch, the compiler will generate IL code to check for integer underflow and overflow. In Visual Studio you set compiler options through dialog boxes. The following steps will guide you through creating a new configuration called **CheckedDebug** that will build a checked version of the program.

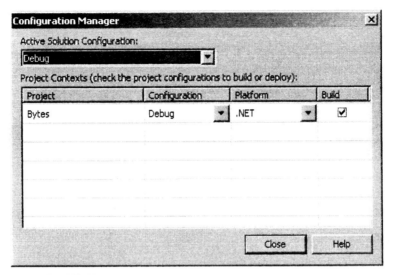

Figure 3–8   *Choosing Release in the Configuration Manager.*

1. Bring up the Configuration Manager dialog.

2. From the Active Solution Configuration: dropdown, choose **<New...>**. The New Solution Configuration dialog will come up.

3. Type **CheckedDebug** as the configuration name. Choose Copy Settings from **Debug**. Check "Also create new project configuration(s)." See Figure 3–9. Click OK.

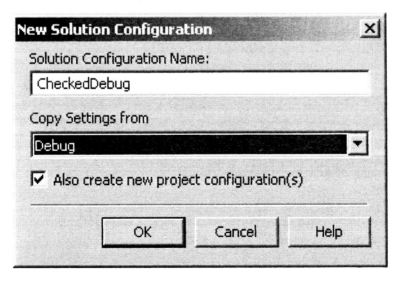

Figure 3–9   *Creating a new configuration.*

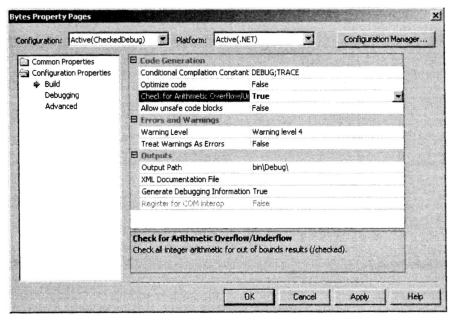

Figure 3-10   *Changing the build settings for a configuration.*

Setting Build Settings for a Configuration

Next we will set the build settings for the new configuration. (You could also set build settings for one of the standard configurations, if you wanted to make any changes from the defaults provided.) Check the toolbar to verify that the new **CheckedDebug** is the currently active configuration.

1. Right-click over **Bytes** in the Solution Explorer and choose Properties. The "Bytes Property Pages" dialog comes up.

2. In Configuration Properties, select Build. Change the setting for "Check for overflow underflow" to **True** (see Figure 3–10). Click OK.

DEBUGGING

In this section we will discuss some of the debugging facilities in Visual Studio. To be able to benefit from debugging at the source code level, you should have built your executable using a Debug configuration, as discussed previously. There are two ways to enter the debugger:

* Just-in-Time Debugging. You run normally, and if an exception occurs you will be allowed to enter the debugger. The program has crashed, so you will not be able to run further from here to single step, set breakpoints, and so on. But you will be able to see the value of variables, and you will see the point at which the program failed.
* Standard Debugging. You start the program under the debugger. You may set breakpoints, single step, and so on.

Just-in-Time Debugging

Build and run (without debugging) the **Bytes** program from the previous section, making sure to use the **CheckedDebug** configuration. This time the program will not run through smoothly to completion, but an exception will be thrown. A "Just-In-Time Debugging" dialog will be shown (see Figure 3–11). Click Yes to debug.

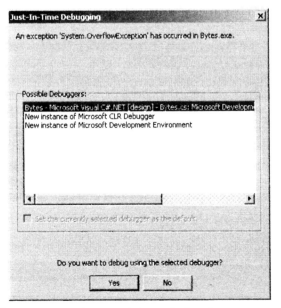

Figure 3–11   *Just-In-Time Debugging dialog is displayed in response to an exception.*

Click OK in the "Attach to Process" dialog and then click Break in the "Microsoft Development Environment" dialog. You will now be brought into a window showing the source code where the problem arose, with an arrow pinpointing the location.

To stop debugging you can use the ■ toolbar button or the menu Debug | Stop Debugging.

Standard Debugging

BREAKPOINTS

The way you typically do standard debugging is to set a breakpoint and then run using the debugger. As an example, set a breakpoint at the first line:

```
bytes = bytes * 1024;
```

The easiest way to set a breakpoint is by clicking in the gray bar to the left of the source code window. You can also set the cursor on the desired line and click the "hand" toolbar button 🖑 to toggle a breakpoint (set if not set, and remove if a breakpoint is set). Now you can run under the debugger, and the breakpoint should be hit. A yellow arrow over the red dot of the breakpoint shows where the breakpoint has been hit. See Figure 3–12.

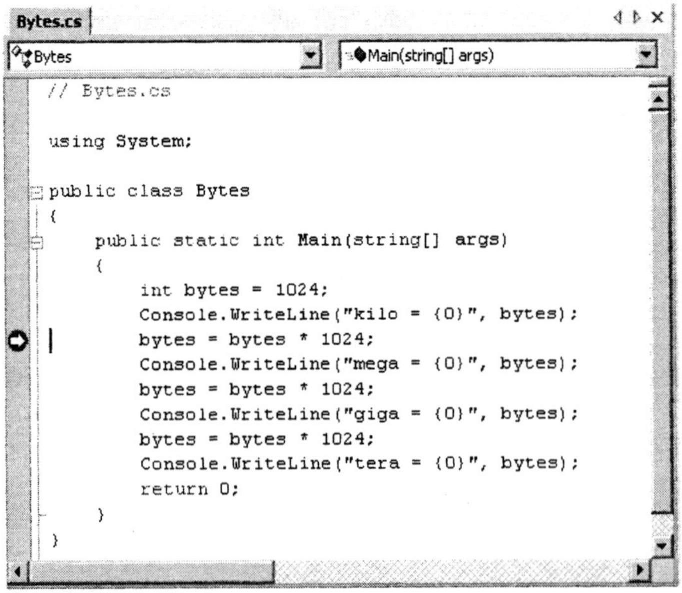

```
// Bytes.cs

using System;

public class Bytes
{
    public static int Main(string[] args)
    {
        int bytes = 1024;
        Console.WriteLine("kilo = {0}", bytes);
        bytes = bytes * 1024;
        Console.WriteLine("mega = {0}", bytes);
        bytes = bytes * 1024;
        Console.WriteLine("giga = {0}", bytes);
        bytes = bytes * 1024;
        Console.WriteLine("tera = {0}", bytes);
        return 0;
    }
}
```

Figure 3–12   *A breakpoint has been hit.*

When you are done with a breakpoint, you can remove it by clicking again in the gray bar or by toggling with the hand toolbar button. If you want to remove all breakpoints, you can use the menu Debug | Clear All Breakpoints, or you can use the toolbar button .

WATCHING VARIABLES

At this point you can inspect variables. The easiest way is to slide the mouse over the variable you are interested in, and the value will be shown as a yellow tool tip. You can also right-click over a variable and choose Quick Watch (or use the eyeglasses toolbar button). Figure 3–13 shows a typical Quick Watch window. You can also change the value of a variable from this window.

When you are stopped in the debugger, you can add a variable to the Watch window by right-clicking over it and choosing Add Watch. The Watch window can show a number of variables, and the Watch window stays open as the program executes. When a variable changes value, the new value is

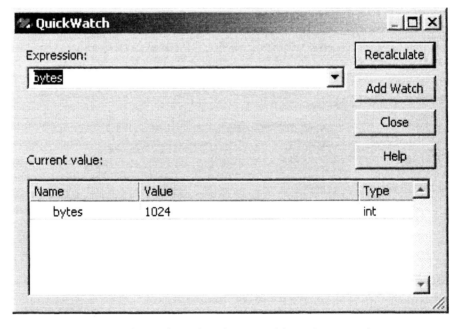

Figure 3–13   *Quick Watch window shows variable, and you can change it.*

shown in red. Figure 3–14 shows the Watch window (note that the display has been changed to hex, as described in the next section).

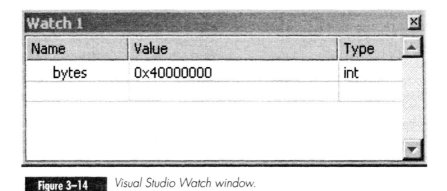

Name	Value	Type
bytes	0x40000000	int

Figure 3–14   *Visual Studio Watch window.*

DEBUGGER OPTIONS

You can change debugger options from the menu Tools | Options, and select Debugging from the list. Figure 3–15 illustrates setting a hexadecimal display. If you then go back to a Watch window, you will see a hex value such as **0x400** displayed.

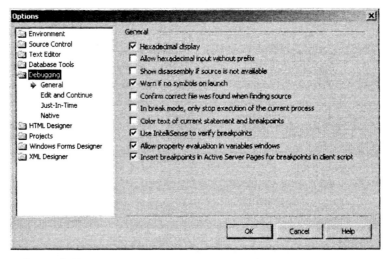

Figure 3–15   *Setting hexadecimal display in Debugging Options.*

SINGLE STEPPING

When you are stopped in the debugger, you can single step. You can also begin execution by single stepping. There are a number of single step buttons. ⊊ ⌊ ⌊ The most common are (in the order shown on the toolbar):

* Step Into
* Step Over
* Step Out

There is also a Run to Cursor button ⊊ .

With Step Into you will step into a function, if the cursor is positioned on a call to a function. With Step Over you will step to the next line (or statement or instruction, depending on the selection in the dropdown next to the step buttons `Line    ▾`). To illustrate Step Into, build the **Bytes\Step2** project, where the multiplication by 1,024 has been replaced by a function call to the static method **OneK**. Set a breakpoint at the first function call, and then Step Into. The result is illustrated in Figure 3–16. Note the red dot at the breakpoint and the yellow arrow in the function.

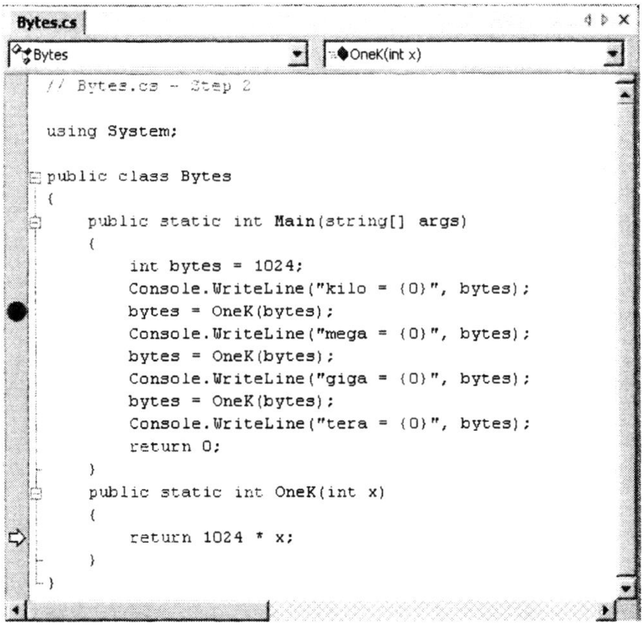

```
// Bytes.cs - Step 2

using System;

public class Bytes
{
    public static int Main(string[] args)
    {
        int bytes = 1024;
        Console.WriteLine("kilo = {0}", bytes);
        bytes = OneK(bytes);
        Console.WriteLine("mega = {0}", bytes);
        bytes = OneK(bytes);
        Console.WriteLine("giga = {0}", bytes);
        bytes = OneK(bytes);
        Console.WriteLine("tera = {0}", bytes);
        return 0;
    }
    public static int OneK(int x)
    {
        return 1024 * x;
    }
}
```

Figure 3–16   *Stepping into a function.*

When debugging, Visual Studio maintains a Call Stack. In our simple example the Call Stack is just two deep. See Figure 3–17.

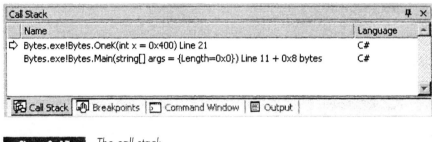

Figure 3–17   *The call stack.*

SUMMARY

Visual Studio.NET is a very rich integrated development environment (IDE), with many features to make programming more enjoyable. In this chapter we covered the basics of using Visual Studio to edit, compile, run, and debug programs, so that you will be equipped to use Visual Studio in the rest of the book. A project can be built in different configurations, such as Debug and Release. Visual Studio.NET has a vast array of features for building database applications, Web applications, components, and many other kinds of projects. It supports many different languages. In this book we are using only a tiny fraction of the capabilities of this powerful tool, but the simple features we employ are very useful, and will certainly make your life as a C# programmer easier.

C # AS A LANGUAGE
IN THE C FAMILY

C# AS A LANGUAGE
IN THE C FAMILY

The new language C# takes its basic structure from the programming language C. The core features are shared by C, C++, Java, and various scripting languages. Thus if you know any of these C-like languages, you will have a definite leg up in learning C#. Part 2 describes these core features in C#. If you are already familiar with C or a similar language, you can quickly skim this section, paying attention to the information in the sidebars. A sidebar will alert you the first time a concept new to C# is introduced. Then you will know to look for further elaborations where they occur later. For example, the **decimal** data type is introduced **in Chapter 4** and flagged with a sidebar. There is further discussion about **decimal** later—for example, operations on **decimal** are discussed in **Chapter 5**—but this later discussion will not have a sidebar, since you have already been alerted in **Chapter 4.**

If you are not familiar with C or a similar language, this section is for you. It will quickly bring you up to speed on the core topics of data types, operators, and control structures.

Simple Data Types

*D*ata typing is fundamental in modern programming languages. C# is a strongly typed language, a feature that contributes to greater reliability in C# programs. In this chapter we discuss the simple data types of integer, floating-point, decimal, character, and boolean. We also examine conversions between these simple types. We will look at the rest of the C# type system, including its relationship to the underlying .NET Common Type System, in Chapter 9.

DATA TYPES

Data in a computer is fundamentally just a string of bits. Associating a type with the bits turns the bit string into meaningful data. Some examples of data types in C# are

- **short** (a 16-bit integer)
- **char** (a 16-bit character)
- **float** (a 32-bit floating-point number)

The same bit string can represent different data, depending on the type. For example, the bit string representation of the character '7' in C# is

```
0037 (hex)
0000 0000 0011 0111 (binary)
```

That same bit string as a **short** (integer) is 55 in decimal. Many programming errors can occur if the two are confused.

Strong Typing

Some programming languages, such as the scripting language VBScript, are untyped. You do not declare a data type for variables. The runtime engine will detect errors, but there is no notion of compile type checking for types. Most modern programming languages are typed, and there is some checking done for types at the time the program is compiled. But the degree of checking varies among languages. In this section we will compare C# with two other popular languages, C++ and Visual Basic 6. We will see that the three languages are quite different in how they handle a common programming situation in which we have both a number and a corresponding character or string.

TYPING IN C#

C# is a strongly typed language. Every constant and variable in C# has an associated type. Variables and constants of different types cannot be mixed except according to strict rules. Consider the following C# program (see **Seven\CSharp**):

```
// Seven.cs

using System;

public class Seven
{
    public static int Main(string[] args)
    {
        char seven = '7';
        short number;
        number = seven;
        Console.WriteLine("seven = " + seven);
        Console.WriteLine("number = " + number);
        return 0;

    }
}
```

If you run this program, you will find that the program is illegal! C# is not a mind reader, so it flags an error on the assignment (different types on each side):

```
        number = seven;
```

You will get the error message "Cannot implicitly convert type 'char' to 'short'".

TYPING IN C++

Consider a similar program in C++ (see **Seven\Cpp**):

```
// seven.cpp

#include <iostream>
using namespace std;

int main()
{
    char seven = '7';
    short number;
    number = seven;
    cout << "seven = " << seven << endl;
    cout << "number = " << number << endl;
    return 0;
}
```

The compiler will not complain, and the following output is obtained:

```
seven = 7
number = 55
```

In C++ **char** is an integer data type, as is **short,** and so the assignment is legal. The internal representation of '7' is the number 55, which gets assigned to **number.**

TYPING IN VISUAL BASIC 6

Consider a similar program in Visual Basic 6 (see **Seven\Vb6**). The program has a GUI interface. The relevant code is contained at the bottom of the file **Form1.frm.**

```
Private Sub Command1_Click()
    Dim seven As String
    Dim number As Integer
    seven = "7"
    number = seven
    MsgBox seven
    MsgBox number
End Sub
```

Visual Basic also does not complain, and what you see displayed in each message box is 7! Unlike C++, Visual Basic has silently performed a conversion for you. Visual Basic was designed as a language that is easy to use, and so a number of "natural" conversions are performed automatically.

CONCLUSION

Each of these languages is typed: You declare a variable as having a certain data type before using it. However, when you do an assignment between two variables of different types, their behavior is very different. C# is a strongly typed language, and the compiler will generate an error message for certain kinds of type conversions. (We will see later that C# will implicitly perform some conversions for you, such as "widening" a 16-bit integer to a 32-bit integer, etc.). You can override the compiler in such cases, a topic we will discuss later in the chapter. C++ is a lower level language and regards **char** as just another integer data type. In the assignment, the code generated by the C++ compiler will simply copy the ASCII code of '7' into the **short** variable. (But you do get warnings in C++ with certain conversions.) Visual Basic 6 is a higher level language designed especially to make it easy to do GUI programming. In VB6 you frequently have string data (e.g., typed by a user into a textbox control), and VB6 makes it easy to write programs without having to do explicit conversions.

There is no "best" way for a language to handle data typing issues. It can be argued that the C# approach is the safest and will result in more reliable programs, especially in large projects. But this safety comes at a price, and as a programmer you have to be explicitly concerned with doing some conversions that you might be used to being done for you automatically in other languages, such as VB6. When you are starting out in C# you may find this aspect of the language to be somewhat of a pain, but once you are fluent in the conversion features of C# it should not be a problem. We discuss conversion among the simple data types later in this chapter, and we discuss more general conversion and formatting issues in Chapter 15.

INTEGER TYPES

In the C family of languages, there is a greater variety of integer data types than in many languages. There are different *sizes* of integer data types, and there are also *signed* and *unsigned* versions of each size of integer type. This flexibility allows you to choose the appropriate integer data type for your situation, and you can conserve memory by using a smaller size integer when it fits your needs. If your data will not have negative values, you can extend its range without increasing its size by using the unsigned version of the type. Table 4–1 summarizes all the integer data types available in C#. The types in C# programs can be represented by keywords in the C# language. These keywords are aliases for types in the **System** namespace. The types in the **System** namespace are important, because these types are not associated with any particular language and are the types used in the intermediate language generated by compilers. It is this common type system that enables .NET languages to interoperate with each other so seamlessly.

Table 4–1	*Integer Data Types in C#*		
C# Keyword	**Size**	**Signed/Unsigned**	**Type in System Namespace**
sbyte	8 bits	signed	SByte
byte	8 bits	unsigned	Byte
short	16 bits	signed	Int16
ushort	16 bits	unsigned	UInt16
int	32 bits	signed	Int32
uint	32 bits	unsigned	UInt32
long	64 bits	signed	Int64
ulong	64 bits	unsigned	UInt64

Integer Types Are of Exact Size in C#

In C and C++ the exact size of the integer data types are not specified but are supposed to conform to the "natural" size on a particular machine. The intent is for **short** and **long** to provide different lengths of integers where practical, but it is not required by the language. In C# (as in Java) the exact sizes are specified by the language.

Ranges of Integer Types

You can easily determine the ranges of the integer data types by using the **MinValue** and **MaxValue** properties of the corresponding types in the **System** namespace. The program **IntegerRange** does this for you.

A New Way to Find Limits

C programmers are familiar with the header file **limits.h** to find the smallest and largest numbers of different data types. In C# you use the **MinValue** and **MaxValue** properties of the types like **Int16** from the **System** namespace.

```
// IntegerRange.cs

using System;

public class IntegerRange
{
```

```
public static int Main(string[] args)
{
    Console.WriteLine("min sbyte = " + SByte.MinValue);
    Console.WriteLine("max sbyte = " + SByte.MaxValue);
    Console.WriteLine("min byte = " + Byte.MinValue);
    Console.WriteLine("max byte = " + Byte.MaxValue);
    Console.WriteLine("min short = " + Int16.MinValue);
    Console.WriteLine("max short = " + Int16.MaxValue);
    Console.WriteLine("min ushort = " + UInt16.MinValue);
    Console.WriteLine("max ushort = " + UInt16.MaxValue);
    Console.WriteLine("min int = " + Int32.MinValue);
    Console.WriteLine("max int = " + Int32.MaxValue);
    Console.WriteLine("min uint = " + UInt32.MinValue);
    Console.WriteLine("max uint = " + UInt32.MaxValue);
    Console.WriteLine("min long = " + Int64.MinValue);
    Console.WriteLine("max long = " + Int64.MaxValue);
    Console.WriteLine("min ulong = " + UInt64.MinValue);
    Console.WriteLine("max ulong = " + UInt64.MaxValue);
    return 0;
}
}
```

Running the program, you can see the numeric ranges of the various integer data types. Note that the unsigned types always start at 0, and can represent a positive number twice as large as can be represented by the corresponding signed type.

```
min sbyte = -128
max sbyte = 127
min byte = 0
max byte = 255
min short = -32768
max short = 32767
min ushort = 0
max ushort = 65535
min int = -2147483648
max int = 2147483647
min uint = 0
max uint = 4294967295
min long = -9223372036854775808
max long = 9223372036854775807
min ulong = 0
max ulong = 18446744073709551615
```

Integer Literals

A *literal* is used when you explicitly write a value for a variable in a program. An integer literal is represented by either an ordinary decimal integer or by a hexadecimal integer. A hexadecimal representation is preceded by

0x or **0X.** The following are equivalent ways of assigning the number of squares on a chessboard to the **int** variable **squaresChess.**

```
squaresChess = 64;
squaresChess = 0x40;
```

Although the above literal will fit in a single byte, in C# integer literals are always stored as 32-bit or 64-bit values. You may influence the type that is used for storing a literal by a suffix. The following suffixes are available. They are not case sensitive.

* **L** (or **l**) for **long**

* **U** (or **u**) for unsigned, i.e. **uint** or **ulong**

* **UL** (or any variation in the case and order, such as **ul, LU,** etc.) for **ulong**

The type of an integer literal is always the smallest of the allowed values in which it will fit, with preference given to signed over unsigned. The basic rule can be overridden by the use of suffixes. Thus in the example above, the literal is stored as an **int,** and there is no type conversion in assigning the literal to the variable. If you wanted to force the literal to be stored as a **uint,** for example, you would write it as **64U** or **0x40U.**

The precise rules for literals, and all aspects of the C# language, are described in detail in *Microsoft C# Language Specifications,* which is available with the online documentation for C#.

FLOATING-POINT TYPES

While integer data types represent whole numbers, floating-point data types can be used to represent decimal fractions, where an exponent can be used to represent very large and very small values. Like the other C family of languages, there are two floating-point data types in C#, corresponding to single and double precision. Floating-point numbers sacrifice precision to achieve a great range, from very small to very large. There is also a **decimal** data type in C#, which can be used to represent decimal numbers exactly, as may be used in financial calculations. The **decimal** data type is discussed in the next section. Table 4–2 summarizes the floating-point data types available in C#. The types in C# programs can be represented by keywords in the C# language. These keywords are aliases for types in the **System** namespace.

Table 4-2	Floating Data Types in C#	
C# Keyword	**Size**	**Type in System Namespace**
float	32 bits	Single
double	64 bits	Double

Ranges of Floating Types

You can easily determine the ranges of the floating-point data types by using the **MinValue** and **MaxValue** properties of the corresponding types in the **System** namespace. The program **FloatRange** does this for you.

```
// FloatRange.cs

using System;

public class FloatRange
{
   public static int Main(string[] args)
   {
      Console.WriteLine("min float = " + Single.MinValue);
      Console.WriteLine("max float = " + Single.MaxValue);
      Console.WriteLine("min double = " + Double.MinValue);
      Console.WriteLine("max double = " + Double.MaxValue);
      return 0;
   }
}
```

Running the program, you can see the numeric ranges of the various floating-point data types. Note the way that very small and very large numbers are represented by exponential notation.

```
min float = -3.40282347E38
max float = 3.40282347E38
min double = -1.7976931348623157E308
max double = 1.7976931348623157E308
```

Floating-Point Literals

Floating-point literals can use either decimal or exponential notation. A floating-point literal without a suffix is stored in memory as a **double.** To specify a **float** use the suffix **F** or **f.** You may use the suffix **D** or **d** to make clear that a literal is a **double.**

```
double pi = 3.14;
float e = 2.72F;
double earthFromSun = 9.3E7
```

IEEE Floating-Point

C# uses the IEEE 754 floating-point standard (see *www.ieee.org*) for floating-point numbers and operations. This standard is now supported by almost all processors. Under this standard, operations such as division by zero do not produce an exception but instead create a special value, such as Infinity or NaN (Not a Number). For an example of these special floating-point values, see the program **SpecialFloat.**

```
// SpecialFloat.cs

using System;

public class SpecialFloat
{
   public static int Main(string[] args)
   {
      Console.WriteLine("1.0/0.0 = " + 1.0/0.0);
      Console.WriteLine("0.0/0.0 = " + 0.0/0.0);
      return 0;
   }
}
```

   Here is the output from this program:

```
1.0/0.0 = Infinity
0.0/0.0 = NaN
```

DECIMAL TYPE

Although floating-point numbers can be written as decimals and can represent both very small and very large quantities, an inherent limitation in the floating-point data types is that they are not precise. This is not acceptable in, for example, financial calculations. C# introduces a simple, built-in data type **decimal,** which can represent precisely any decimal number with up to 28 significant digits. The **decimal** data types (see Table 4–3) use 96 bits, and more of these bits are used for precision as opposed to range, as in the floating-point types.

Table 4–3   *Decimal Data Types in C#*

C# Keyword	Size	Type in System Namespace
decimal	96 bits	Decimal

C# Has New Decimal Data Type

The **decimal** data type in C# is something new that is not built into C or C++. Those languages require library support for the equivalent.

Range of Decimal Type

As with the integer and floating-point types, we can write a simple program to show the range of decimal values. See **DecimalRange.**

```
// DecimalRange.cs

using System;

public class DecimalRange
{
        public static int Main(string[] args)
        {
                Console.WriteLine(
                        "min decimal = " + Decimal.MinValue);
                Console.WriteLine(
                        "max decimal = " + Decimal.MaxValue);
                Console.WriteLine(
                        "min decimal = {0:E}", Decimal.MinValue);
                Console.WriteLine(
                        "max decimal = {0:E}", Decimal.MaxValue);
                return 0;
        }
}
```

In this program, we have previewed some simple formatting of output, a topic we will discuss in Chapter 15. Here is the output from this program:

```
min decimal = -79228162514264337593543950335
max decimal = 79228162514264337593543950335
min decimal = -7.922816E+028
max decimal = 7.922816E+028
```

Decimal Literals

As with floating-point, **decimal** literals can use either decimal or exponential notation. A **decimal** literal is specified by the suffix **M** or **m** (think of money).

```
decimal mySalary = 199.50M;
decimal nationalDebit = 7E12M
```

The program **DecimalLiterals** illustrates use of both floating-point and **decimal** literals.

CHARACTER TYPE

Individual characters are represented by the **char** data type, which in C# is 16 bits wide and corresponds to a Unicode character. The corresponding type in the **System** namespace is **Char.** See Table 4–4.

Table 4–4	Character Data Type in C#	
C# Keyword	**Size**	**Type in System Namespace**
char	16 bits	Char

C# Uses Unicode

In C and C++ the character width is not defined but is typically 8 bits and uses the ASCII character set. The "wide" character type **wchar_t** is also available. In C#, as in Java, characters are always 16 bits wide and are represented by the Unicode character set.

Character Literals

A **char** literal represents a single character. It can consist of a character in single quotes, or a Unicode character in hex (with prefix **\x** or **\u**), or an escape character (to represent something like a quote or backslash). Some examples include the following:

```
'7'        // character in quotes
\x0055     // same character in hex
\u0055     // same character in Unicode
'\''       // single quote
```

Table 4–5 shows all the escape characters recognized by C#.

Table 4-5	Escape Characters in C#	
Escape Character	**Name**	**Value**
\'	Single quote	0x0027
\"	Double quote	0x0022
\\	Backslash	0x005C
\0	Null	0x0000
\a	Alert	0x0007
\b	Backspace	0x0008
\f	Form feed	0x000C
\n	New line	0x000A
\r	Carriage return	0x000D
\t	Horizontal tab	0x0009
\v	Vertical tab	0x000B

The program **CharacterLiterals** illustrates using character literals. Note that the method **Write** from the **System** class does not write out a new line.

```
// CharacterLiterals.cs

using System;

public class CharacterLiterals
{
   public static int Main(string[] args)
   {
      Console.Write('7');
      Console.Write('\t');
      Console.Write('\x0037');
      Console.Write('\t');
      Console.Write('\u0037');
      Console.Write('\n');
      Console.Write('\'');
      Console.Write('7');
      Console.Write('\'');
      Console.WriteLine();
      return 0;
   }
}
```

Tabs are output using the escape character '**\t**'. A new line can be generated either by use of the escape character '**\n**' or by using the **WriteLine** method. Here is the output from this program:

```
7       7       7
'7'
```

BOOLEAN TYPE

C# has a boolean data type **bool** that is used to represent logical values. A variable of type **bool** can have either the value **true** or the value **false,** which are the two literals that are of this type. A **bool** value has size of 8 bits. The corresponding type in the **System** namespace is **Boolean.** See Table 4–6.

Table 4–6	Boolean Data Type in C#	
C# Keyword	**Size**	**Type in System Namespace**
bool	8 bits	Boolean

CONVERSIONS

Frequently in programming you will have occasion to use a value of one data type in a situation where a different data type is called for. Since C# is a strongly typed language, there must be a *conversion* in these situations. There are two kinds of conversions:

* An *implicit* conversion is done silently by the compiler, where required.
* An *explicit* conversion must be called for explicitly by the programmer.

There are a number of rules about conversions, but rather than try to memorize these, it is easier to reason from general principles. The basic principle is that it is safe to convert from one type to a "wider" type, such as from **short** to **int** or from **float** to **double.** Such a conversion will be done for you implicitly by the compiler.

But sometimes you will perform a conversion that the compiler cannot tell is inherently safe. You may know that the actual possible values for a variable are within an acceptable range, or you may deliberately be willing to accept some loss of precision. In such cases, you can perform a *cast* operation, which is simply to enclose the new type in parentheses in front of the value that is being converted. For example,

```
float pi = 3.14;         // compiler error
float pi = (float) 3.14;   // cast - OK
```

The first line produces an error message because floating-point literals are always **double.** The cast operation makes the error message go away (and it is clear in this case that there is no loss of precision, as the number does not have many significant digits).

As a second example, consider the program **Seven.cs** from earlier in the chapter (see **Seven\CSharp**).

```
char seven = '7';
short number;
number = seven;
```

There is a problem with the third line, because a **char** cannot be implicitly converted to a **short.** The reason is that **short** is signed and has maximum value 32767, while **char** is unsigned and has maximum value 65535. There are two ways to resolve this problem. One is to perform a cast, and the other is to use the **ushort** data type in place of **short** for the variable **number.**

The program **Conversions** illustrates a number of implicit and explicit conversions. The last part of the program converts the **bool** values of **true** and **false** to an integer data type, showing (as one might expect) that the numerical value corresponding to **true** is 1, while **false** corresponds to zero. Note that in this case casting does not work, and we must perform the conversion by another technique, which we will discuss in Chapter 15. Casting is applicable to similar data types, but **bool** and **int** are conceptually completely different kinds of data types. For example, you cannot perform arithmetic operations on **bool.** (You do perform logical operations, which we will discuss in Chapter 5.)

```
// Conversions.cs

using System;

public class Conversions
{
    public static int Main(string[] args)
    {
        // float pi = 3.14;            // compiler error
        float pi = (float) 3.14;
        Console.WriteLine("pi = " + pi);
        // short seven = '7';          // compiler error
        short seven = (short) '7';     // cast
        ushort useven = '7';           // ok
        Console.WriteLine("seven = " + seven);
        Console.WriteLine("useven = " + useven);
        // int itrue = (int) true;     // cast fails
        int itrue = Convert.ToInt32(true);
        int ifalse = Convert.ToInt32(false);
        Console.WriteLine("itrue = " + itrue);
        Console.WriteLine("ifalse = " + ifalse);
        return 0;
    }
}
```

Here is the output from the program:

```
pi = 3.14
seven = 55
useven = 55
itrue = 1
ifalse = 0
```

SUMMARY

This chapter discussed the important topic of data types. C# is a strongly typed language, which contributes to program reliability, but also means that you, as a programmer, sometimes have to be concerned with explicit instructions to the compiler. We looked at the five simple data types in C#: integer, floating-point, decimal, character, and boolean. We concluded with a discussion of conversion among the simple data types, including conversion that is done implicitly and conversion that is done by casting. In Chapter 5 we will look at operations that can be performed on these simple data types. In Chapter 9 we will discuss the rest of the data types in C#, and in Chapter 15 we will consider more issues in conversion among data types and in formatting.

Operators and Expressions

The C family of languages is blessed with an exceptionally rich set of operators, including unary and binary operators and a special ternary operator. This chapter surveys all the important operators in C# that are applied to simple data types: arithmetic, relational, logical, bitwise, and assignment. We also discuss expressions and the associativity and precedence rules for operators in C#, and present the complete C# precedence table. During our discussion of individual operations, we look at some exceptional conditions (e.g., division by zero and overflow) and we describe checked and unchecked arithmetic.

OPERATOR CARDINALITY

Operators in C# can be classified by the number of operands to which they apply, a property that is sometimes known as *operator cardinality*.

- *Unary* operators take a single operand. A simple example is unary minus, which changes the sign of a number.
- *Binary* operators are the most common and take two operands. Examples include simple arithmetic such as addition and subtraction.
- C# has one *ternary* operator, which produces one of two results, depending on the value of a boolean expression.

ARITHMETIC OPERATORS

The arithmetic operators include the four classic operations of addition, subtraction, multiplication, and division, and the remainder operator. These operations may be applied to any of the numerical data types of integer, floating-point, and decimal. We will first examine each of these operators in the "pure" case, where the operands are of the same data type, and then we'll look at the "mixed" case, where operands are of different data types and some kind of conversion must be performed before the operation can be carried out. As we go along, we will also look at a few exceptional conditions, such as overflow (result too big), underflow (result too small), and division by zero.

Our order of discussion begins with the multiplicative operators (multiplication, division, and remainder), which have a higher precedence than the additive operators (addition and subtraction). We discuss precedence in detail later in this chapter.

Multiplicative Operators

There are three multiplicative operators, * (multiplication), / (division), and % (remainder). These are all binary operators and can be applied to all the numerical data types. We will look at these individually and examine some of the exceptional conditions.

MULTIPLICATION

The most important thing to remember about integer multiplication is that the actual multiply operation is applied to 32-bit or 64-bit integers. The compiler will silently convert to a wider type if necessary. Floating-point multiplication can be done between two floats or two doubles (mixed case is discussed later). And of course there is only one **decimal** data type.

The only real pitfall in multiplication is the case of overflow, where the result exceeds the size of the operands, and the three data types all behave differently in this regard! Integer multiply will silently drop bits and not warn you. Floating-point will produce the special result **Infinity**, as discussed in Chapter 4. Decimal overflow will throw an **OverflowException**. The program **Multiply** illustrates all three cases. (Exceptions are breaks in the normal flow of program execution, which can be caught by special pieces of code called exception handlers. We will discuss C# exception handling in Chapter 16.)

```
// Multiply.cs

using System;

public class Multiply
{
   public static int Main(string[] args)
   {
      int x = 99999;
      int y = 99999;
      int z = x * y;
      Console.WriteLine("{0} * {1} = {2}", x, y, z);

      float f1 = 1.0E20f;
      float f2 = 1.0E20f;
      Console.WriteLine("{0} * {1} = {2}", f1, f2, f1*f2);

      decimal d1 = 1.0E15m;
      decimal d2 = 1.0E15m;
      Console.WriteLine("{0} * {1} = {2}", d1, d2, d1*d2);
      return 0;
   }
}
```

Here is the result of running the program:

```
99999 * 99999 = 1409865409
1E20 * 1E20 = Infinity

Exception occurred: System.OverflowException: Value was
either too large or too small for a Decimal.
   at System.Decimal.Multiply(Decimal d1, Decimal d2)
   at System.Decimal.op_Multiply(Decimal d1, Decimal d2)
   at Multiply.Main(String[] args) in
c:\oi\csharp\chap5\multiply\multiply.cs:line 20
```

DIVISION

Integer division will also be carried out as a 32-bit or 64-bit operation. Since the result must be an integer, the result will be truncated if it does not come out even. The rounding will always be in the direction of zero. Thus,

```
17/5 is 3
17/-5 is -3
```

Division by zero will result in a **DivideByZeroException.** If you happen to divide the largest negative integer by negative one, you will get an **OverflowException,** because the most negative number is one greater in magnitude than the most positive number. The program **IntegerDivision** illustrates some of these examples.

```
// IntegerDivision.cs

using System;

public class IntegerDivision
{
   public static int Main(string[] args)
   {
      Console.WriteLine("{0} / {1} = {2}", 17, 5, 17/5);
      Console.WriteLine("{0} / {1} = {2}", 17, -5, 17/-5);
      int zero = 0;
      Console.Write("{0} / {1} = ", 17, zero);
      Console.WriteLine("{2}", 17/zero);
      return 0;
   }
}
```

Here is the output:

```
17 / 5 = 3
17 / -5 = -3
17 / 0 =
Exception occurred: System.DivideByZeroException: Attempted
to divide by zero.
   at IntegerDivision.Main(String[] args) in
c:\oi\csharp\chap6\integerdivision\integerdivision.cs:line
13
```

Floating point division can be carried out as either **float** or **double**. The result is carried out according to the rules of IEEE 754 arithmetic, and the result may be a number, positive or negative infinity, or NaN, as discussed in Chapter 4.

Decimal division is carried out as **decimal**. Division by zero results in a **DivideByZeroException**. If the result is too large, there is an **OverflowException**. If the result is too small, it is made zero.

REMAINDER

Integer remainder will also be carried out as a 32-bit or 64-bit operation. The remainder is calculated by multiplying the integer quotient by the divisor and subtracting from the original number. Thus,

```
x % y is x - (x/y) * y
17%5 is 2
17%-5 is -2
```

The remainder operation can also be applied to floating-point and decimal numbers and is defined in a similar manner.

Additive Operators

There are two binary operators, **+** (addition) and **−** (subtraction). There are also unary **+** (plus) and unary **−** (minus). Finally there are two operators unique to the C family, the unary increment (**++**) and decrement (**--**) operators. These can be applied to all the numerical data types. We will look at these individually and examine the one possible exceptional condition (overflow).

BINARY ADDITION AND SUBTRACTION

Integer addition and subtraction is always on 32-bit or 64-bit integers. In a **checked** context an overflow will generate an **OverflowException**. In an **unchecked** context any overflow bits will be silently truncated.

Floating-point arithmetic is computed according to the rules of IEEE 754 arithmetic. The result may be an ordinary number, positive or negative infinity, or NaN.

The result of **decimal** arithmetic will throw an **OverflowException** if the result is too large. If the result is too small, it will be made zero.

UNARY PLUS AND MINUS

The unary minus operator (–) is equivalent to subtracting the operand from zero. The unary plus operator (+) is equivalent to a no-op.

INCREMENT AND DECREMENT

The increment and decrement operators are unary and come in two versions, postfix and prefix. Let's look at postfix increment:

```
y = x++;
```

This is equivalent to the following:

```
y = x;
x = x + 1;
```

y is assigned to the current value of **x**, and as a side effect, the value of **x** is incremented. The prefix operation

```
y = ++x;
```

is equivalent to the following:

```
x = x + 1;
y = x;
```

x is incremented first, and this incremented value is assigned to **y**.

The postfix and prefix decrement operators behave in a similar manner.

A Practical Example

Let us use C# to build a little calculator. You can extend what you know now with the **Math** class, which has methods for many mathematical functions, such as exponents, logarithms, and trigonometry. You can take a formula, write an expression for it using C# operators and **Math** methods, and then display the result.

As an illustration, let's compute accumulations in an Individual Retirement Account under compound interest. The program will accept the following inputs:

- Annual Deposit = A
- Interest Rate = R
- Number of Years = N

Assume that a deposit is made at the end of each year and that interest is compounded annually. Use the following formula:

```
Total Accumulation = A * ((1 + R) N - 1) / R
```

Input will be done using the **InputWrapper** class from Chapter 2. The only thing in the formula we can't handle from straight operators is the exponent, raising a quantity to the power N. Investigating the **Math** class (in the **System** namespace), we find the **Pow** method to be what we need. Here is the program:

```
// Ira.cs
//
// Interactive program to compute the total accumulation
// in an Individual Retirement Account under compound
// interest. Assume that a deposit is made at the end of
// each year and that interest is compounded annually.

using System;

public class Ira
{
    public static int Main(string[] args)
    {
        InputWrapper iw = new InputWrapper();
        double amount;   // annual deposit amount
        double rate;     // interest rate
        int years;       // number of years
        double total;    // total accumulation
        amount = iw.getDouble("amount: ");
        rate = iw.getDouble("rate: ");
        years = iw.getInt("years: ");
        total =
            amount * (Math.Pow(1 + rate, years) - 1) / rate;
        long total_in_cents = (long) Math.Round(total * 100);
```

```
        total = total_in_cents /100.0;
        Console.WriteLine("total = {0}", total);
        return 0;
    }
}
```

Here is the output of a sample run.

```
amount: 1000
rate: .05
years: 10
total = 12577.89
```

RELATIONAL OPERATORS

C# has the usual operators for testing equality, inequality, less than, and so on, as shown in Table 5–1. Note that the result of a relational operator is a **bool** value.

| **Table 5–1** | C# Relational Operators |

Operation	Returns true if...
x == y	x equals y
x != y	x is not equal to y
x < y	x is less than y
x <= y	x is less than or equal to y
x > y	x is greater than y
x >= y	x is greater than or equal to y

The key syntactical feature here is the *double equal* for testing equality. It is an error to use a single equal sign.

Equality Relation in C# and in C/C++

A bugbear of programming in C/C++ is the double equal operator. If the programmer uses a single equal operator, the compiler may not complain. (Recent compilers may give a warning.) For example, the following code compiles in C/C++.

```
if (x = y)
{
    ...
```

When the program runs, x will be assigned to the value y, and the result will be used to evaluate the **if** condition. If the value is non-zero, it evaluates to true, otherwise to false. This problem does not arise in C#, because **if** tests and similar constructs apply to a **bool**, and there is no implicit conversion from a numerical data type to a **bool** data type.

This classic problem has disappeared in C#!

The program **Relational** demonstrates use of the relational operators in C#. Note that the line that is commented out will not compile in C#. In C/C++ that line will compile, but will produce a logic error.

```
// Relational.cs

using System;

public class Relational
{
    public static int Main(string[] args)
    {
        int x = 17;
        int y = 5;
        //bool result = (x = y);
        Console.WriteLine("{0} == {1} = {2}", x, y, x == y);
        Console.WriteLine("{0} != {1} = {2}", x, y, x != y);
        Console.WriteLine("{0} < {1} = {2}", x, y, x < y);
        Console.WriteLine("{0} <= {1} = {2}", x, y, x <= y);
        Console.WriteLine("{0} > {1} = {2}", x, y, x > y);
        Console.WriteLine("{0} >= {1} = {2}", x, y, x >= y);
        return 0;
    }
}
```

Here is the output from the program:

```
17 == 5 = False
17 != 5 = True
17 < 5 = False
17 <= 5 = False
17 > 5 = True
17 >= 5 = True
```

CONDITIONAL LOGICAL OPERATORS

You can combine **bool** values by means of the logical operators **&&** (AND), **||** (inclusive OR), and ! (NOT). The first two operators are binary, and the third is unary. You can exhaustively specify the outcome of a logical operation by means of a truth table. The following truth tables apply to AND (Table 5–2), inclusive OR (Table 5–3), and NOT (Table 5–4).

Table 5–2   *Truth Table for AND*

x	y	x && y
false	false	false
false	true	false
true	false	false
true	true	true

Table 5–3   *Truth Table for OR*

x	y	x || y
false	false	false
false	true	true
true	false	true
true	true	true

Table 5–4   *Truth Table for NOT*

x	! x
false	true
true	false

Short Circuit Evaluation

An important feature of the logical operations is that they are evaluated from left to right, and evaluation stops as soon as the truth or falsity is determined. As an example, consider the program **ShortCircuit.**

```
// ShortCircuit.cs

using System;

public class ShortCircuit
{
   public static int Main(string[] args)
   {
      int x = 4;
      int y = 5;
      Console.WriteLine("x = {0}, y = {1}", x, y);
      bool result = true || (++x == y);
      Console.WriteLine("result = {0}", result);
      Console.WriteLine("x = {0}, y = {1}", x, y);

      result = true && (++x == y);
      Console.WriteLine("result = {0}", result);
      Console.WriteLine("x = {0}, y = {1}", x, y);
      return 0;
   }
}
```

Before running the program, try to reason out what the output will be. Your first job is to figure out what the first **result** will be. You may be puzzling over pre-increment and post-increment to determine the truth or falsity of **(++x == y)**, but wait! It doesn't matter! You are doing an OR with **true,** and the result is always **true,** no matter what the second operand is. (See Table 5–3). Thus the second operand is not evaluated, and there is no side effect changing the value of **x.** You should now be able to understand the output:

```
x = 4, y = 5
result = True
x = 4, y = 5
result = True
x = 5, y = 5
```

Ternary Conditional Operator

C# has kept the unusual C **ternary** operator **?:** that takes three operands. This "conditional" operator is used to assign a value based on a condition (true or false). A conditional expression is written as

```
expr1 ? expr2 : expr3
```

The **bool** expression **expr1** is evaluated first. If it evaluates to **true**, the overall expression evaluates to **expr2**; otherwise, to **expr3**. The program **AbsoluteValue** will calculate the absolute value of a number:

```
// AbsoluteValue.cs

using System;

public class AbsoluteValue
{
   public static int Main(string[] args)
   {
      int x = 5;
      int abs = (x < 0) ? -x : x;
      Console.WriteLine("x = {0}, abs = {1}", x, abs);
      x = -x;
      abs = (x < 0) ? -x : x;
      Console.WriteLine("x = {0}, abs = {1}", x, abs);
      return 0;
   }
}
```

Here is the output:

```
x = 5, abs = 5
x = -5, abs = 5
```

BITWISE OPERATORS

C# has a number of *bitwise* operators that can be used for bit manipulation. This feature is a heritage of the original problem domain of the programming language C—systems programming—where bit twiddling was an important requirement. There are two kinds of bitwise operators:

- Bitwise logical AND, OR, XOR (exclusive or), and NOT, sometimes called "masking" operators
- Shift operators (right shift and left shift).

Table 5–5 summarizes the bitwise operators in C#.

Table 5–5	Truth Table for XOR
Operation	**Description**
~	Bitwise NOT
&	Bitwise AND
|	Bitwise OR
^	Bitwise XOR
<<	Left Shift
>>	Right Shift

Bitwise Logical Operators

Unlike the conditional logical operators, which apply only to the **bool** data type, the bitwise logical operators apply to the integer data types as well as **bool**. When applied to **bool** operands, the truth table definitions for the bitwise logical operations are identical to those for the conditional logical operations. The difference is that the conditional logical operators do short circuit evaluation, and the bitwise logical operators do not. The exclusive or XOR operator ^ is only available in bitwise form.

When applied to an integer data type, the operation is applied to each individual bit, with 0 equivalent to **false** and 1 equivalent to **true**. The truth table for the XOR operator ^ is shown in Table 5–6.

Table 5–6	Truth Table for XOR	
x	**y**	**x ^ y**
0	0	0
0	1	1
1	0	1
1	1	0

Shift Operators

The shift operators take two operands. The first operand specifies the value whose bits are to be shifted, and the second operand specifies how many positions to shift.

```
a = b << n;    // shift n positions to the left,
               // equivalent to multiplying by 2 n times

a = b >> n;    // shift n positions to right and extend
               // sign, equivalent to dividing by 2
               // n times
```

The first operand is a 32-bit or 64-bit integer, and the second operand is an **int.** If a shift operator is applied to a shorter integer data type, the first operand is promoted to a 32-bit integer prior to shifting.

The program **Shift** illustrates shifting to the left and to the right for both positive and negative numbers. The helper method **WriteBinary** makes use of a simple loop. (We discuss loops in Chapter 6). Note that negative numbers have the leading bit ("sign bit") 1, and positive numbers have the leading bit 0.

```csharp
// Shift.cs

using System;

public class Shift
{
    public static int Main(string[] args)
    {
        int x = 30;
        Console.WriteLine("Original Number");
        WriteBinary(x);
        Console.WriteLine("   {0}", x);

        Console.WriteLine("Shifting Left");
        WriteBinary(x << 1);
        Console.WriteLine("   {0}", x << 1);
        WriteBinary(x << 2);
        Console.WriteLine("   {0}", x << 2);
        WriteBinary(x << 3);
        Console.WriteLine("   {0}", x << 3);

        Console.WriteLine("Shifting Right");
        WriteBinary(x >> 1);
        Console.WriteLine("   {0}", x >> 1);
        WriteBinary(x >> 2);
        Console.WriteLine("   {0}", x >> 2);
        WriteBinary(x >> 3);
        Console.WriteLine("   {0}", x >> 3);

        x = -30;
        Console.WriteLine("Original Number");
        WriteBinary(x);
        Console.WriteLine("   {0}", x);

        Console.WriteLine("Shifting Left");
        WriteBinary(x << 1);
        Console.WriteLine("   {0}", x << 1);
        WriteBinary(x << 2);
        Console.WriteLine("   {0}", x << 2);
        WriteBinary(x << 3);
        Console.WriteLine("   {0}", x << 3);
```

```
        Console.WriteLine("Shifting Right");
        WriteBinary(x >> 1);
        Console.WriteLine("    {0}", x >> 1);
        WriteBinary(x >> 2);
        Console.WriteLine("    {0}", x >> 2);
        WriteBinary(x >> 3);
        Console.WriteLine("    {0}", x >> 3);
        return 0;
    }
    private static void WriteBinary(int x)
    {
        for (int i = 0; i < 32; i++)
        {
            if (x < 0)
                Console.Write("1");
            else
                Console.Write("0");
            x <<= 1;
        }
    }
}
```

Here is the output:

```
Original Number
00000000000000000000000000011110    30
Shifting Left
00000000000000000000000000111100    60
00000000000000000000000001111000    120
00000000000000000000000011110000    240
Shifting Right
00000000000000000000000000001111    15
00000000000000000000000000000111    7
00000000000000000000000000000011    3
Original Number
11111111111111111111111111100010    -30
Shifting Left
11111111111111111111111111000100    -60
11111111111111111111111110001000    -120
11111111111111111111111100010000    -240
Shifting Right
11111111111111111111111111110001    -15
11111111111111111111111111111000    -8
11111111111111111111111111111100    -4
```

ASSIGNMENT OPERATORS

The basic assignment operator in C# is = and is used to assign a value to a variable. It has the form

```
variable = expression;
```

The expression is formed by combining operators with constant and variable operands, and can become quite complicated. We will discuss the rules for evaluating expressions in the next section. Once the expression is evaluated, its value is assigned to the variable.

Note that an assignment is itself an expression and can be used on the right-hand side of another assignment or in other usages. Thus evaluating an assignment can change a variable as a side effect. As an example, consider the following:

```
int x = 30;
int y = 5;
int z = 1;
x = (y = z++) + 60;
```

What will be the value of x, y, and z after the assignment? The program **Assign** illustrates. Here is the output:

```
x = 30, y = 5, z = 1
After x = (y = z++) + 60;
x = 61, y = 1, z = 2
```

Compound Assignment

A *compound assignment* performs a binary operation as part of the assignment. Here is an example:

```
x = 5;
x += 2;        // equivalent to x = x + 2;
```

There are 10 compound assignment operators in all, as shown in Table 5–7.

Table 5–7	Compound Assignment Operators
Description	**Operators**
Arithmetic	*=, /=, %=, +=, -=
Shift	<<=, >>=
Bitwise	&=, ^=, |=

EXPRESSIONS

Expressions are built up by combining constants and variables, using operators. The result of one operation can be an operand in another operation, and in this way expressions of great complexity can be created. When evaluating expressions, the C# compiler follows rules as to the order of operations, and these rules are summarized in a *precedence* table. A simple example of precedence is addition and multiplication. Multiplication is done first. If you want the order done in another way, you can use parentheses to override the standard order. Here is a simple example:

```
x = 5 * 8 + 13;          // result is 53, multiply first
x = 5 * (8 + 13);        // result is 105, add first
```

As a practical matter, in your programs you should learn to use a few of the most common precedence rules. Good use of precedence allows clearer code. Don't feel that you must memorize all of the precedence rules. When in doubt, put in parentheses.

Associativity

When an operand occurs between two operators at the same precedence level, the *associativity* of the operator controls the order of evaluation. Most operators associate left-to-right. Here is an example:

```
int n = 60 / 5 / 2;      // first 60/5 = 12, then 12/2 = 6
int n = 60 / (5 / 2);    // first 5/2 = 2, then 60/2 = 30
```

The only operators that are right-associative are the assignment operators and the conditional operator **?:**. For example,

```
x = y = z;     // evaluates as x = (y = z);
```

Precedence Table

Table 5–8 gives the complete precedence table for all of C#. It includes operators we have not discussed yet. The table summarizes all operators in precedence order, from highest to lowest. Operations at the same level are performed in the order of their associativity, normally left-to-right, as discussed previously. You may override the precedence order via parentheses.

Table 5–8	*Operator Precedence in C#*
Category	**Operators**
Primary	(x) x.y f(x) a[x] x++ x-- new typeof sizeof checked unchecked
Unary	= - ! ~ ++x --x (T)x
Multiplicative	* / %
Additive	+ -
Shift	<< >>
Relational	< > <= >= is as
Equality	== !=
Logical AND	&
Logical XOR	^
Logical OR	|
Conditional AND	&&
Conditional OR	||
Conditional	?:
Assignment	= *= /= %= += -= <<= >>= &= ^= |=

CHECKED AND UNCHECKED

C# allows you to control compile and runtime checking of various arithmetic operations. As an example, consider integer multiply and the possibility of overflow. The default behavior is to do compile time checking but not runtime checking. You can turn off compile time checking with the **unchecked** operator applied to an expression computed at compile time. The program **Unchecked** provides an illustration. Two large numbers are multiplied together, and the result overflows the 32-bit **int** data type, but no compile time or runtime error messages are issued.

```csharp
// Unchecked.cs

using System;

public class Unchecked
{
    public static int Main(string[] args)
    {
        int x = 99999;
        int y = 99999;
```

```
        int z = unchecked (99999 * 99999);
        Console.WriteLine("compiled: {0}*{1} = {2}",x,y,z);
        z = x * y;
        Console.WriteLine("runtime: {0}*{1} = {2}",x,y,z);
        return 0;
    }
}
```

Here is the output:

```
compiled: 99999*99999 = 1409865409
runtime: 99999*99999 = 1409865409
```

Compile time checking has been turned off, and by default the compiler does not generate code to check for integer overflow. You may use the **/checked+** compile option to turn on runtime overflow checking. Here is the result of compiling and running the same program with this compiler switch:

```
C:\OI\CSharp\Chap5\Unchecked>csc unchecked.cs /checked+
Microsoft (R) Visual C# Compiler Version 7.00.9030 [CLR ver-
sion 1.00.2204.21]
Copyright (C) Microsoft Corp 2000. All rights reserved.


C:\OI\CSharp\Chap5\Unchecked>unchecked
compiled: 99999*99999 = 1409865409

Exception occurred: System.OverflowException: An exception
of type System.OverflowException was thrown.
    at Unchecked.Main(String[] args)
```

Using the **/checked+** compiler switch turns on runtime overflow checking everywhere. You can selectively turn on overflow checking for selected computations, using the **checked** operator:

```
z = checked (x * y);
```

A complete illustration is provided by the **Checked** program. When you build this program, notice the error message of an overflow at compile time.

You can also use **checked** and **unchecked** as statements, applying to a group of statements within a block:

```
checked

{
    z = x + 1;
    z = x * y;
}
```

SUMMARY

This chapter discussed the simple operators in C#, which is a rather large subject, as there are so many of them, including unary and binary operators and a special ternary operator. We looked at all the important operators in C# that are applied to simple data types: arithmetic, relational, logical, bitwise, and assignment. We also discussed expressions and the associativity and precedence rules for operators in C#, and presented the complete C# precedence table. We examined some of the exceptional conditions, such as overflow, that can arise. In the next chapter we will conclude our survey of the C-like features of C# by discussing C# control structures. We will also look at the C# exception-handling mechanism.

Control Structures

*The C family of languages has a fairly standard set of control structures that are common to languages supporting structured programming. In this chapter we survey these structures, which include if tests, while loops, for loops, and do loops. We preview arrays, which will be used in several of our example programs. For easy programming of arrays, we introduce the C# **foreach** loop, which is available in Visual Basic but not in most C family languages. There are also break, continue, and goto statements for altering control flow. Finally we discuss the **switch** statement, which is somewhat more robust than in classic C/C++.*

If you are experienced with any structured programming language, you should be able to breeze through this chapter (but as usual, pay attention to the sidebars). If you are at an early stage in your programming career (or are a college student), you should find the step-by-step descriptions and example programs very helpful.

IF TESTS

In an *if* test a **bool** expression is evaluated, and depending on the result, the "true branch" or "false branch" is executed.

```
if (expression)
      statement 1;
else
      statement 2;
statement 3;
```

If expression evaluates to true, statement 1 will be executed (true branch). If expression evaluates to false, statement 2 will be executed (false branch). In either case statement 3 will be subsequently executed. This example of an if test is a particular case of "control structures," which alter the flow of control in a program.

If tests are sometimes represented in a flowchart, by using a diamond symbol. See Figure 6–1.

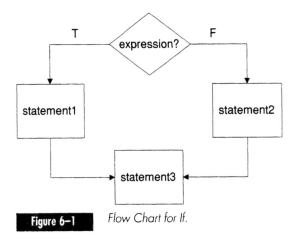

Figure 6–1   *Flow Chart for If.*

As an example, consider a C# program **LeapYear** that will read a year and determine whether it is a leap year. The basic algorithm is that years divisible by 4 are leap years. There are two exceptions: years divisible by 100 are not leap years, except years divisible by 400, which are leap years.

```
// LeapYear.cs
//
// Leap year program with accurate algorithm
// We say that N is a leap year if N is divisible by 4
// AND (N is divisible by 400 OR N is not divisible by 100)

using System;

public class LeapYear
{
    public static int Main(string[] args)
    {
```

```
        InputWrapper iw = new InputWrapper();
        int year = iw.getInt("year: ");
        if ((year % 4 == 0) &&
            ((year % 400 == 0) || (year % 100 != 0)))
            Console.WriteLine("{0} is a leap year", year);
        else
            Console.WriteLine("{0} is not a leap year", year);
        return 0;
    }
}
```

Here is some output from running the program four times, with sets of years that will exercise all the cases:

```
year: 2001
2001 is not a leap year
year: 1996
1996 is a leap year
year: 1900
1900 is not a leap year
year: 2000
2000 is a leap year
```

Single Branch If

A variation of the if statement is the case where there is only one branch:

```
if (expression)
        statement 1;
statement 2;
```

If expression evaluates to true, statement 1 will be executed, followed by statement 2. If expression evaluates to false, statement 2 will be executed directly.

Blocks

The "statement" after **if** or **else** may in fact be several statements inside a *block*, or a *compound statement*. In C# a block is delimited by curly braces. Inside the block there may be several statements separated by semicolons. The block itself appears from outside like a single statement.

A variable declared inside a block is visible only within that block and is said to have *block scope*. Local variables inside a block are allocated on the stack (see sidebar) and are popped from the stack and deallocated when leaving the block.

Variables of Value Type

In C# there are variables of *value* type and variables of *reference* type. Variables of value type are allocated on the stack and are automatically deallocated when the *stack* is popped, but variables of reference type are allocated on the *heap* and will not be deallocated until done so by the system garbage collector. Value types and reference types are discussed in Chapter 9.

The program **Swap** illustrates a block and the declaration of a local variable **temp** within the block. An attempt to use the variable outside the block is a compiler error.

```
// Swap.cs

using System;

public class Swap
{
    public static int Main(string[] args)
    {
        int x = 5;
        int y = 12;
        Console.WriteLine("Before: x = {0}, y = {1}", x, y);
        if (x < y)
        {
            int temp = x;
            x = y;
            y = temp;
        }
        Console.WriteLine("After: x = {0}, y = {1}", x, y);
        // Console.WriteLine("temp = {0}", temp);
        return 0;
    }
}
```

The block is shown in bold. An attempt to access the variable **temp** outside the block produces a compiler error message. Here is the output:

```
Before: x = 5, y = 12
After: x = 12, y = 5
```

LOOPS

Loops are a fundamental part of computer programming. A loop enables a program to perform actions repetitively. Since a computer can perform a single action with great speed, being able to repeat actions gives a computer great power. Loops are enabled at the machine code level by means of a branch statement. You branch to an earlier part of your code, and thus a segment of code gets repeated. Loops are enabled in a high-level language like C# by special loop constructs such as **while** and **for.**

While Loop

The most basic type of loop in C# is a **while** loop.

```
while (expression)
{
      statements;
      . . .
}
more statements;
```

The **(bool)** expression is evaluated. If the expression evaluates to **false,** the loop is exited immediately. If the expression evaluates to **true,** the statements in the curly brace are executed, followed by a branch back to the **while** statement.

This looping behavior continues until the expression evaluates to **false,** and then the loop exits, and execution continues with the statements after the loop. Note that there must be code within the curly braces to change the value of the expression, or you will have an *infinite loop.*

As an example, consider the program **LeapYearLoop**, which reads years and determines whether the year is a leap year. After one year is processed, another year is entered. You enter –1 to terminate the program.

```
// LeapYearLoop.cs
//
// Loop to read in years and determine whether year
// entered is a leap year.
// -1 is entered to terminate the program
using System;

public class LeapYearLoop
{
  public static int Main(string[] args)
  {
    InputWrapper iw = new InputWrapper();
    int year = iw.getInt("year: ");
    while (year != -1)
    {
      if ((year % 4 == 0) &&
          ((year % 400 == 0) || (year % 100 != 0)))
        Console.WriteLine("{0} is a leap year", year);
      else
        Console.WriteLine("{0} is not a leap year", year);
```

```
        year = iw.getInt("year: ");
    }
    return 0;
  }
}
```

INFINITE LOOPS

The **LeapYearLoop** example is not an infinite loop, because at the bottom of the body of the loop, there is an input of new year. As an experiment, comment out the input statement at the bottom of the loop, recompile, and run again.

```
while (year != -1)
{
  if ((year % 4 == 0) &&
      ((year % 400 == 0) || (year % 100 != 0)))
      Console.WriteLine("{0} is a leap year", year);
  else
      Console.WriteLine("{0} is not a leap year", year);
  // year = iw.getInt("year: ");
}
```

To get out of the infinite loop, try Ctrl+C. Another approach (in Windows) is to use Task Manager to exit out of the Command Prompt, or (last resort) reboot the system. You should always save your source files before testing your program!

FLOWCHARTING A WHILE LOOP

Figure 6–2 shows a flowchart for a while loop. You keep looping while the expression is true, and you exit when the expression becomes false. Note that the statement can be a simple statement or a block.

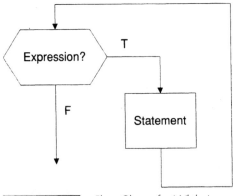

Figure 6-2   *Flow Chart of a While Loop.*

INDENTING AND CURLY BRACES

As a good programming practice, you should indent statements inside a loop. But indenting by itself does not group the statements together.

```
int number = 3;
while (number >= 3)
      Console.WriteLine("number = {0}", number);
      --number;
...
```

The above is an infinite loop, because the decrement is not inside the loop. Use curly braces!

```
int number = 3;
while (number >= 3)
{
      Console.WriteLine("number = {0}", number);
      --number;
}
...
```

SENTINELS

There are two common ways to exit a loop. The first method is to use a special input value called a *sentinel* to test for "end-of-file." Our **LeapYearLoop** program used –1 as a sentinel.

```
while (year != -1)
{
   if ((year % 4 == 0) &&
       ((year % 400 == 0) || (year % 100 != 0)))
       Console.WriteLine("{0} is a leap year", year);
   else
       Console.WriteLine("{0} is not a leap year", year);
   year = iw.getInt("year: ");
}
```

COUNTED LOOPS

The second way to exit a loop is to use a *counter.*

* Initialize the counter (usually to 0).
* Loop test compares counter to the number of iterations desired.
* Counter is incremented each time through the loop.

```
counter = 0;
while (counter < number_of_iterations)
{
```

```
      . . .
   ++counter;
}
```

   The program **LeapYearCounter** illustrates using a counter with a while loop. The user is prompted for a count of how many years to test.

```
// LeapYearCounter.cs
//
// Loop to read in years and determine whether year
// entered is a leap year.
// A counter is used to control number of years processed

using System;

public class LeapYearCounter
{
  public static int Main(string[] args)
  {
    InputWrapper iw = new InputWrapper();
    int count = iw.getInt("count: ");
    int i = 0;
    while (i < count)
    {
      int year = iw.getInt("year: ");
      if ((year % 4 == 0) &&
          ((year % 400 == 0) || (year % 100 != 0)))
          Console.WriteLine("{0} is a leap year", year);
      else
          Console.WriteLine("{0} is not a leap year", year);
      i++;
    }
    return 0;
  }
}
```

For Loops

C# has a special kind of loop called a **for** loop that is convenient for counters. The **for** loop is very flexible, but we will focus on using it to implement a counted loop.

```
for (initialization; test; iteration)
{
      statements;
      . . .
}
more statements;
```

1. Initialization is performed (e.g., **counter = 0**).

2. Test is made for loop termination (e.g., **counter < num_iter**).

3. Body of loop is executed.

4. Iteration is performed (e.g., **++counter**) and branch back to top of loop.

The iteration step could be either an increment or a decrement.

The example program **ForUp** illustrates calculating the sum of the numbers from 1 to 100 using a **for** loop with the counter going up. Notice that in this loop the variable **i** is defined within the loop and hence is not available outside the loop.

```
// ForUp.cs

using System;

public class ForUp
{
    public static int Main(string[] args)
    {
        int sum = 0;
        for (int i = 1; i <= 100; i++)
        {
            sum += i;
        }
        Console.WriteLine("sum = {0}", sum);
        // Console.WriteLine("i = {0}", i);
        // i is not defined outside the for loop
        return 0;
    }
}
```

The example **ForDown** illustrates calculating the sum of the numbers from 1 to 100 using a **for** loop with the counter going down. Notice that in this loop the variable **i** is defined before the loop and hence is available outside the loop.

```
// ForDown.cs

using System;

public class ForDown
{
    public static int Main(string[] args)
    {
        int sum = 0;
        int i;
        for (i = 100; i >= 1; i--)
        {
```

```
        sum += i;
    }
    Console.WriteLine("sum = {0}", sum);
    Console.WriteLine("i = {0}", i);
    // i is defined outside the for loop
    return 0;
    }
}
```

Do Loops

A variation of the **while** loop is the **do** loop, with a **while** test at the bottom of the loop.

```
do
{
        . . .
} while (expression);
```

The body of the loop is always executed at least once. If the **bool** expression after the **while** at the bottom evaluates to **true**, the loop will be executed again.

The **do** loop is used less frequently than **while** and **for**, because you usually want to allow for the special case of "empty" execution, which is provided naturally by **while** and **for.**

PREVIEW OF ARRAYS AND FOREACH

We will discuss arrays in detail in Part 3. Arrays are a very common and easy-to-use data structure in many programming languages, and they are useful for illustrating programs involving loops. Hence we will give a brief preview here, so that we can provide more interesting examples for the rest of the chapter.

An array is declared using square brackets [] after the type, not after the variable.

```
int [] a;      // declares an array of int
```

Note that the size of the array is not part of its type. The variable declared is a reference to the array. You create the array elements and establish the size of the array using the **new** operator.

```
a = new int[10];          // creates 10 array elements
```

The new array elements start out with the appropriate default values for the type (0 for **int**). You may both declare and initialize array elements using curly brackets, as in C/C++.

```
int a[] = {2, 3, 5, 7, 11};
```

As our first example, we will populate a 10-element array with the first 10 Fibonacci numbers. The Fibonacci sequence is defined as follows:

```
fib[0] = 1
fib[1] = 1
fib[i] = fib[i-1] + fib[i-2] for i >= 2
```

The program **Fibonacci** populates the array and then prints out the first 10 Fibonacci elements all on one line, followed by printing them out in reverse order on the next line.

```
// Fibonacci.cs

using System;

public class Fibonacci
{
    public static int Main(string[] args)
    {
        int [] fib;
        fib = new int[10];
        fib[0] = fib[1] = 1;
        for (int i = 2; i < 10; i++)
            fib[i] = fib[i-1] + fib[i-2];

        for (int i = 0; i < 10; i++)
            Console.Write("{0} ", fib[i]);
        Console.WriteLine();

        for (int i = 9; i >= 0 ; i--)
            Console.Write("{0} ", fib[i]);
        Console.WriteLine();
        return 0;
    }
}
```

Here is the output:

```
1 1 2 3 5 8 13 21 34 55
55 34 21 13 8 5 3 2 1 1
```

Foreach

Visual Basic programmers are used to a handy kind of loop called **foreach**. This special loop is used for iterating through *collections*. In .NET, collections are available as part of the .NET Framework, and the **foreach** loop is available in some of the .NET languages, including C#. An array is a special kind of collection, so you can use **foreach** to iterate through an array. Note that **foreach** does not give you control over the direction in which you iterate. The example program **ForEachLoop** initializes an array with some fixed elements, and then displays the elements and calculates their sum. Note how concise the syntax is, without need for any subscripts.

Foreach Loop in C#

If you are a C/C++ programmer, the **foreach** loop may be new to you. It is very convenient! If you are a Visual Basic programmer, you will recognize **foreach** as an old friend.

```csharp
// ForEachLoop.cs

using System;

public class ForEachLoop
{
    public static int Main(string[] args)
    {
        int [] primes = {2, 3, 5, 7, 11, 13};
        int sum = 0;
        foreach (int prime in primes)
        {
            Console.Write("{0} ", prime);
            sum += prime;
        }
        Console.WriteLine();
        Console.WriteLine("sum = {0}", sum);
        return 0;
    }
}
```

Here is the output:

```
2 3 5 7 11 13
sum = 41
```

MORE ABOUT CONTROL FLOW

In this section we will look at several more features of C# that pertain to control flow. The **break** statement allows us to exit a loop prematurely. The **continue** statement bypasses the remaining statements in the body of a loop and causes processing to resume with the next iteration. Finally, we discuss the infamous **goto** statement.

break

The **break** statement allows you to immediately exit a loop. As an example consider the program **BreakSearch**. An array is initialized, and a linear search is made for a target. If the target is found, the loop is exited. At the end, a test is made of the loop index to see the reason for exiting the loop. A normal exit will occur if the loop index is equal to **primes.Length**, the number of elements in the array. (Note the use of the **Length** property of an array. We will discuss the most useful properties and methods of arrays in Chapter 12.) A normal exit means the target was not found. If the target was found, we print out the index at which it was found.

```
// BreakSearch.cs

using System;

public class BreakSearch
{
    public static int Main(string[] args)
    {
        int [] primes = {2, 3, 5, 7, 11, 13};
        foreach (int prime in primes)
            Console.Write("{0} ", prime);
        Console.WriteLine();
        int target = 7;
        int i;
        for(i = 0; i < primes.Length; i++)
        {
            if (target == primes[i])
                break;
        }
        if (i == primes.Length)
            Console.WriteLine("{0} not found", target);
        else
            Console.WriteLine("{0} found at {1}", target,i);
        return 0;
    }
}
```

Here is the output:

```
2 3 5 7 11 13
7 found at 3
```

continue

The **continue** statement allows you to bypass the remaining statements in the loop body and get on with the next iteration. Unlike **break,** this statement does not cause an immediate exit from the loop.

goto

The most primitive form of control in computer programs is the **goto** statement, which corresponds to an unconditional branch in machine code. In early programming languages **goto** was used extensively, which led to complex "spaghetti" code that was hard to understand and hard to maintain. With the emergence of structured programming and higher level control structures such as **if...else** and **while,** it became possible to write programs without **goto,** and the resulting structured programs are generally much easier to understand and to maintain. Some modern languages, such as Java, do not contain a **goto** statement.

   C# has a **goto,** but you should use it rarely, if at all. It could be used to jump all the way out of a nested loop (**break** only exits a single loop). But it is always possible to program without a **goto.** In the next section, we will illustrate a more structured approach. The syntax of **goto** is very simple:

```
goto label;
       ...
label:
       ...
```

The program **GotoSearch** illustrates the syntax of using **goto.**

```
// GotoSearch.cs

using System;

public class GotoSearch
{
   public static int Main(string[] args)
   {
      int [] primes = {2, 3, 5, 7, 11, 13};
      foreach (int prime in primes)
         Console.Write("{0} ", prime);
      Console.WriteLine();
      int target = 7;
      int i;
```

```
        for(i = 0; i < primes.Length; i++)
        {
            if (target == primes[i])
                goto found;
        }
        Console.WriteLine("{0} not found", target);
        return 0;
    found:
        Console.WriteLine("{0} found at {1}", target,i);
        return 0;
    }
}
```

Structured Programming

Although a program like the one shown in the preceding section is easy to understand on a small scale, the structure of such a program is problematical if the same style is carried over to larger programs. The basic difficulty is that there are many execution paths, and so it becomes difficult to verify that the program is correct.

Structured programming imposes certain discipline. Programs are built out of basic components, such as blocks (compound statements), and simple control structures like **if...else** and **while.** Each of these components has a single entrance and a single exit. The program in the preceding section violates these principles in several places. The **Main** function has two exits (**return** statements). The loop can be exited in two ways, normally and via the **goto**. Such a program can become difficult to maintain. If some task needs to always be done before exiting a loop, you may have to place duplicate code, which can become out of synch when this common code is updated in one place.

The program **StructuredSearch** illustrates a more structured programming approach to our simple linear search than either of our previous solutions. Both **break** and **goto** can be replaced by a simple **while** loop and use of a suitable **bool** flag.

```
// StructuredSearch.cs

using System;

public class StructuredSearch
{
    public static int Main(string[] args)
    {
        int [] primes = {2, 3, 5, 7, 11, 13};
        foreach (int prime in primes)
            Console.Write("{0} ", prime);
        Console.WriteLine();
```

```
int target = 7;
int i = 0;
bool found = false;
while (!found && i < primes.Length)
{
   if (target == primes[i])
      found = true;
   else
      i++;
}
if (found)
   Console.WriteLine("{0} found at {1}", target,i);
else
   Console.WriteLine("{0} not found", target);
return 0;
   }
}
```

The **bool** expression in the **while** loop illustrates use of the operator precedence rules. Review Table 5–8 in Chapter 5 to make sure you understand why the expression evaluates properly as written. Also, the example illustrates short-circuit evaluation, because when **found** becomes true, the first part of the AND expression becomes false, and so the whole expression must become **false,** whatever the second part.

SWITCH STATEMENT

You can always use a sequence of **if** statements to distinguish among a group of alternatives, but this situation can sometimes be handled more easily by the **switch** statement. As a simple illustration, consider the following problem: An array contains a series of scores in the range 1 to 5. You are to classify the scores as follows:

* 1 is "Very Low."
* 2 is "Low."
* 3 is "Medium."
* 4 and 5 are "High."
* Any other score is "Special Case."

The program **SwitchDemo** demonstrates the use of the **switch** statement to solve this problem.

```
// SwitchDemo.cs

using System;
```

```
public class SwitchDemo
{
    public static int Main(string[] args)
    {
        int [] scores = {2, 3, 5, 9, 1, 2, 4};
        foreach (int score in scores)
            Console.Write("{0} ", score);
        Console.WriteLine();
        for (int i = 0; i < scores.Length; i++)
        {
            switch(scores[i])
            {
                case 1:
                    Console.Write("Very ");
                    goto case 2;
                case 2:
                    Console.WriteLine("Low");
                    break;
                case 3:
                    Console.WriteLine("Medium");
                    break;
                case 4:
                case 5:
                    Console.WriteLine("High");
                    break;
                default:
                    Console.WriteLine("Special Case");
                    break;
            }
        }
        return 0;
    }
}
```

Here is the output:
```
2 3 5 9 1 2 4
Low
Medium
High
Special Case
Very Low
Low
High
```

The basic structure is to have an expression after **switch** and a series of **case** statements. Control passes to the appropriate case, depending on the value of the expression. After the code for this case, you must have a **break** statement (you will get a compiler error if you forget). If the value of the expression is not among the case values, control will pass to **default.** If rather than exiting the switch after executing one case, you would like to do further processing with code from another case, use a **goto** (illustrated with a score of 1 in our example). If two cases are treated the same, you can simply have no code after the first case (as illustrated with scores 4 and 5).

In C# the **switch** statement expression can be any of the integer data types, **char** and **string**.

C# Improves the Switch Statement Over C/C++

A classic programming error with the class C style **switch** statement is to forget the **break.** This is not a compiler error, but at runtime execution will simply flow to the next case. The C# compiler will catch this problem for you, and if you deliberately want to flow to the next case, you can use a **goto.** Another virtue of the C# **switch** statement is that it allows the switch expression to be of type **string** (which we will discuss later in this book).

SUMMARY

This chapter surveyed all the control structures of C#, including **if, while, do, for,** and **switch.** We also discussed alternative ways of exiting or continuing iteration in a loop, including **break, continue,** and **goto.** We reviewed the principles of structured programming, which avoids use of **goto** and leads to programs that are easier to understand and maintain. We previewed the use of arrays in C#, and used arrays in several of our example programs. We presented a special kind of loop in C#, called the **foreach** loop, that makes it very easy to write concise code for iterating through an array or another collection.

With this chapter, we come to the end of our discussion of the elements of C# that are common to the C family of languages. In Part 3 we take up the object-oriented and component features of C#, beginning with the fundamental concept of *class.*

C# PROGRAMMING FUNDAMENTALS

C # PROGRAMMING
FUNDAMENTALS

Building on its C foundations, C# is a modern, object-oriented language. To be successful with C# or any other object-oriented language, you need to start "thinking in objects," which may not be easy if you are an experienced procedural programmer. Part Three is the core of the book, systematically covering the features of the C# programming language that go beyond C. The object-oriented features of C# are covered gradually and thoroughly, making this part of the book accessible to readers without OOP background. A case study is used, illustrating how the object-oriented features of C# work in combination. This case study is progressively built from chapters 12 to 18. The C# data types, based on the .NET Common Type System, are explored in detail. We cover features new in C#, such as properties and indexers. We cover practical issues of formatting and conversions, and we discuss the important topic of exceptions. We conclude this part with a study of interfaces, which provide a better level of abstraction in expressing system functionality. We will see in Part Four the importance of interfaces in the .NET Framework.

Object-Oriented Programming

The most important feature of C# is that it is a thoroughly object-oriented language, built that way from the ground up. C# enjoys the benefits of other object-oriented languages, such as C++ and Java, and has some additional features that enhance the OOP experience. Beyond being object-oriented, C# is also designed to facilitate the creation of components, *which can be thought of as black-box entities that can be easily reused in creating software systems. In this chapter we look at the big picture of what is object-oriented programming. We discuss objects and classes, abstraction and encapsulation, inheritance, and polymorphism. We provide a survey of some of the more important object-oriented languages, and we see where C# fits in this picture. We conclude with an introduction to components, which extend the ideas of object-oriented programming in a manner that facilitates software reuse.*

OBJECTS

Objects have both a real-world and a software meaning, and an object model can describe a relationship between the two. This section summarizes the key terminology of objects.

Objects in the Real World

The term *object* has an intuitive real-world meaning. There are concrete, tangible objects, such as a ball, an automobile, and an airplane. There are also more abstract objects that have a definite intellectual meaning, such as a committee, a patent, or an insurance contract.

Objects have both attributes (or characteristics) and operations that can be performed upon them. A ball has a size, a weight, a color, and so on. Operations may be performed on the ball, such as throw, catch, and drop.

There can be various relationships among classes of objects. For example, one relationship is a specialization relationship, such as an automobile is a special kind of vehicle. Another relationship is a whole/part relationship, such as an automobile consists of an engine, a chassis, wheels, and other parts.

Object Models

Objects can also be used in programs. Objects are useful in programming because you can set up a software model of a real-world system. Software objects correspond to objects in the real world. Explicitly describing the real-world system in terms of objects helps you to understand the system more explicitly and precisely. The model can then be implemented as actual software using a programming language. A software system implemented in this way tends to be more faithful to the real system, and it can be changed more readily when the real system is changed.

There are formal languages for describing object models. The most popular language is UML (Unified Modeling Language), which is a synthesis of several earlier modeling languages. Formal modeling languages are beyond the scope of this book, but we will find that informal models are useful.

Reusable Software Components

Another advantage of objects in software is that they can facilitate reusable software components. Hardware has long enjoyed significant benefits from reusable hardware components. For example, computers can be created from power supplies, printed circuit boards, and other components. Printed circuit boards in turn can be created from chips. The same chip can be reused in many different computers, and new hardware designs do not have to be done from scratch.

With appropriate software technology, similar reuse is feasible in software systems. Objects provide the foundation for software reuse.

Objects in Software

An *object* is a software entity containing data and related functions as a self-contained module. Objects hold *state* and specify *behavior*. Figure 7–1 illustrates a bank account object. The state of the object consists of the owner of the account, an ID for the account, and the account balance. The behavior of the account consists of functions to deposit or withdraw an amount, to change the owner of the account, and to obtain an account statement. Objects provide the means for *abstraction, encapsulation,* and *instantiation.*

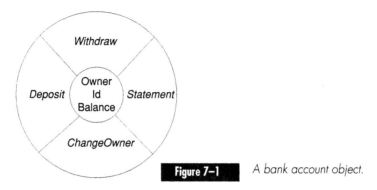

Figure 7–1   *A bank account object.*

State and Behavior

An object has data—a set of properties, or attributes—which are its essential characteristics. The state of an object is the value of these attributes at any point in time. The behavior of an object is the set of operations or responsibilities it must fulfill for itself and for other objects.

The data and operations are packaged together, as illustrated in Figure 7–2. As part of software design, this packaging aids conceptualization and abstraction. Related items are turned into a conceptual unit.

Figure 7–2   *Data and operations are packaged together.*

Abstraction

An *abstraction* captures the essential features of an entity, suppressing unnecessary details. All instances of an abstraction share these common features. Abstraction helps us deal with complexity.

Encapsulation

The implementation of an abstraction should be hidden from the rest of the system, or *encapsulated*. Objects have a public and a private side, as illustrated in Figure 7–3.

```
Public Interface

      Private
```

Figure 7–3   *Objects have a public and a private side.*

The public side is what the rest of the system knows, while the private side implements the public side. Data itself is private, walled off from the rest of the program. Data can only be accessed through functions (or *methods*) with a public interface.

There are two kinds of protection:

* Internal data is protected from corruption.
* Users of the object are protected from changes in the representation.

ENCAPSULATION EXAMPLE

Consider a *Bank* object that has a list of *Account* objects. How do we represent this list of accounts? You could use an array, or a linked list, or several other representations. If you pick a specific representation, say a linked list, and expose this representation to the rest of the system, you will have an overly complicated system. Moreover, the system will be brittle, because with several parts of the system accessing the linked list, it would be possible for a piece of code to make an error in manipulating the links, leaving the list in a corrupted state.

A much better solution is to encapsulate the list within the Bank object and define public methods such as **AddAccount** and **DeleteAccount.** The rest of the system then does not need to be concerned with the details of representation of the list, but simply goes through these public methods.

CLASSES

A *class* groups all objects with common behavior and common structure. A class allows production of new objects of the same type. An object is an instance of some class. We refer to the process of creating an individual object as *instantiation*.

Classes can be related in various ways, such as by *inheritance* and by *containment*.

Inheritance

Inheritance is a key feature of the object-oriented programming paradigm. You abstract out common features of your classes and put them in a high-level base class. You can add or change features in more specialized derived classes, which "inherit" the standard behavior from the base class. Inheritance facilitates code reuse and extensibility.

Consider **Account** as a base class, with derived classes **CheckingAccount** and **SavingsAccount.** All accounts share some characteristics, such as a balance. Different kinds of accounts differ in other respects. For example, a checking account has a monthly fee, while a savings account pays interest at a certain rate. Figure 7–4 illustrates the relationship among these different kinds of accounts.

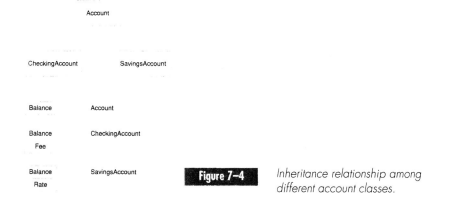

Figure 7–4   *Inheritance relationship among different account classes.*

Relationships Among Classes

Classes may be related to each other in various ways.

* The inheritance (IS-A) relationship specifies how one class is a special case of another class. A **CheckingAccount** (subclass or derived class) is a special kind of **Account** (superclass or base class).
* The composition (HAS-A) relationship specifies how one class (the whole) is made up of other classes (the parts). A **Bank** (whole) has a list of **Account** objects.
* A weaker kind of relationship (USES-A) can be identified when one class merely makes use of some other class when carrying out its responsibilities.

POLYMORPHISM

Consider the problem of generating monthly statements for different kinds of accounts. Checking and savings accounts differ, with one possibly resulting in a fee and the other in a posting of interest.

A traditional approach is to maintain a type field in an account structure and to perform processing in a switch statement, with cases for each type. Such use of switch statements is error prone and requires much maintenance when adding a new account type.

An alternative is to localize the intelligence to generate a statement in each account class, which will support its own **GetStatement** method. Generic monthly statement code can then be written that will handle different types of accounts and will not have to be modified to support an additional account type. Provide a **GetStatement** method in the base class and an override of this method in each derived class. Call **GetStatement** through an object reference to a general **Account** object. Depending on the actual account class referred to, the appropriate **GetStatement** method will be called.

The ability for the same method call to result in different behavior depending on the object through which the method is invoked is referred to as *polymorphism*. Although somewhat advanced, polymorphism can greatly simplify complex systems and is an important part of the object-oriented paradigm.

OBJECT-ORIENTED LANGUAGES [1]

How do you write programs that make use of objects? So-called "data hiding" to achieve encapsulation can be implemented fairly easily in many programming languages. For example, in C you can declare data to be static and thus have file scope. Then you implement various functions in this source file that may access the data. The functions can be called from functions in other source files (they are public), but the data itself is private to the file where it is declared.

It is not quite so easy in C to implement class type behavior, where you can create objects as instances of a class. It can be done through the concept of an opaque "handle" that is used to represent a data object. A special "CreateXXXX" function is implemented to create a particular type of object and return a handle. Internally, a handle table is maintained, which associates a pointer to actual data with a handle. Outside, there is no access to the

---

1. The sections Object-Oriented Languages and Components are taken from the author's book *Understanding and Programming COM+*, Prentice Hall, 2000.

pointer to the data, only to the handle. All functions that manipulate these "objects" take a handle as a parameter. This type of handle architecture is used extensively in the Windows C style API, including extension systems such as ODBC.

Simula and C++

The first use of the class construct in a programming language occurred in 1967 in Norway, in the language Simula, which was derived from Algol. Bjarne Stroustrup, the inventor of C++, used the language Simula in his doctoral research for coding simulation programs he wrote to model computer systems. He found that the Simula language was very expressive and permitted him to work at a high level of abstraction. But when it came time to run the programs to get the numerical results he needed for his thesis, he found that the performance was far too slow, and he would never be able to complete the work in time. So he recoded his programs in C. But he did something very intelligent. In place of handcoding, he wrote a translator program that would take a C-like program with extensions for classes (modeled after Simula) and translate to pure C. The result was a language initially called "C with Classes," later to become C++. The translator program became the AT&T "cfront" compiler, which would translate C++ to C, thus facilitating the creation of C++ compilers for many different kinds of computers (because C itself is implemented on many machines). Later C++ compilers translated directly to machine language for the particular machine. Whether the translation is via a preliminary translation to C via cfront or directly, the end result is compiled machine language code for the target platform. Besides being compiled code, the design of C++ (remember Stroustrup and his need to complete his thesis!) in several ways was steered towards *efficiency*.

Smalltalk

Another important object-oriented language was Smalltalk. Unlike C++, which derived from C, Smalltalk (designed at the Xerox Parc research facility) was created from the ground up as a "pure" object-oriented language. In Smalltalk, everything, even numbers, was implemented as objects. There was an extensive standard class library that was part of the language. There were also very rich program development tools, such as class browsers and debuggers. The result was a very capable program development environment. Smalltalk code was not as efficient as C++, and the programming language quite different from what most programmers were used to. Smalltalk has remained as a niche language. There have been other object-oriented languages that have remained even more as niche players, such as Objective C and Eiffel.

Java

A very popular current language is Java. Java is object-oriented from the ground up but, unlike Smalltalk, takes a more pragmatic approach to native data types, implementing them directly and not as objects. Java compiles into a portable intermediate language called "byte-code" that runs on a Java Virtual Machine, which interprets the bytecode on a particular platform. The result is that the same compiled Java program will run unchanged on many different computers—a feature very desirable in Internet applications. Java comes with a large and rapidly expanding standard class library. A downside of Java is lower performance.

Visual Basic

Visual Basic is not commonly thought of as an object-oriented language, but in fact modern versions of the language are quite object-oriented. The Visual Basic object model is tied closely to Microsoft's Component Object Model (COM) and works very well in a COM environment, both for using COM objects and for creating COM objects. Originally, Visual Basic was interpreted, but later versions can produce compiled code. Visual Basic is exceptionally easy to program.

The newest version of Visual Basic, Visual Basic.NET, is a fully object-oriented language and conforms to the same object model as C#.

C#

The new programming language C# is fully object-oriented and in many respects combines the best elements of C++, Smalltalk, Java, and Visual Basic. C# is closest to Java among other programming languages, and the basic structure of the .NET environment is rather close to the Java environment, with C# and other .NET languages generating an intermediate language, which executes on a virtual machine (the Common Language Runtime). But C# contains some important enhancements. The most significant is that in C# "everything is an object," as in Smalltalk. This uniformity greatly simplifies use of the language, enabling numbers to be treated like objects, stored in collections, and so on. But whereas Smalltalk paid a heavy performance penalty for such uniformity, C# has a unique concept of "boxing" and "unboxing," in which a primitive value like a number can be "boxed" into an object wrapper when there is need for the value to be treated as an object. But for usages where an object is not required, simple values can be efficiently manipulated directly.

Another important innovation of C# is its support of *components*.

COMPONENTS

A few years ago the magazine *BYTE* ran a cover story entitled "Is Object-Oriented Programming Dead?" Inside, they made the point that in many ways "objects" have not lived up to their hype. People had talked about how objects would facilitate code reuse. In fact, objects have been compared to hardware "chips." Great economy is now achieved in hardware engineering by creating computers from chips rather than implementing custom circuitry. It was hoped that similar reuse could be achieved by software objects. But it never happened.

Meanwhile, Microsoft created a language called Visual Basic to simplify programming Windows applications. Central to the Visual Basic approach was drawing various graphical user interface (GUI) elements, or "controls" (like text boxes, list boxes, buttons, etc.) onto a form. These various controls could be attached to little pieces of code that would handle associated events. From the beginning, Microsoft recognized that the built-in controls were nowhere near comprehensive enough to satisfy the needs of Visual Basic programmers. So Microsoft defined a specification for a "VBX" (Visual Basic Extension) custom control. A VBX would plug into the VB development environment and behave just like an ordinary built-in control, but would do the special features designed for it. Like an ordinary control, a VBX had *properties* that could be set and *events* that could be handled by VB code.

Soon there were hundreds and then thousands of VBXs created and sold by independent software vendors. A VBX could be a simple graphical "widget" of some sort or could implement complex functionality such as Windows sockets. Any VBX could be easily plugged into a Visual Basic program.

The *BYTE* article highlighted VBXs as more successful than objects in implementing the dream of reuse. The article raised the hackles of many in the object-oriented community. VBXs were not object-oriented (they lacked even the concept of a method, and they certainly did not support features such as inheritance and polymorphism). But they did facilitate reuse. They were commercially successful.

A VBX can be considered an example (albeit a somewhat crude one) of a software *component*. Loosely, a software component can be thought of as a piece of binary code that can be easily plugged into different applications.

C# and Components

Beyond supporting classical object-oriented programming, C# is designed as a *component-oriented* language. In C# properties, methods, and events are all supported directly by the language, enabling the creation of the easy-to-use pluggable components that have been a characteristic of the Visual Basic environment. Combined with the RAD characteristics of Visual Studio.NET, C# development does indeed offer much of the ease and speed of development of Visual Basic. At the same time, C# is completely object-oriented (even more so than C++), and so C# is extremely powerful.

We will discuss the component-oriented features of C# as we elaborate the features of the language in the coming chapters, and in Chapter 21 we will show how to create the black-box class libraries that are components in the .NET world.

SUMMARY

C# is a thoroughly object-oriented language, built that way from the ground up. In this chapter we surveyed the principal concepts of object-oriented programming, including objects and classes, abstraction and encapsulation, inheritance, and polymorphism. We looked at a number of object-oriented languages and saw the position of C# in this picture. Finally, we briefly examined components, which can be thought of as black-box entities that can be easily reused in creating software systems. C# is a language that is object-oriented and also facilitates creating components. In Chapter 8 we begin our detailed discussion of object-oriented programming in C# with a careful discussion of classes in C#.

Classes

We have seen the important role of classes in object-oriented programming. In this chapter we explain the use of classes in C# for representing structured data, and we review the distinction between objects and classes. C# classes support encapsulation through fields and methods in conjunction with the public and private access specifiers. The **new** operator is used to instantiate objects from classes. We describe the use of references in C# and explain the role of garbage collection. In C# constructors are used to initialize objects. We discuss static members, which apply to the entire class rather than to a particular instance. We examine the use of **const** and **readonly** to specify constants in C# programs.

CLASSES AS STRUCTURED DATA

C# defines primitive data types that are built in to the language, as discussed in Chapter 4. Data types such as **int, decimal,** and **bool** can be used to represent simple data. C# provides the *class* mechanism to represent more complex forms of data. Through a class, you can build up structured data out of simpler elements, which are called data members, or *fields*. (See **TestAccount\Step1.**)

125

```
// Account.cs

public class Account
{
    public int Id;
    public decimal Balance;
}
```

Account is now a new data type. An account has an **Id** (e.g., 1) and a **Balance** (e.g., 100.00).

Classes and Objects

A class represents a "kind of," or type of, data. It is analogous to the built-in types like **int** and **decimal.** A class can be thought of as a template from which individual instances can be created. An instance of a class is called an object. Just as you can have several individual integers that are instances of **int,** you can have several accounts that are instances of **Account**. The fields, such as **Id** and **Balance** in our example, are sometimes also called *instance variables.*

References

There is a fundamental distinction between the primitive data types and the extended data types that can be created using classes. When you declare a variable of a primitive data, you are allocating memory and creating the instance.

```
int x;    // 4 bytes of memory have been allocated
```

When you declare a variable of a class type (an *object reference*), you are only obtaining memory for a *reference* to an object of the class type. No memory is allocated for the object itself, which may be quite large.

```
Account acc;  // acc is a reference to an Account object
              // The object itself does not yet exist
```

Instantiating and Using an Object

You instantiate an object by the **new** operator.

```
acc = new Account();    // Account object now exists
                        // and acc is a reference to it
```

Once an object exists, you work with it, including accessing its fields and methods. Our simple **Account** class at this point has no methods, only two fields. You access fields and methods using a dot.

```
acc.Id = 1;
acc.Balance = 100;      // Fields have now been assigned
Console.WriteLine("Account id {0} has balance {1}",
                     acc.Id, acc.Balance);
```

Here is the complete test program to exercise the **Account** class (you can find the program in the directory **TestAccount\Step1** in the current chapter).

```
// TestAccount.cs

using System;

public class TestAccount
{
   public static void Main(string[] args)
   {
      Account acc;// acc is a reference to an Account object
                  // The object itself does not yet exist
      acc = new Account();  // Account object now exists
                            // and acc is a reference to it
      acc.Id = 1;
      acc.Balance = 100;    // Fields have now been assigned
      Console.WriteLine("Account id {0} has balance {1}",
   acc.Id, acc.Balance);
   }
}
```

Here is the output from running the program:

```
Account id 1 has balance 100
```

Assigning Object References

Figure 8–1 shows the object reference **acc** and the data it refers to after the assignment:

```
acc.Id = 1;
acc.Balance = 100;      // Fields have now been assigned
```

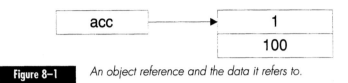

Figure 8-1   *An object reference and the data it refers to.*

Now consider a second object variable referencing a second object, as illustrated in Figure 8–2, after the assignment:

```
Account acc2 = new Account();
acc2.Id = 2;
acc2.Balance = 200;
```

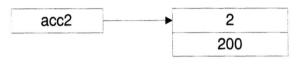

Figure 8-2   *A second object reference and the data it refers to.*

When you assign an object variable, you are only assigning the reference; *there is no copying of data*. Figure 8–3 shows both object references and their data after the assignment:

```
acc2 = acc;   // acc2 now refers to same object acc does
```

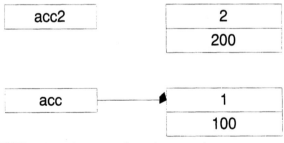

Figure 8-3   *Two references refer to the same data.*

Garbage Collection

Through the assignment of a reference, an object may become orphaned. Such an orphan object (or "garbage") takes up memory in the computer, which can now never be referenced. In Figure 8–3 the account with **Id** of 2 is now garbage.

The Common Language Runtime automatically reclaims the memory of unreferenced objects. This process is known as *garbage collection*. Garbage collection takes up some execution time, but it is a great convenience for programmers, helping to avoid a common program error known as a *memory leak.*

Sample Program

An illustration of assigning object references is provided in **TestAccount\Step2.** We print out the contents of **acc** and **acc2** before and after assigning **acc2** to refer to the same object as **acc.** Once these two references refer to the same object, changing the value of a field will affect them both. Here is the program:

```
// TestAccount.cs - Step2

using System;

public class TestAccount
{
    public static void Main(string[] args)
    {
        Account acc;
        acc = new Account();
        acc.Id = 1;
        acc.Balance = 100;
        Account acc2 = new Account();
        acc2.Id = 2;
        acc2.Balance = 200;
        Console.WriteLine("acc  id {0} has balance {1}",
                          acc.Id, acc.Balance);
        Console.WriteLine("acc2 id {0} has balance {1}",
                          acc2.Id, acc2.Balance);
        acc2 = acc;
        Console.WriteLine("----After acc2 = acc----");
        Console.WriteLine("acc  id {0} has balance {1}",
                          acc.Id, acc.Balance);
        Console.WriteLine("acc2 id {0} has balance {1}",
                          acc2.Id, acc2.Balance);
        acc.Balance = 150;
        Console.WriteLine("----After acc.Balance = 150----");
        Console.WriteLine("acc  id {0} has balance {1}",
                          acc.Id, acc.Balance);
        Console.WriteLine("acc2 id {0} has balance {1}",
                          acc2.Id, acc2.Balance);
    }
}
```

Here is the output:

```
acc  id 1 has balance 100
acc2 id 2 has balance 200
```

```
-----After acc2 = acc-----
acc  id 1 has balance 100
acc2 id 1 has balance 100
-----After acc.Balance = 150-----
acc  id 1 has balance 150
acc2 id 1 has balance 150
```

METHODS

Typically, a class will specify *behavior* as well as data. A class *encapsulates* data and behavior in a single entity. A method consists of

- An access specifier, typically **public** or **private**
- A return type (can be **void** if the method does not return data)
- A method name, which can be any legal C# identifier
- A parameter list, enclosed by parentheses, which specifies data that is passed to the method (can be empty if no data is passed)
- A method body, enclosed by curly braces, which contains the C# code that the method will execute

```
public void Deposit(decimal amount)
{
   balance += amount;
}
```

In this example the return type is **void** (no data is passed back), method name is **Deposit,** parameter list consists of a single parameter of type **decimal,** and the body contains one line of code that increments the member variable **balance** by the value that is passed in.

Public and Private

Fields and methods of a C# class can be specified as **public** or **private.** Normally, you declare fields as **private.** A private field can only be accessed from within the class, not from outside.

```
public class Account
{
   private int id;
   private decimal balance;
   . . .
```

Methods may be declared as either **public** or **private.** Public methods are called from outside the class and are used to perform calculations and to manipulate the private data. You may also provide public "accessor" methods to provide access to private fields.

```
public decimal GetBalance()
{
    return balance;
}
public int GetId()
{
    return id;
}
```

You may also have private methods, which can be thought of as "helper functions" for use within the class. Rather than duplicating code in several places, you may create a private method, which will be called wherever it is needed.

Abstraction

An abstraction captures the essential features of an entity, suppressing unnecessary details. There are many possible features of an account, but for our purposes, the only essential things are its id, its balance, and the operations of making a deposit and a withdrawal. All instances of an abstraction share these common features. Abstraction helps us deal with complexity.

Encapsulation

The implementation of an abstraction should be hidden from the rest of the system, or *encapsulated*. Objects have a public and a private side. The public side is what the rest of the system knows, while the private side implements the public side. Figure 8–4 illustrates the public method **Deposit,** which operates on the private field **balance.**

Deposit   ▶ balance

Figure 8–4   *Public method operates on private data.*

Data itself is private and can only be accessed through methods with a public interface. Such encapsulation provides two kinds of protection:
* Internal data is protected from corruption.
* Users of the object are protected from changes in the representation.

CONSTRUCTORS AND INITIALIZATION

Another important issue for classes is *initialization*. When an object is created, what initial values are assigned to the instance data? A classical problem in programming is uninitialized variables. When you run the program, you may get unpredictable results, depending on what happened to be in memory at the time you ran the program.

C# helps prevent such unpredictable behavior by performing a default initialization. Variables of numerical data types are initialized to 0.

In general you will want to perform your own initialization. There are two approaches. One is for the user of the class to perform the initialization. That is the approach followed in Steps 1 and 2 of the **TestAccount** program. That approach was feasible because we made the fields public, and so the class user could initialize them.

A second approach is to provide initialization code in the class itself. You could assign instance data in the class definition, as illustrated in **InitialAccount\Step1**.

```
public class Account
{
    private int id = 7;
    private decimal balance = 700;
    ...
    public decimal GetBalance()
    {
        return balance;
    }
    public int GetId()
    {
        return id;
    }
}
```

With this approach, *all* instances of **Account** will start out with the same initial values. We would like to find a way for the class to initialize its instance data appropriately, in a way that can be specified when the object is created. This capability is provided in C# by *constructors.*

Constructors

Through a constructor, you can initialize individual objects in any way you wish. Besides initializing instance data, you can perform other appropriate initializations (e.g., open a file).

A constructor is like a special method that is automatically called when an object is created via **new**. A constructor

* has no return type
* has the same name as the class
* should usually have **public** access
* may take parameters, which are passed when invoking **new**

```
public Account(int i, decimal bal)
{
    id = i;
    balance = bal;
}
```

In the calling program, you use **new** to instantiate object instances, and you pass desired values as parameters. This example is illustrated in **InitialAccount\Step2.**

```
// InitialAccount.cs

using System;

public class InitialAccount
{
    public static void Main(string[] args)
    {
        Account acc1 = new Account(1, 100);
        Console.WriteLine("balance of {0} is {1}",
                acc1.GetId(), acc1.GetBalance());
        Account acc2 = new Account(2, 200);
        Console.WriteLine("balance of {0} is {1}",
                acc2.GetId(), acc2.GetBalance());
    }
}
```

Here is the output:

```
balance of 1 is 100
balance of 2 is 200
```

Default Constructor

If you do not define a constructor in your class, C# will implicitly create one for you, called the *default constructor*, which takes no arguments. The default constructor will assign instance data, using any assignments in the class definition. **InitialAccount\Step1** provides an illustration. The default constructor is called when an object instance is created with **new** and no parameters.

Add the following code to the **Step2** test program shown previously:

```
Account acc3 = new Account();
Console.WriteLine("balance of {0} is {1}",
        acc3.GetId(), acc3.GetBalance());
```

Where this worked fine in **Step1** when there was no explicit constructor at all, we now get a compiler error:

```
error CS1501: No overload for method 'Account' takes '0'
arguments
```

In C# you may *overload* methods, including constructors, in which you have several methods with the same name but different argument lists. (We will discuss method overloading in Chapter 10.) We can fix this problem by defining a second constructor with no arguments. We may leave the body empty. **InitialAccount\Step3** illustrates.

```
public class Account
{
    private int id = 7;
    private decimal balance = 700;
    public Account()
    {
    }
    public Account(int i, decimal bal)
    {
        id = i;
        balance = bal;
    }
    ...
```

If we run the test program, performing two explicit initializations and one default initialization, we will get the following output:

```
balance of 1 is 100
balance of 2 is 200
balance of 7 is 700
```

this

Sometimes it is convenient within code for a method to be able to access the current object reference. C# defines a keyword **this,** which is a special variable that always refers to the current object instance. With **this** you can then refer to instance variables. If you examine the code for the constructor above, you will see that we made a point to use different names for the parameters than for the instance variables. We can make use of the same names and avoid ambiguity by using the **this** variable. Here is alternate code for the constructor:

```
public Account(int id, decimal balance)
{
    this.id = id;
    this.balance = balance;
}
```

Sample Program

The program **TestAccount\Step3** illustrates all the features we have discussed so far. Here is the class definition:

```
// Account.cs - Step3

public class Account
{
    private int id;
    private decimal balance;
    public Account()
    {
    }
    public Account(int id, decimal balance)
    {
        this.id = id;
        this.balance = balance;
    }
    public void Deposit(decimal amount)
    {
        balance += amount;
    }
    public void Withdraw(decimal amount)
    {
        balance -= amount;
    }
    public decimal GetBalance()
    {
        return balance;
    }
    public int GetId()
    {
        return id;
    }
}
```

Here is the test program:

```
// TestAccount.cs - Step3

using System;

public class TestAccount
```

```
{
    public static void Main(string[] args)
    {
        Account acc;
        acc = new Account(1, 100);
        Console.WriteLine("balance of {0} is {1}",
                            acc.GetId(), acc.GetBalance());
        acc.Deposit(25);
        acc.Withdraw(50);
        Console.WriteLine("balance of {0} is {1}",
                            acc.GetId(), acc.GetBalance());
        acc = new Account();
        Console.WriteLine("balance of {0} is {1}",
                            acc.GetId(), acc.GetBalance());
    }
}
```

Here is the output:

```
balance of 1 is 100
balance of 1 is 75
balance of 0 is 0
```

STATIC FIELDS AND METHODS

In C# a field normally is assigned on a *per-instance* basis, with a unique value for each object instance of the class. Sometimes it is useful to have a single value associated with the entire class. Such a field is called a **static** field. Like instance data members, static data members can be either **public** or **private.** To access a public static member, you use the dot notation, but in place of an object reference before the dot, you use the name of the class.

Static Methods

A method may also be declared **static**. A static method can be called without instantiating the class. You use the dot notation, with the class name in front of the dot. Because you can call a static method without an instance, a static method can only use static data members and not instance data members.

Static methods may be declared **public** or **private**. A private static method, like other private methods, may be used as a helper function within a class, but not called from outside.

Sample Program

Our previous **Account** classes relied on the user of the class to assign an id for the account. A better approach is to encapsulate assigning an id within the class itself, so that a unique id will be automatically generated every time an **Account** object is created. It is easy to implement such a scheme by using a static field **nextid,** which is used to assign an id. Every time an id is assigned, **nextid** is incremented. The program **StaticAccount** demonstrates this solution, and also illustrates use of private static helper functions. Here is the code defining the **Account** class:

```
// Account.cs

public class Account
{
    private int id;
    private decimal balance;
    private static int nextid = 1;
    public Account()
    {
        this.id = nextid++;
    }
    public Account(decimal balance)
    {
        this.id = nextid++;
        this.balance = balance;
    }
    public static int GetNextId()
    {
        return nextid;
    }
    public void Deposit(decimal amount)
    {
        balance = Add(balance, amount);
    }
    public void Withdraw(decimal amount)
    {
        balance -= amount;
    }
    public decimal GetBalance()
    {
        return balance;
    }
    public int GetId()
    {
        return id;
    }
    static private decimal Add(decimal x, decimal y)
    {
```

```
            return x + y;
        }
    }
```

Here is the test program:

```
// StaticAccount.cs

using System;

public class StaticAccount
{
    public static void Main(string[] args)
    {
        Console.WriteLine("nextid = {0}",
                          Account.GetNextId());
        Account acc1, acc2, acc3;
        acc1 = new Account(100);
        acc1.Deposit(25);
        acc2 = new Account(200);
        acc3 = new Account();
        WriteAccount(acc1);
        WriteAccount(acc2);
        WriteAccount(acc3);
        Console.WriteLine("nextid = {0}",
                          Account.GetNextId());
        //Console.WriteLine("nextid = {0}", acc3.GetNextId());
        // illegal
    }
    private static void WriteAccount(Account acc)
    {
        Console.WriteLine("balance of {0} is {1}",
                          acc.GetId(), acc.GetBalance());
    }
}
```

Note that the static method **GetNextId** is accessed through the class **Account** and not through an object reference such as **acc3**. This program also illustrates the fact that **Main** is a static method and is invoked by the runtime without an instance of the **StaticAccount** class being created. Since there is no instance, any method called from within **Main** must also be declared **static**, as illustrated by **WriteAccount.**

Here is the output:

```
nextid = 1
balance of 1 is 125
balance of 2 is 200
balance of 3 is 0
nextid = 4
```

Static Constructor

Besides having static fields and static methods, a class may also have a *static constructor*. A static constructor is called only once, before any object instances have been created. A static constructor is defined by prefixing the constructor with **static.** A static constructor can take no parameters and has no access modifier. The program **StaticConstructor** illustrates a static constructor for the **Account** class. All constructors write a line of text when they are called, so it will be easy to understand just when the various constructors are called.

```
// Account.cs

using System;

public class Account
{
    private int id;
    private decimal balance;
    private static int nextid = 1;
    static Account()
    {
        Console.WriteLine("Static constructor");
    }
    public Account()
    {
        Console.WriteLine("Account() constructor");
        this.id = nextid++;
    }
    public Account(decimal balance)
    {
        Console.WriteLine("Account(decimal) constructor");
        this.id = nextid++;
        this.balance = balance;
    }
    public decimal GetBalance()
    {
        return balance;
    }
    public int GetId()
    {
        return id;
    }
}
```

Here is the test program:

```
// StaticConstructor.cs

using System;
```

```
public class StaticConstructor
{
    public static void Main(string[] args)
    {
        Account acc1, acc2, acc3;
        acc1 = new Account(100);
        acc2 = new Account(200);
        acc3 = new Account();
        WriteAccount(acc1);
        WriteAccount(acc2);
        WriteAccount(acc3);
    }
    private static void WriteAccount(Account acc)
    {
        Console.WriteLine("balance of {0} is {1}",
                          acc.GetId(), acc.GetBalance());
    }
}
```

Here is the output:

```
Static constructor
Account(decimal) constructor
Account(decimal) constructor
Account() constructor
balance of 1 is 100
balance of 2 is 200
balance of 3 is 0
```

CONSTANT AND READONLY FIELDS

If you want to make sure that a variable always has the same value, you can assign the value via an initializer and use the **const** modifier. Such a constant is automatically static, and you will access it from outside the class through the class name.

Another situation may call for a one-time initialization at runtime, and after that the value cannot be changed. You can achieve this effect through a **readonly** field. Such a field may be either an instance member or a static member. In the case of a instance member, it will be assigned in an ordinary constructor. In the case of a static member, it will be assigned in a static constructor.

The program **ConstantAccount** illustrates the use of both **const** and **readonly.** In both cases, you will get a compiler error if you try to modify the value.

```
// Account.cs

public class Account
{
    public const decimal FEE = 5.00m;
    public readonly int FreeChecks;
    public Account(int num)
    {
        FreeChecks = num;
    }
}
```

Here is the test program:

```
// ConstantAccount.cs

using System;

public class ConstantAccount
{
    public static void Main(string[] args)
    {
        Console.WriteLine("FEE = {0}", Account.FEE);
        // Account.FEE = 7.00m;     // illegal
        Account acc = new Account(10);
        Console.WriteLine("{0} free checks", acc.FreeChecks);
        // acc.FreeChecks = 20;     // illegal
    }
}
```

Here is the output:

```
FEE = 5
10 free checks
```

SUMMARY

In this chapter we explored the use of classes in C# for representing structured data. A class can be thought of as a template from which individual instances can be created. An instance of a class is called an object. Classes support encapsulation through *fields* and *methods*. Typically, fields are private and methods are public. The **new** operator is used to instantiate objects from classes. When you declare a variable of a primitive data, you are allocating memory and creating the instance. When you declare a variable of a class type (an "object reference"), you are only obtaining memory for a *reference* to an object of the class type. No memory is allocated for the object itself until **new** is invoked. Through the assignment of a reference, an object may become orphaned. The Common Language Runtime automatically reclaims the memory of such orphaned or unreferenced objects. This process is known as *garbage collection*. Initialization of objects can be performed in constructors. Static members apply to the entire class rather than to a particular instance. **const** and **readonly** can be used to specify constants in C# programs.

The C# Type System

*I*n C# there is a fundamental distinction between value *types*, *whose storage is allocated immediately when the variable is declared and* reference *types, where storage is allocated elsewhere and the variable is only a reference to the actual data. In the previous chapter we looked at classes, which define reference types. In this chapter we survey the entire C# type system, including a review of the simple types, which were discussed in Chapter 4. In C# a* **struct** *has many similarities to a* **class** *but is a value type. Another important kind of value type in C# is an* **enum.** *We provide a survey of several other important types, which will be examined in detail later, including string, array, interface, and delegate. We discuss the default values that get assigned to variables when there is not an explicit initialization. We will see that all types in C# are rooted in a fundamental base class called* **object.** *In C# "everything is an object," and simple types are transparently converted to objects as needed through a process known as* boxing. *The inverse process,* unboxing, *returns an object to the simple value from which it came.*

OVERVIEW OF TYPES IN C#

In C# there are three kinds of types:

- Value types
- Reference types
- Pointer types

Value Types

Value types directly contain their data. Each variable of a value type has its own copy of the data. Value types are typically allocated on the stack and are automatically destroyed when the variable goes out of scope. Value types include the simple types discussed in Chapter 4, structures, and enumeration types.

Reference Types

Reference types do not contain data directly but only refer to data. Variables of reference types store references to data, called objects. Two different variables can reference the same object. Reference types are allocated on the *managed heap* and eventually get destroyed through a process known as *garbage collection.*

Reference types include **string, object,** class types, array types, interfaces, and delegates.

Pointer Types

Pointer types are only used in unsafe code and will be discussed in Chapter 20.

VALUE TYPES

In this section we will survey all the value types, beginning with a review of the simple data types discussed in Chapter 4. We will see that there is a correspondence between these C# types and types in the Common Language Runtime, as expressed by classes in the **System** namespace. We will also discuss structures and enumeration types.

Simple Types

The simple data types are general-purpose value data types, including numeric, character, and Boolean.

* The **sbyte** data type is an 8-bit signed integer.
* The **byte** data type is an 8-bit unsigned integer.
* The **short** data type is a 16-bit signed integer.
* The **ushort** is a 16-bit unsigned integer.
* The **int** data type is a 32-bit signed integer.
* The **uint** is a 32-bit unsigned integer.
* The **long** data type is a 64-bit signed integer.
* The **ulong** is a 64-bit unsigned integer.
* The **char** data type is a Unicode character (16 bits).
* The **float** data type is a single-precision floating point.
* The **double** data type is a double-precision floating point.
* The **bool** data type is a Boolean (**true** or **false**).
* The **decimal** data type is a decimal type with 28 significant digits (typically used for financial purposes).

Types in System Namespace

There is an exact correspondence between the simple C# types and types in the **System** namespace. C# reserved words are simply aliases for the corresponding type in the **System** namespace. Table 9–1 shows this correspondence.

Table 9-1 Types in C# and the System Namespace

C# Reserved Word	Type in System Namespace
sbyte	System.SByte
byte	System.Byte
short	System.Int16
ushort	System.UInt16
int	System.Int32
uint	System.UInt32
long	System.Int64
ulong	System.UInt64
char	System.Char
float	System.Single
double	System.Double
bool	System.Boolean
decimal	System.Decimal

Structures

A **struct** is a value type which can group inhomogeneous types. It can also have constructors and methods. These basic features are illustrated in the program **HotelCreate**. There are fields **city, name, rooms,** and **cost.** There is a constructor, and there is a method **Show.**

```csharp
// Hotel.cs

public struct Hotel
{
    public Hotel(string city, string name, int rooms,
                 decimal cost)
    {
        Console.WriteLine("Hotel struct instance");
        this.city = city;
        this.name = name;
        this.rooms = rooms;
        this.cost = cost;
    }
    public void Show()
    {
        Console.WriteLine("{0} {1} {2} {3:C}",
                          city, name, rooms, cost);
    }
    public string city;
    public string name;
    public int rooms;
    public decimal cost;
}
```

A **struct** object is created using the **new** operator.

```csharp
Hotel ritz = new Hotel("Boston", "Ritz", 100, 200.00m);
```

A **struct** object can also be created without **new**, but then the fields will be unassigned, and the object cannot be used until the fields have been initialized.

```csharp
Hotel flop;
flop.city = "Podunk";
// Now it is OK to use the city field
flop.name = "Flop";
flop.rooms = 50;
flop.cost = 30.00m;
// Now it is OK to use the complete object
flop.Show();
```

UNINITIALIZED VARIABLES

The C# compiler will detect attempts to use uninitialized variables. A **struct** object cannot be used until its fields have been assigned. A simple local variable must be initialized before it can be used.

```
int x;
Console.WriteLine("x = {0}", x);     // error
```

TEST PROGRAM

Here is the test program from **HotelCreate** that exercises the **Hotel** structure.

```
// HotelCreate.cs

using System;

public class HotelCreate
{
    public static void Main()
    {
        Hotel ritz = new Hotel("Boston", "Ritz", 100,
                            200.00m);
        ritz.Show();
        Hotel flop;
        flop.city = "Podunk";
        // Now it is OK to use the city field
        flop.name = "Flop";
        flop.rooms = 50;
        flop.cost = 30.00m;
        // Now it is OK to use the complete object
        flop.Show();
        // Attempt to use an uninitialized variable
        int x;
        x = 5;       // NEED this initialization
        Console.WriteLine("x = {0}", x);
    }
}
```

Here is the output:

```
Hotel struct instance
Boston Ritz 100 $200.00
Podunk Flop 50 $30.00
x = 5
```

Note that a constructor is invoked for **new,** but no constructor is involved when a **struct** object is created simply by declaring it.

COPYING A STRUCTURE

When you assign one **struct** variable to another, you will get two independent copies of the same data. If you subsequently change one copy, the two copies will be different. This is in contrast to a class, where if you do an assignment, you will have two references to the same data. The program **HotelCopy** illustrates a number of aspects of copying structures. The class definition now has a special constructor for making a copy of a **Hotel** object. When do you think it will be invoked?

```
// Hotel.cs

using System;

public struct Hotel
{
    public Hotel(Hotel hotel)
    {
        Console.WriteLine("Copy Hotel struct instance");
        this.city = hotel.city;
        this.name = hotel.name;
        this.rooms = hotel.rooms;
        this.cost = hotel.cost + 1m;   // not quite a copy
    }
    public Hotel(string city, string name, int rooms,
                 decimal cost)
    {
        Console.WriteLine("Hotel struct instance");
        this.city = city;
        this.name = name;
        this.rooms = rooms;
        this.cost = cost;
    }
    public void Show()
    {
        Console.WriteLine("{0} {1} {2} {3:C}", city, name,
                          rooms, cost);
    }
    public string city;
    public string name;
    public int rooms;
    public decimal cost;
}
```

Here is the test program:

```
// HotelCopy.cs

using System;
```

```
public class HotelCopy
{
    public static void Main()
    {
        Hotel ritz = new Hotel("Boston", "Ritz", 100,
                                200.00m);
        Console.Write("ritz: ");
        ritz.Show();
        Hotel flop = ritz;                      // #1
        Console.Write("flop: ");
        flop.Show();
        // Change price of flop
        flop.cost = 10.00m;
        Console.Write("flop: ");
        flop.Show();
        Console.Write("ritz: ");
        ritz.Show();
        Hotel fancy = new Hotel(ritz);      // #2
        Console.Write("fancy: ");
        fancy.Show();
    }
}
```

Two new objects, **flop** and **fancy,** are created by copying, shown by the comments #1 and #2 in the previous listing. In both cases an independent copy is made, and changing the value of one copy will not affect the value of the other copy. Copy #1 does not involve any constructor; there is simply an implicit memberwise copy of all the elements of the **struct.** In the case of #2, we explicitly invoke the additional constructor by using the **new** operator, and any copying that gets done is performed within that constructor. To demonstrate, we did not perform a perfect copy, but incremented the cost by $1 for the copy. Here is the output:

```
Hotel struct instance
ritz: Boston Ritz 100 $200.00
flop: Boston Ritz 100 $200.00
flop: Boston Ritz 100 $10.00
ritz: Boston Ritz 100 $200.00
Copy Hotel struct instance
fancy: Boston Ritz 100 $201.00
```

CLASSES AND STRUCTS

While in C++ the concepts of **class** and **structs** are very close, there is more fundamental difference in C#. In C++ a class has default visibility of **private** and a struct has default visibility of **public,** and that is the *only* difference.

In C# the key difference between a class and a struct is that a class is a *reference* type and a struct is a *value* type. A class must be instantiated explicitly using **new**. The new instance is created on the heap, and memory is managed by the system through a garbage collection process. A struct instance may simply be declared, or you may use **new**. For a struct the new instance is created on the stack, and the instance will be deallocated when it goes out of scope.

There are different semantics for assignment, whether done explicitly or via call by value mechanism in a method call. For a class, you will get a second object reference, and both object references refer to the same data. For a struct, you will get a completely independent copy of the data in the struct.

Enumeration Types

The final kind of value type is an *enumeration* type. An enumeration type is a distinct type with named constants. Every enumeration type has an underlying type, which is one of the following.

* **byte**
* **short**
* **int**
* **long**

An enumeration type is defined through an **enum** declaration.

```
public enum BookingStatus : byte
{
    HotelNotFound,          // 0 implicitly
    RoomsNotAvailable,      // 1 implicitly
    Ok = 5                  // explicit value
}
```

If the type is not specified, **int** is used. By default, the first **enum** member is assigned the value 0, the second member 1, and so on. Constant values can be explicitly assigned.

You can make use of an enumeration type by declaring a variable of the type indicated in the **enum** declaration (e.g., **BookingStatus**). You can refer to the enumerated values by using the dot notation. Here is some illustrative code:

```
BookingStatus status;
status = hotel.ReserveRoom(name, date);
if (status == BookingStatus.HotelNotFound)
    Console.WriteLine("Hotel not found");
...
```

REFERENCE TYPES

A variable of a reference type does not directly contain its data, but instead provides a *reference* to the data stored elsewhere (the heap). In C# there are the following kinds of reference types:

* Class
* Array
* Interface
* Delegate

Reference types have a special value **null,** which indicates the absence of an instance.

Class Types

A class type defines a data structure that has fields, methods, constants, and other kinds of members. Class types support *inheritance*. Through inheritance a derived class can extend or specialize a base class. We introduced C# classes in the previous chapter, and we will discuss inheritance and other details about classes in later chapters.

There are two classes in the .NET Framework Class Library that are so important that they have C# reserved words as aliases for them: **object** and **string.**

OBJECT

The **object** class type is the ultimate base type for all types in C#. Every C# type derives directly or indirectly from **object.** The **object** keyword in C# is an alias for the predefined **System.Object** class. **System.Object** has methods such as **ToString, Equals,** and **Finalize,** which we will study later.

STRING

The **string** class encapsulates a Unicode character string. The **string** keyword is an alias for the predefined **System.String** class. The string type is a *sealed* class. (A sealed class is one that cannot be used as the base class for any other classes.)

The **string** class inherits directly from the root **object** class. String literals are defined using double quotes. There are useful built-in methods for **string.** For now, note that the **Equals** method can be used to test for equality of strings.

```
string a = "hello";
if (a.Equals("hello"))
      Console.WriteLine("equal");
else
```

```
    Console.WriteLine("not equal");
```

There are also overloaded operators:

```
if (a == "hello")
        ...
```

We will study **string** in detail in Chapter 11.

Arrays

An array is a collection of elements that are all of the same type. Arrays are accessed using a square bracket and an index. In C# array indices start at 0, as in other C family languages. We previewed arrays in Chapter 6 and will study arrays in detail in Chapter 12.

Interfaces

The purpose of an interface is to specify a contract independently of implementation. Like a class, an interface has *methods*. But whereas a class provides an implementation of its methods, an interface only specifies them. A class may implement one or more interfaces, specified by using a colon notation.

```
public class Acme : ICustomer, IHotelInfo, IHotelReservation
{
...
```

We will study interfaces in detail in Chapter 17.

Delegates

The purpose of a delegate is to provide a "callback" behavior in an object-oriented, type-safe manner. Whereas in C or C++ you would use a function pointer, in C# you can encapsulate a reference to a method inside a delegate object. You can then pass this delegate object to other code, which can then call your method. The code which calls your method does not have to know at compile time which method is being called. We will study delegates in detail in Chapter 19.

DEFAULT VALUES

Several kinds of variables are automatically initialized to default values:

* Static variables
* Instance variables of class and struct instances
* Array elements

Local variables are *not* automatically initialized, as we saw earlier in the chapter.

The default value of a variable of reference type is **null.**

The default value of a variable of value type is the value assigned in the default constructor. For simple types this value corresponds to a bit pattern of all zeros:

- For integer types, the default value is 0
- For **char,** the default value is '\u0000'
- For **float,** the default value is 0.0f
- For **double,** the default value is 0.0d
- For **decimal,** the default value is 0.0m
- For **bool,** the default value is **false**

For an **enum** type, the default value is 0. For a **struct** type, the default value is obtained by setting all value type fields to their default values, as described above, and all reference type fields to **null.**

BOXING AND UNBOXING

One of the strong features of C# is that it has a unified type system. Every type, including the simple built-in types such as **int,** derive from **System.Object**. In C# "everything is an object."

A language such as Smalltalk also has such a feature, but pays the price of inefficiency for simple types. Languages such as C++ and Java treat simple built-in types differently than objects, thus obtaining efficiency but at loss of a unified type system.

C# enjoys the best of both worlds through a process known as *boxing.* Boxing converts a value type such as **int** or a **struct** to an object reference, and is done implicitly. *Unboxing* converts a boxed value type (stored on the heap) back to an unboxed simple value (stored on the stack). Unboxing is done through a type cast.

```
int x = 5;
object o = x;        // boxing
x = (int) o;         // unboxing
```

SUMMARY

In this chapter we discussed the overall type system of C#. There is a fundamental distinction between *value* types, whose storage is allocated immediately when the variable is declared, and *reference types,* where storage is allocated elsewhere and the variable is only a reference to the actual data. We looked at the various kinds of value types, including the simple types discussed in Chapter 4, **struct,** which is somewhat similar to **class** but different due to being a value type, and **enum.** We then surveyed several other important types, including string, array, interface, and delegate, which will be examined in detail later. The default value of value types is a bit pattern of all zeros, and the default value of reference types is **null.** We saw that all types in C# are rooted in a fundamental base class called **object.** In C# "everything is an object," and simple types are transparently converted to objects as needed through a process known as boxing. The inverse process, unboxing, returns an object to the simple value from which it came.

Methods, Properties, and Operators

raditionally, a very important way of structuring programs has been through functional decomposition. Object-oriented programming is a more powerful organizing principle, in which data and functions are grouped together in objects. But functions remain an important building block of software systems. In C# all functions are methods *belonging to classes. In this chapter we examine methods in detail. We look at how methods are defined and used, how parameters are passed to and from methods, and how the same method name can be overloaded, with different versions having different parameter lists. You can also implement methods in C# that take a variable number of parameters. C# has a special syntax for paired get/set methods for accessing data. This* property *syntax was popularized by Visual Basic and simplifies programming. Finally we see how we can overload operators in C#, which makes invoking certain methods more natural and intuitive.*

METHODS

We have seen that classes can have different kinds of members, including fields, constants, and *methods*. A method implements behavior that can be performed by an object or a class. Ordinary methods, sometimes called *instance methods*, are invoked through an object instance.

```
Account acc = new Account();
acc.Deposit(25);
```

Static methods are invoked through a class, and do not depend upon the existence of any instances.

```
int sum = SimpleMath.Add(5, 7);
```

Methods have a list of parameters, which may be empty. Methods either return a value or have a **void** return. Multiple methods may have the same name, so long as they have different *signatures*, a feature known as *method overloading*. Methods have the same signature if they have the same number of parameters, and these parameters have the same types and modifiers (such as **ref** or **out**). The return type does not contribute to defining the signature of a method.

By default, parameters are *value* parameters, which means a copy is made of the parameter. The keyword **ref** designates a *reference* parameter, in which case the parameter inside the method and the corresponding actual argument refer to the same object. The keyword **out** refers to an *output* parameter, which is the same as a reference parameter, except that on the calling side, the parameter need not be assigned prior to the call.

We will study parameter passing and method overloading in more detail later in this chapter.

The most important thing to understand right now is that in C# *all* functions are methods and so are associated with a class. There is no such thing as a freestanding function, as in C and C++. "All functions are methods" is rather similar to "everything is an object" and reflects the fact that C# is a pure object-oriented language. The advantage of all functions being methods is that classes become a natural organizing principle. Methods are nicely grouped together.

Classes with All Static Methods

Sometimes part of the functionality of your system may not be tied to any data but may be purely functional in nature. In C# you would organize such functions into classes that have all static methods and no fields. The program **TestSimpleMath** provides an elementary example. Here is the definition of the class:

```
// SimpleMath.cs

public class SimpleMath
{
    public static int Add(int x, int y)
    {
        return x + y;
    }
    public static int Multiply(int x, int y)
```

```
    {
        return x * y;
    }
}
```

Here is the test program:

```
// TestSimpleMath.cs

using System;

public class TestSimpleMath
{
    public static void Main(string[] args)
    {
        int sum = SimpleMath.Add(5, 7);
        int product = SimpleMath.Multiply(5, 7);
        Console.WriteLine("sum = {0}", sum);
        Console.WriteLine("product = {0}", product);
    }
}
```

Here is the output:

```
sum = 12
product = 35
```

PARAMETER PASSING

Programming languages have different mechanisms for passing parameters. In the C family of languages the standard is "call by value." This means that the actual data values themselves are passed to the method. Typically, these values are pushed onto the stack, and the called function obtains its own independent copy of the values. Any changes made to these values will not be propagated back to the calling program. C# provides this mechanism of parameter passing as the default, but C# also supports "reference" parameters and "output" parameters. In this section we will examine all three of these mechanisms, and we will also look at the ramifications of passing class and struct data types.

Some terminology will help us in the following discussion. Storage is allocated on the stack for method parameters. This storage area is known as the *activation* record. It is popped when the method is no longer active. The *formal parameters* of a method are the parameters as seen within the method. They are provided storage in the activation record. The *actual parameters* of a method are the expressions between commas in the parameter list of the method call.

```
int sum = SimpleMath.Add(5, 7);    // actual parameters are
                                   // 5 and 7
...
public static int Add(int x, int y)
{                                  // formal parameters are
                                   // x and y
   ...
}
```

Value Parameters

Parameter passing is the process of initializing the storage of the formal parameters by the actual parameters. The default method of parameter passing in C# is *call-by-value*, in which the values of the actual parameters are copied into the storage of the formal parameters. Call-by-value is "safe," because the method never directly accesses the actual parameters, only its own local copies. But there are drawbacks to call-by-value:

* There is no direct way to modify the value of an argument. You may use the return type of the method, but that only allows you to pass one value back to the calling program.
* There is overhead in copying a large object.

The overhead in copying a large object is borne when you pass a struct instance. If you pass a class instance, or an instance of any other reference type, you are passing only a reference and not the actual data itself. This may sound like "call-by-reference," but what you are actually doing is passing a reference by value. Later in this section we will discuss the ramifications of passing struct and class instances.

Reference Parameters

Consider a situation in which you want to pass more than one value back to the calling program. C# provides a clean solution through *reference parameters*. You declare a reference parameter with the **ref** keyword, which is placed before both the formal parameter and the actual parameter. A reference parameter does not result in any copying of a value. Instead, the formal parameter and the actual parameter refer to the same storage location. Thus changing the formal parameter will result in the actual parameter changing, as both are referring to exactly the same storage location.

The program **ReferenceMath** illustrates using **ref** parameters. The two methods **Add** and **Multiply** are replaced by a single method **Calculate,** which passes back two values as reference parameters.

```
// ReferenceMath.cs

public class ReferenceMath
```

```
{
   public static void Calculate(int x, int y,
                                ref int sum, ref int prod)
   {
      sum = x + y;
      prod = x * y;
   }
}
```

Notice the use of the **ref** keyword in front of the third and fourth parameters. Here is the test program:

```
// TestReferenceMath.cs

using System;

public class TestReferenceMath
{
   public static void Main(string[] args)
   {
      int sum = 0, product = 0;
      MultipleMath.Calculate(5, 7, ref sum, ref product);
      Console.WriteLine("sum = {0}", sum);
      Console.WriteLine("product = {0}", product);
   }
}
```

Again we need to have the **ref** keyword in front of the parameters. It is also necessary to initialize the variables before using them as reference parameters.

Output Parameters

A reference parameter is really designed for two-way communication between the calling program and the called program, both passing data in and getting data out. Thus there is a requirement that reference parameters be initialized before their use. In the case we just looked at, where we are only obtaining output, initializing the variables only for them to be assigned new values is rather pointless. C# provides for this case with *output parameters*. Use the keyword **out** wherever you would use the keyword **ref**. Then you do not have to initialize the variable before use. Naturally, you could not use an **out** parameter inside the method; you can only assign it. The program **OutputMath** illustrates the use of output parameters.

Structure Parameters

A struct is a value type, so if you pass a struct as a value parameter, the struct instance in the called method will be an independent copy of the struct in the calling method. The program **HotelStruct** illustrates passing an instance of a **Hotel** struct by value. Here is the definition of the struct:

```
// Hotel.cs

using System;

public struct Hotel
{
   public Hotel(string city, string name, int rooms,
                decimal cost)
   {
      Console.WriteLine("Hotel struct instance");
      this.city = city;
      this.name = name;
      this.rooms = rooms;
      this.cost = cost;
   }
   public void Show()
   {
      Console.WriteLine("{0} {1} {2} {3:C}", city, name,
                        rooms, cost);
   }
   public string city;
   public string name;
   public int rooms;
   public decimal cost;
}
```

Here is the test program, which has a method **RaisePrice** that passes a **Hotel** instance by value. Before running the test program, figure out the expected output.

```
// HotelTest.cs

using System;

public class HotelTest
{
   public static void Main()
   {
      Hotel ritz = new Hotel("Boston", "Ritz", 100,
                             200.00m);
      // The Ritz before and after
      Console.WriteLine("Before price hike");
```

```
      ritz.Show();
      RaisePrice(ritz, 50.00m);
      Console.WriteLine("After price hike");
      ritz.Show();
   }
   private static void RaisePrice(Hotel hotel,
                                  decimal delta)
   {
      hotel.cost += delta;
      Console.WriteLine("new cost = {0:C}", hotel.cost);
   }
}
```

Here is the output:

```
Hotel struct instance
Before price hike
Boston Ritz 100 $200.00
new cost = $250.00
After price hike
Boston Ritz 100 $200.00
```

The object **hotel** in the **RaisePrice** method is an independent copy of the object **ritz** in the **Main** method. Figure 10–1 shows the values in both structures after the price has been raised for **hotel.** Thus the change in price does not propagate back to **Main**.

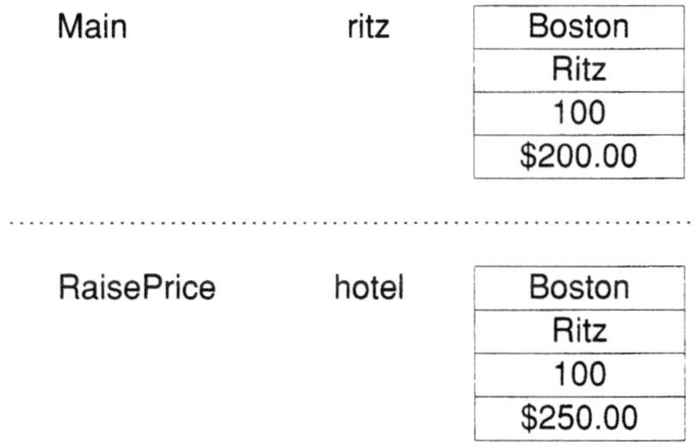

Main	ritz	Boston
		Ritz
		100
		$200.00

RaisePrice	hotel	Boston
		Ritz
		100
		$250.00

Figure 10–1 *Passing a struct instance by value.*

The program **HotelStructRef** has the same struct definition, but the test program passes the **Hotel** instance by reference. Now the change does propagate, as you would expect.

Class Parameters

A class is a reference type, so if you pass a class instance as a value parameter, the class instance in the called method will refer to the same object as the reference in the calling method. The program **HotelClass** illustrates passing an instance of a **Hotel** class by value. Figure 10–2 illustrates how the

hotel reference in the **RaisePrice** method refers to the same object as the **ritz** reference in **Main**. Thus when you change the price in the **RaisePrice** method, the object in **Main** is the same object and shows the new price.

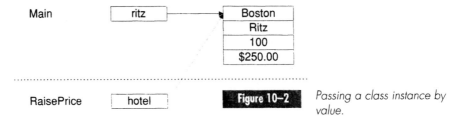

Figure 10–2   *Passing a class instance by value.*

METHOD OVERLOADING

In a traditional programming language such as C, you need to create unique names for all your methods. If methods do basically the same thing but only apply to different data types, it becomes tedious to create unique names. For example, suppose you have a **FindMax** method that can find the maximum of two **int** or two **long** or two **string**. If we need to come up with a unique name for each method, we would have to create method names such as **FindMaxInt, FindMaxLong,** and **FindMaxString.**

In C#, as in other object-oriented languages such as C++ and Java, you may *overload* method names. That is, different methods can have different names, if they have different *signatures*. Two methods have the same signature if they have the same number of parameters, the parameters have the same data types, and the parameters have the same modifiers (none, **ref,** or **out**). The return type does not contribute to defining the signature of a method.

At runtime the compiler will resolve a given invocation of the method by trying to match up the actual parameters with formal parameters. A match occurs if the parameters match exactly or if they can match through an implicit conversion. For the exact matching rules, consult the *C# Language Specification.*

The program **OverloadDemo** illustrates method overloading. The method **FindMax** is overloaded to take either **long** or **string** parameters. The method is invoked three times, for **int, long,** and **string** parameters. There is an exact match for the case of **long** and **string**. The call with **int** actual parameters can resolve to the **long** version, because there is an implicit conversion of **int** into **long**. You may wish to review the discussion of conversions of data types at the end of Chapter 4. The program uses the ternary operator **?:,** which we covered in Chapter 5. We will cover the **string** data type and the **Compare** method in Chapter 11.

```
// OverloadDemo.cs

using System;

public class OverloadDemo
{
   public static void Main()
   {
      int x1 = 5, x2 = 7;
      long y1 = 5000000000L, y2 = 7000000000L;
      string s1 = "fifteen", s2 = "seven";
      Console.WriteLine("max of {0}, {1} = {2}",
                     x1, x2, FindMax(x1,x2));
      Console.WriteLine("max of {0}, {1} = {2}",
                     y1, y2, FindMax(y1,y2));
      Console.WriteLine("max of {0}, {1} = {2}",
                     s1, s2, FindMax(s1,s2));    }
   static long FindMax(long a, long b)
   {
      return a < b ? b : a;
   }
   static string FindMax(string a, string b)
   {
      return String.Compare(a,b) <= 0 ? b : a;
   }
}
```

Here is the output:

```
max of 5, 7 = 7
max of 5000000000, 7000000000 = 7000000000
max of fifteen, seven = seven
```

MODIFIERS AS PART OF THE SIGNATURE

It is important to understand that if methods have identical types for their formal parameters, but differ in a modifier (none, **ref**, or **out**), then the methods have different signatures. The program **OverloadHotel** provides an illustration. We have two **RaisePrice** methods. In the first method, the hotel is passed as a value parameter. In the second version, the hotel is passed as a reference parameter. These methods have different signatures.

```
// HotelTest.cs

using System;

public class HotelDemo
{
   public static void Main()
```

```
{
    Hotel ritz = new Hotel("Boston", "Ritz", 100,
                            200.00m);
    Hotel flop = new Hotel("Podunk", "Flop", 50, 20.00m);
    // The Ritz before and after
    Console.WriteLine("Before price hike");
    ritz.Show();
    RaisePrice(ritz, 50.00m);
    Console.WriteLine("After price hike");
    ritz.Show();
    // The Flop before and after -- use ref version
    Console.WriteLine("Before price hike");
    flop.Show();
    RaisePrice(ref flop, 50.00m);
    Console.WriteLine("After price hike");
    flop.Show();
}
private static void RaisePrice(Hotel hotel,
                              decimal delta)
{
    hotel.cost += delta;
    Console.WriteLine("new cost = {0:C}", hotel.cost);
}
private static void RaisePrice(ref Hotel hotel,
                              decimal delta)
{
    hotel.cost += delta;
    Console.WriteLine("new cost = {0:C}", hotel.cost);
}
}
```

VARIABLE LENGTH PARAMETER LISTS

Our **FindMax** methods in the previous section were very specific with
respect to the number of parameters—there were always exactly two parameters. Sometimes you may want to be able to work with a variable number of parameters, for example, to find the maximum of two, three, four, or
more numbers. C# provides a **params** keyword, which you can use to
indicate that an array of parameters is provided. Sometimes you may want
to provide both a general version of your method that takes a variable
number of parameters and also one or more special versions that take an
exact number of parameters. The special version will be called in preference, if there is an exact match. The special versions are more efficient.
The program **VariableMax** illustrates a general **FindMax** method that
takes a variable number of parameters. There is also a special version that

takes two parameters. Each method prints out a line identifying itself, so you can see which method takes precedence. Here is the program:

```csharp
// VariableMax.cs

using System;

public class VariableMax
{
    public static void Main()
    {
        Console.WriteLine("max of {0}, {1} = {2}",
                        5,7,FindMax(5,7));
        Console.WriteLine("max of {0}, {1}, {2} = {3}",
                        500,5,7,FindMax(500,5,7));
        Console.WriteLine("max of {0}, {1}, {2}, {3} = {4}",
                        500,5,7,80,FindMax(500,5,7,80));
    }
    static int FindMax(int a, int b)
    {
        Console.WriteLine("FindMax with Two Parameters");
        return a < b ? b : a;
    }
    static int FindMax(params int[] args)
    {
        Console.WriteLine(
                "FindMax with Variable Number of Parameters");
        int imax = Int32.MinValue;
        for (int i = 0; i < args.Length; i++)
        {
            if (args[i] > imax)
                imax = args[i];
        }
        return imax;
    }
}
```

Here is the output:

```
FindMax with Two Parameters
max of 5, 7 = 7
FindMax with Variable Number of Parameters
max of 500, 5, 7 = 500
FindMax with Variable Number of Parameters
max of 500, 5, 7, 80 = 500
```

PROPERTIES

The encapsulation principle leads us to typically store data in private fields and to provide access to this data through public accessor methods that allow us to set and get values. For example, in the **Account** class we used as an illustration in Chapter 8, we provided a method **GetBalance** to access the private field balance. You don't need any special syntax; you can simply provide methods and call these methods what you want, typically **GetXXX** and **SetXXX**.

C# provides a special *property* syntax that simplifies user code. Rather than using methods, you can simply use an object reference followed by a dot followed by a property name. Here are some hypothetical examples of a **Balance** property (that we assume for the sake of argument is both read/write) of a hypothetical **Account** class. We show in comments the corresponding method code.

```
Account acc = new Account();
decimal bal;
bal = acc.Balance;          // bal = acc.GetBalance();
acc.Balance = 100m;         // acc.SetBalance(100m);
acc.Balance += 1m; // acc.SetBalance(acc.GetBalance() + 1m);
```

As you can see, the syntax using the property is a little more concise. Properties were popularized in Visual Basic, and are now part of .NET and available in selected other .NET languages, such as C#. The program **AccountProperty** illustrates implementing and using several properties, **Balance, Id,** and **Owner.** The first two properties are read-only (only **get** defined), and the third property is read/write (both **get** and **set**). It is also possible to have a write-only property (only **set** defined). Here is the code for the **Account** class, where the properties are defined. Notice the syntax and the special C# keyword **value.**

```
// Account.cs

public class Account
{
    private int id;
    private static int nextid = 1;
    private decimal balance;
    private string owner;
    public Account(decimal balance, string owner)
    {
        this.id = nextid++;
        this.balance = balance;
        this.owner = owner;
    }
    public void Deposit(decimal amount)
```

```
    {
        balance += amount;
    }
    public void Withdraw(decimal amount)
    {
        balance -= amount;
    }
    public decimal Balance
    {
        get
        {
            return balance;
        }
    }
    public int Id
    {
        get
        {
            return id;
        }
    }
    public string Owner
    {
        get
        {
            return owner;
        }
        set
        {
            owner = value;
        }
    }
}
```

Here is the test program:

```
// TestAccount.cs

using System;

public class TestAccount
{
    public static void Main(string[] args)
    {
        Account acc;
        acc = new Account(100, "Bob");
        ShowAccount(acc);
        acc.Deposit(25);
        acc.Withdraw(50);
        ShowAccount(acc);
        acc.Owner = "Carl";
```

```
        ShowAccount(acc);
        acc = new Account(200, "Mary");
        ShowAccount(acc);
    }
    private static void ShowAccount(Account acc)
    {
        Console.WriteLine("id: {0} owner: {1} balance: {2:C}",
                        acc.Id, acc.Owner, acc.Balance);
    }
}
```

Here is the output:

```
id: 1 owner: Bob balance: $100.00
id: 1 owner: Bob balance: $75.00
id: 1 owner: Carl balance: $75.00
id: 2 owner: Mary balance: $200.00
```

OPERATOR OVERLOADING

Another kind of syntactic simplification that can be provided in C# is *operator overloading*. The idea is that certain method invocations can be implemented more concisely using operators rather than method calls. Suppose we have a class **Matrix** that has static methods to add and multiply matrices. Using methods, we could write a matrix expression like this:

```
Matrix a, b, c, d;
// code to initialize the object references
d = Matrix.Multiply(a, (Matrix.Add(b, c)));
```

If we overload the operators + and *, we can write this code more succinctly:

```
d = a * (b + c);
```

You cannot create a brand new operator, but you can overload many of the existing C# operators to be an alias for a static method. For example, given the static method **Add** in the **Matrix** class:

```
class Matrix
{
...
    public static Matrix Add(Matrix x, Matrix y)
    {
```

you could write instead:

```
    public static Matrix operator+(Matrix x, Matrix y)
```

All of the rest of the class implementation code stays the same, and you can then use operator notation in client code. Operator declarations, such as **operator+** shown above, must obey the following rules:

* Operators must be **public** and **static,** and may not have any other modifiers.
* Operators take only value parameters, and not reference or output parameters.
* Operators must have a signature that differs from the signatures of all other operators in the class.

There are three categories of operators that can be overloaded. Table 10–1 shows the unary and binary operators that can be overloaded. A third category of operators is user-defined conversions, which will be discussed in Chapter 15.

Table 10–1   *Unary and Binary Operators That Can Be Overloaded*

Type	Operators
Unary	+ - ! ~ ++ -- true false
Binary	+ - * / % & | ^ << >> == != > < >= <=

If you overload a binary operator **op**, the corresponding compound assignment operator **op=** will be overloaded for you by the compiler. For example, if you overload **+** you will automatically have an overload of **+=**.

The relational operators must be overloaded in pairs:

* **operator==** and **operator!=**
* **operator>** and **operator<**
* **operator>=** and **operator<=.**

Sample Program

As an illustration of operator overloading, consider the program **TestClock,** which has a class **Clock** that does "clock arithmetic." The legal values of **Clock** are integers between 1 and 12 inclusive. Addition is performed modulo 12. Thus 9 + 7 is 16 modulo 12, or 4. We overload the plus operator to do this special kind of addition operation. We have two different versions of the plus operator. One adds two **Clock** values, and the other adds a **Clock** and an **int.**

```
// Clock.cs

public class Clock
{
    private int hour;
    public Clock(int h)
    {
```

```
      hour = h % 12;
      if (hour == 0)
         hour = 12;
   }
   public int Hour
   {
      get
      {
         return hour;
      }
      set
      {
         hour = value;
      }
   }
   public static Clock operator+(Clock c1, Clock c2)
   {
      int h = c1.hour + c2.hour;
      Clock c3 = new Clock(h);
      return c3;
   }
   public static Clock operator+(Clock c1, int h2)
   {
      int h = c1.hour + h2;
      Clock c3 = new Clock(h);
      return c3;
   }
}
```

Here is the test program. Note that we are able to use **+=** even though we have not explicitly provided such an overload. The compiler automatically furnishes this overload for us by virtue of our overloading **+**.

```
// TestClock.cs

using System;

public class TestClock
{
   public static void Main(string[] args)
   {
      Clock c1 = new Clock(17);
      Console.WriteLine("c1 = {0}", c1.Hour);
      Clock c2 = new Clock(10);
      Console.WriteLine("c2 = {0}", c2.Hour);
      Clock c3 = c1 + c2;
      Console.WriteLine("c3 = {0}", c3.Hour);
      c3 += 1;
      Console.WriteLine("c3 + 1 = {0}", c3.Hour);
   }
}
```

Here is the output:

```
c1 = 5
c2 = 10
c3 = 3
c3 + 1 = 4
```

Operator Overloading in the Class Library

Although you may rarely have occasion to overload operators in your own classes, you will find that a number of classes in the .NET Framework Class Library make use of operator overloading. In Chapter 11 you will see how **+** is used for concatenation of strings. In Chapter 19 you will see how **+=** is used for adding an event handler to an event.

SUMMARY

In this chapter we examined a number of features of methods. In C# there is no such thing as a freestanding function. All functions are tied to classes and are called methods. If you do not care about class instances, you can implement a class that has only static methods. By default, parameters are passed by value, but C# also supports reference parameters and output parameters. A method name can be overloaded, with different versions having different parameter lists. You can also implement methods in C# that take a variable number of parameters. C# provides a special property syntax for concisely invoking get/set methods for accessing data. You can overload operators in C#, a feature which makes the C# language inherently more extensible without requiring special coding in the compiler.

Characters and Strings

*Characters and strings are very important data types in practical programming. We already looked briefly at the **char** data type in Chapter 4, and in Chapter 9 we briefly mentioned **string**. In this chapter we will study these two data types in more detail. The C# keyword **string** is an alias for the class **String** in the **System** namespace. We will examine methods of the **String** class. While a **string** is immutable, a special class **StringBuilder** can be used in situations where we want to make changes to a string without creating a new object. Finally we'll look at several common programming situations involving strings, including working with command line arguments, processing a command loop, and splitting a string into constituent parts.*

CHARACTERS

C# provides the primitive data type **char** to represent individual characters. A character literal is represented by a character enclosed in single quotes.

```
char ch1 = 'a';
```

A C# **char** is represented internally as an unsigned two-byte integer. You can cast back and forth between **char** and integer data types.

```
char ch1 = 'a';
int n = (int) ch1;
n++;
```

```
ch1 = (char) n;                    // ch1 is now 'b'
```

The relational operators **==**, **<**, **>**, and so on apply to **char**.

```
char ch1 = 'a';
char ch2 = 'b'
if (ch1 < ch2)                     // expression is true
    ...
```

Sample Program

The program **CharTest** illustrates simple **char** operations.

```
// CharTest.cs
//
//  Test simple operations on characters

using System;

public class CharTest
{
    public static void Main(string[] args)
    {
        char ch1 = 'a';
        char ch2 = 'b';
        Console.WriteLine("ch1 = {0}, ch2 = {1}", ch1, ch2);
        // demonstrate inequality for char
        if (ch1 < ch2)
            Console.WriteLine(ch1 + " < " + ch2);
        else if (ch1 == ch2)
            Console.WriteLine(ch1 + " == " + ch2);
        else
            Console.WriteLine(ch1 + " > " + ch2);

        // demonstrate casting between integers
        int n = (int) ch1;
        n++;
        ch1 = (char) n;
        Console.Write("After increment: ");
        Console.WriteLine("ch1 = {0}, ch2 = {1}", ch1, ch2);
        if (ch1 < ch2)
            Console.WriteLine(ch1 + " < " + ch2);
        else if (ch1 == ch2)
            Console.WriteLine(ch1 + " == " + ch2);
        else
            Console.WriteLine(ch1 + " > " + ch2);
    }
}
```

Here is the output:

```
ch1 = a, ch2 = b
a < b
After increment: ch1 = b, ch2 = b
b == b
```

Character Codes

The integer corresponding to a character is referred to as its *character code*. You can easily write a C# program to display character codes. The program **CharCode** provides an illustration.

```
// CharCode.cs
//
// Shows some character codes

using System;

public class CharCode
{
   public static void Main(string[] args)
   {
      byte nA = (byte) 'A';
      byte nZ = (byte) 'Z';
      for (int i = nA; i <= nZ; i++)
      {
         Console.Write(i + "  ");
         Console.WriteLine((char) i);
      }
      char ch = '\u0041';
      Console.WriteLine(ch);
   }
}
```

The output gives you a table of character codes for 'A' through 'Z'. The last line shows the character 'A' via a special Unicode escape sequence for characters (discussed in the next section).

```
65  A
66  B
67  C
...
88  X
89  Y
90  Z
A
```

ASCII AND UNICODE

Traditionally, a one-byte character code called ASCII has been used to represent characters. ASCII code is simple and compact. But ASCII cannot be used to represent many different alphabets used throughout the world.

Modern computer systems prefer to use a two-byte character code called Unicode. Most modern (and many ancient) alphabets can be represented by Unicode characters. ASCII is a subset of Unicode, corresponding to the first 255 Unicode character codes. For more information on Unicode, you can visit the Web site *www.unicode.org*. C# uses Unicode to represent characters.

ESCAPE SEQUENCES

You can represent any Unicode character in a C# program by using the special escape sequence beginning with \u followed by hexadecimal digits.

```
char A = '\u0041';   // 41 (hex) is 65 (dec) or 'A'
```

Special escape sequences are provided for a number of standard nonprinting characters and for characters like quotation marks that would be difficult to represent otherwise. Table 11–1 (reproduced from Chapter 4) shows the standard escape sequences in C#.

Table 11–1   *Escape Characters in C#*

Escape Character	Name	Value
\'	Single quote	0x0027
\"	Double quote	0x0022
\\	Backslash	0x005C
\0	Null	0x0000
\a	Alert	0x0007
\b	Backspace	0x0008
\f	Form feed	0x000C
\n	New line	0x000A
\r	Carriage return	0x000D
\t	Horizontal tab	0x0009
\v	Vertical tab	0x000B

The program **Escape** illustrates a few escape sequences in a C# program.

```
// Escape.cs
//
// Demonstrates some escape sequences in C#

using System;

public class Escape
{
    public static void Main(string[] args)
```

```
    {
        char A = '\u0041';
        char TAB = '\t';
        char NEWLINE = '\n';
        Console.Write(A);
        Console.Write(A);
        Console.Write(A);
        Console.Write(TAB);
        Console.Write(A);
        Console.Write(A);
        Console.Write(A);
        Console.Write(NEWLINE);
        Console.Write(A);
        Console.Write(A);
        Console.Write(A);
        Console.Write(NEWLINE);
    }
}
```

Here is the output:

```
AAA     AAA
AAA
```

STRINGS

More useful in programs than individual characters are strings of characters. C# provides a **string** type, which is an alias for the **String** class in the **System** namespace. As a class type, **string** is a reference type. Much string functionality, available in all .NET languages, is provided by the **String** class. The C# compiler provides additional support to make working with strings more concise and intuitive. In this section we will first outline the main features of the **String** class. We will then look at string input, at the additional support provided by C#, and at the issues of string equality. The following section surveys some of the useful methods of the **String** class. The section after that discusses the **StringBuilder** class, and the chapter concludes with illustrations of some common programming situations involving strings.

String Class

The **String** class inherits directly from **Object** and is a *sealed* class, which means that you cannot further inherit from **String**. We will discuss inheritance and sealed classes in Chapters 13 and 14. When a class is sealed, the compiler can perform certain optimizations to make methods in the class more efficient.

Instances of **String** are *immutable,* which means that once a string object is created, it cannot be changed during its lifetime. Operations that appear to modify a string actually return a new string object. If, for the sake of efficiency, you need to modify a string-like object directly, you can make use of the **StringBuilder** class, which we will discuss in a later section.

A string has a zero-based index, which can be used to access individual characters in a string. That means that the first character of the string **str** is **str[0]**, the second character is **str[1]**, and so on.

Comparison operations on strings are by default case-sensitive, although there is an overloaded version of the **Compare** method that permits case-insensitive comparisons.

The empty string should be distinguished from **null**. If a string has not been assigned, it will be a null reference. Any string, including the empty string, compares greater than a null reference. Two null references compare equal to each other.

Compiler Support

The C# compiler provides a number of features to make working with strings easier and more intuitive.

STRING LITERALS AND INITIALIZATION

You can define a **string** literal by enclosing a string of characters in double quotes. Special characters can be represented using an escape sequence, as discussed earlier in the chapter. You may also define a "verbatim" string literal using the **@** symbol. In a verbatim string, escape sequences are not converted but are used exactly as they appear. If you want to represent a double quote inside a verbatim string, use two double quotes.

The proper way to initialize a string variable with a literal value is to supply the literal after an equal sign. You do not need to use **new** like you do with other data types. The following provides some examples of string literals and initializing string variables.

```
string s1 = "bat";
string path1 = "c:\\OI\\CSharp\\Chap11\\Concat";
string path = @"c:\OI\CSharp\Chap11\Concat\";
string greeting = @"""Hello, world""";
```

CONCATENATION

The **String** class provides a method **Concat** for concatenating strings. In C# you can use the plus operator **+** to perform concatenation. As we saw in Chapter 10, when **+** is overloaded, you automatically get an overload of the compound operator **+=**. The following program illustrates string literals and concatenation.

```
// Concat.cs

using System;

public class Concat
{
    public static void Main(string[] args)
    {
        string s1 = "bat";
        Console.WriteLine("s1 = {0}", s1);
        string s2 = "man";
        Console.WriteLine("s2 = {0}", s2);
        s1 += s2;
        Console.WriteLine(s1);
        string path1 = "c:\\OI\\CSharp\\Chap11\\Concat";
        Console.WriteLine("path1 = {0}", path1);
        string path = @"c:\OI\CSharp\Chap11\Concat\";
        string file = "Concat.cs";
        path = path + file;
        Console.WriteLine(path);
        string greeting = @"""Hello, world""";
        Console.WriteLine(greeting);
    }
}
```

Here is the output:

```
s1 = bat
s2 = man
batman
path1 = c:\OI\CSharp\Chap11\Concat
c:\OI\CSharp\Chap11\Concat\Concat.cs
"Hello, world"
```

INDEX

You can extract an individual character from a string using a square bracket and a zero-based index.

```
string s1 = "bat";
char ch = s1[0];    // contains 'b'
```

RELATIONAL OPERATORS

In general, for reference types, the **==** and **!=** operators check if the *object references* are the same, not whether the contents of the memory locations referred to are the same. However, the **String** class overloads these operators, so that the textual content of the strings is compared. The program **StringRelation** illustrates using these relational operators on strings. The inequality operators. such as **<**, are *not* available for strings; use the **Compare** method.

String Equality

To fully understand issues of string equality, you should be aware of how the compiler stores strings. When string literals are encountered, they are entered into an internal table of string identities. If a second literal is encountered with the same string data, an object reference will be returned to the existing string in the table; no second copy will be made. As a result of this compiler optimization, the two object references will be the same, as represented in Figure 11–1.

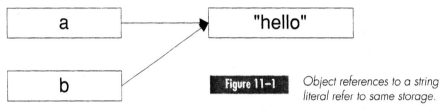

Figure 11–1 *Object references to a string literal refer to same storage.*

You should not be misled by this fact to conclude that two object references to the same string data will always be the same. If the contents of the string get determined at runtime, for example, by the user inputting the data, the compiler has no way of knowing that the second string should have an identical object reference. Hence you will have two distinct object references, which happen to refer to the same data, as illustrated in Figure 11–2.

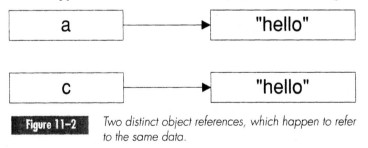

Figure 11–2 *Two distinct object references, which happen to refer to the same data.*

As discussed, when strings are checked for equality, either through the relational operator **==** or through the **Equals** method, a comparison is made of the *contents* of the strings, not of the object references. So in both the previous cases, the strings **a** and **b** will check out as equal. You have to be more careful with other reference types, where reference equality is *not* the same as content equality.

String Comparison

The fundamental way to compare strings for equality is to use the **Equals** method of the **String** class. There are several overloaded versions of this function, including a static version that takes two **string** parameters, and a non-static version that takes one **string** parameter that is compared with the current instance. These methods test if the contents of the strings are identical and are case sensitive. A **bool** value of **true** or **false** is returned.

If you wish to perform a case-insensitive comparison, you may use the **Compare** method. This method has several overloaded versions, all of them static. Two strings, s1 and s2, are compared. An integer is returned expressing the lexical relationship between the two strings, as shown in Table 11–2.

Table 11–2	Return Values of **Compare** Method
Relationship	**Return Value**
s1 less than s2	negative integer
s1 equal to s2	0
s1 greater than s2	positive integer

A third parameter allows you to control the case sensitivity of the comparison. If you use only two parameters, a case-sensitive comparison is performed. The third parameter is a **bool**. A value of **false** calls for a case-sensitive comparison, and a value of **true** calls for ignoring case.

The program **StringCompare** illustrates a number of comparisons, using both the **Equal** and **Compare** methods.

```
// StringCompare.cs

using System;

public class StringCompare
{
   public static void Main(string[] args)
   {
      string a1 = "hello";
      string a2 = "hello";
      string b = "HELLO";
      string c = "goodbye";
      Console.WriteLine("{0}.Equals({1}): {2}",
                  a1, a2, a1.Equals(a2));
      Console.WriteLine("String.Equals({0},{1}): {2}",
                  a1, a2, String.Equals(a1,a2));
      Console.WriteLine("Case sensitive...");
      Console.WriteLine("String.Compare({0},{1}): {2}",
                  a1, b, String.Compare(a1,b));
      Console.WriteLine("Case insensitive...");
```

```
        Console.WriteLine("String.Compare({0},{1},true): {2}",
                        a1, b, String.Compare(a1,b,true));
        Console.WriteLine("Order relation...");
        Console.WriteLine("String.Compare({0},{1}): {2}",
                        a1, c, String.Compare(a1,c));
        Console.WriteLine("String.Compare({0},{1}): {2}",
                        c, a1, String.Compare(c,a1));
    }
}
```

Here is the output:

```
hello.Equals(hello): True
String.Equals(hello,hello): True
Case sensitive...
String.Compare(hello,HELLO): -1
Case insensitive...
String.Compare(hello,HELLO,true): 0
Order relation...
String.Compare(hello,goodbye): 1
String.Compare(goodbye,hello): -1
```

String Input

The **Console** class has methods for inputting characters and strings. The method **Read** will read in a single character (as an **int**). The method **ReadLine** will read in a line of input, terminated by a carriage return, line feed, or combination, and will return a **string**. In general, the **ReadLine** method is the easier to use and synchronizes nicely with **Write** and **WriteLine**. The program **ReadStrings** illustrates reading in a first name, a middle initial, and a last name. All input is done via **ReadLine**. The middle initial as a character is determined by extracting the character at position 0.

```
// ReadStrings.cs

using System;

public class ReadStrings
{
    public static void Main(string[] args)
    {
        Console.Write("First name: ");
        string first = Console.ReadLine();
        Console.Write("Initial: ");
        string initial = Console.ReadLine();
        char ch = initial[0];
        Console.Write("Last name: ");
        string last = Console.ReadLine();
        string name = first + " " + ch + ". " + last;
```

```
        Console.WriteLine("name = {0}", name);
    }
}
```

Here is a sample run of the program:

```
First name: Robert
Initial: J
Last name: Oberg
name = Robert J. Oberg
```

Our **InputWrapper** class, which we introduced in Chapter 2 and have used from time to time, has a method **getString**, which provides a prompt and reads in a string. For an illustration in this chapter of using **InputWrapper** for string input, see the program **StringDemo**.

STRING METHODS

In this section we will survey a few useful methods of the **String** class. Many of the methods have various overloaded versions. We show a representative version. Consult the online documentation for details on these and other methods. The program **StringMethods** demonstrates all the examples that follow.

int Length {get;}

This property returns the length of a string. Notice the convenient shorthand notation that is used for declaring a property.

```
string str = "hello";
int n = str.Length;                    // 5
```

string ToUpper();

This method returns a new string in which all characters of the original string have been converted to uppercase.

```
str = "goodbye";
str = str.ToUpper();                   // GOODBYE
```

string ToLower();

This method returns a new string in which all characters of the original string have been converted to lowercase.

```
str = str.ToLower();                   // goodbye
```

public string Substring(int startIndex, int length);

This method returns a substring that starts from a specified index position in the value and continues for a specified length. Remember that in C# the index of the first character in a string is 0.

```
string sub = str.Substring(4,3);   // bye
```

int IndexOf(string value);

This method returns the index of the first occurrence of the specified string. If the string is not found, -1 is returned.

```
str = "goodbye";
int n1 = str.IndexOf("bye");       // 4
int n2 = str.IndexOf("boo");       // -1
```

STRING BUILDER CLASS

As we have discussed, instances of the **String** class are immutable. As a result, when you manipulate instances of **String** you are frequently obtaining new **String** instances. Depending on your applications, creating all these instances may be expensive. The .NET library provides a special class **StringBuilder** (located in the **System.Text** namespace) in which you may directly manipulate the underlying string without creating a new instance. When you are done, you can create a **String** instance out of an instance of **StringBuilder** by using the **ToString** method.

A **StringBuilder** instance has a capacity and a maximum capacity. These capacities can be specified in a constructor when the instance is created. By default, an empty **StringBuilder** instance starts out with a capacity of 16. As the stored string expands, the capacity will be increased automatically. The program **StringBuilderDemo** provides a simple demonstration of using the **StringBuilder** class. It shows the starting capacity and the capacity after strings are appended. At the end, a **String** is returned.

```
// StringBuilderDemo.cs

using System;
using System.Text;

public class StringBuilderDemo
{
    public static void Main(string[] args)
    {
        StringBuilder build = new StringBuilder();
```

```
        Console.WriteLine("capacity = {0}", build.Capacity);
        build.Append("This is the first sentence.\n");
        Console.WriteLine("capacity = {0}", build.Capacity);
        build.Append("This is the second sentence.\n");
        Console.WriteLine("capacity = {0}", build.Capacity);
        build.Append("This is the last sentence.\n");
        Console.WriteLine("capacity = {0}", build.Capacity);
        string str = build.ToString();
        Console.Write(str);
    }
}
```

Here is the output:

```
capacity = 16
capacity = 34
capacity = 70
capacity = 142
This is the first sentence.
This is the second sentence.
This is the last sentence.
```

PROGRAMMING WITH STRINGS

We conclude this chapter by providing several common examples of programming with strings.

Command Line Arguments

The **Main** method contains a **string** array. The elements of this array are the arguments passed to the program when the program is started from the command line. The program **EchoArguments** writes out each argument on a separate line. We previewed arrays and the **foreach** loop in Chapter 6, and we will discuss arrays in more detail in Chapter 12.

```
// EchoArguments.cs

using System;

public class EchoArguments
{
    public static void Main(string[] args)
    {
        foreach (string arg in args)
            Console.WriteLine(arg);
    }
}
```

Here is the result of running the program from the command line and entering three arguments. (If you are using Visual Studio, the executable file **EchoArguments.exe** will be found in the directory **c:\OI\ CSharp\Chap11\EchoArguments\bin\Debug.**)

```
>echoarguments one two three
one
two
three
```

Command Loops

A common pattern for console programs is for there to be a "command loop." Commands are entered at the keyboard in response to a prompt, the command typed in is compared to the supported commands, and the appropriate code is executed for each command. This command processing continues in a loop until an appropriate command such as "quit" is entered to stop the processing.

```
Console.WriteLine("Enter command, 'quit' to exit");
cmd = iw.getString("> ");
while (! cmd.Equals("quit"))
{
   if (cmd.Equals("length"))
      // process "length" command
   else if (cmd.Equals("new"))
      // process " new " command
   else if (cmd.Equals("show"))
      // process " show " command
...
   else
      help();
   cmd = iw.getString("> ");
}
```

The program **StringDemo** illustrates such a command loop. This program provides an interactive demonstration of a number of methods of the **String** class. Here is a sample run of this program (from within the Visual Studio development environment):

```
Enter string to work on: hello
Enter command, 'quit' to exit
> length
length = 5
> new
new string: goodbye
> show
current string = goodbye
> quit
Press any key to continue
```

Splitting a String

The **String** class provides a very useful method, **Split**, that can be used for splitting a string into substrings, based on specified characters that are used as separators.

```
string[] Split(char[] separator);
```

The separators (such as blank, comma, tab, and new line) are placed in an array of characters, which is passed to the **Split** method. The substrings that are delimited by these separators are returned as an array of strings. If the separators do not occur, the whole string is returned as a one-element array.

The program **StringSplit** provides an illustration of the use of this method.

```
// StringSplit.cs

using System;

public class StringSplit
{
    public static void Main(string[] args)
    {
        string all = "San Francisco\tHilton\t150\t89.95";
        char[] seps = {'\t'};
        string[] pieces = all.Split(seps);
        foreach (string piece in pieces)
            Console.WriteLine(piece);
    }
}
```

If you are not accustomed to the **foreach** loop, you may wish to refer to Chapter 6. Here is the output:

```
San Francisco
Hilton
150
89.95
```

SUMMARY

In this chapter we studied the C# data types **char** and **string**. In C# characters are represented in Unicode and take up 16 bits. The C# **string** data type is an alias for the **String** class, which has a number of useful methods. The C# compiler makes working with strings somewhat easier, allowing you to use operators for concatenation and testing for equality. Instances of **String** are immutable once they have been created. A special class **StringBuilder** can be used in situations where we want to make changes to a string without creating a new object. We concluded the chapter by looking at several common programming situations involving strings, including working with command line arguments, processing a command loop, and splitting a string into constituent parts.

Arrays and Indexers

*rrays are another important data type in practical program-ming. We previewed arrays in Chapter 6 and have been using sim-ple arrays in some of our examples. In this chapter we provide a systematic discussion of this important data type. In C# arrays are objects. They are a reference data type. They are based on the class **System.Array** and so inherit the properties and methods of this class. We will introduce the **Random** class as a convenient way to populate arrays with test data. After examining one-dimensional arrays, we examine two varieties of higher dimen-sional arrays. A "jagged" array is an array of arrays, and each row can have a different number of elements. In "rectangular" arrays, all rows have the same number of elements. Arrays are a special kind of collection, which means that the **foreach** loop can be used in C# for iterating through array elements. At this point we have covered enough C# to write some interesting programs, and we introduce Step 1 of our banking system case study, where a bank is created that holds an array of accounts. We conclude the chapter with a discussion of indexers, which provides a way to access encapsulated data in a class with an array notation.*

ARRAYS

An array is a collection of elements with the following characteristics.

⊕ All array elements must be of the same type. The element type of an array can be any type, including an array type. An array of arrays is often referred to as a *jagged* array.

⊕ An array may have one or more dimensions. For example, a two-dimensional array can be visualized as a table of values. The number of dimensions is known as the array's *rank*.

⊕ Array elements are accessed using one or more computed integer values, each of which is known as an *index*. A one-dimensional array has one index.

⊕ In C# an array index starts at 0, as in other C family languages.

⊕ The elements of an array are created when the array object is created. The elements are automatically destroyed when there are no longer any references to the array object.

One-Dimensional Arrays

An array is declared using square brackets [] after the type, not after the variable.

```
int [] a;                    // declares an array of int
```

Note that the size of the array is not part of its type. The variable declared is a *reference* to the array.

You create the array elements and establish the size of the array using the **new** operator.

```
a = new int[10];             // creates 10 array elements
```

The new array elements start out with the appropriate default values for the type (0 for **int**).

You may both declare and initialize array elements using curly brackets, as in C/C++.

```
int a[] = {2, 3, 5, 7, 11};
```

You can indicate you are done with the array elements by assigning the array reference to **null**.

```
a = null;
```

The garbage collector is now free to deallocate the elements.

SYSTEM.ARRAY

Arrays are objects. **System.Array** is the abstract base class for all array types.

Accordingly, you can use the properties and methods of **System.Array** for any array. Here are some examples:

- **Length** is a property that returns the number of elements currently in the array.
- **Sort** is a static method that will sort the elements of an array.
- **BinarySearch** is a static method that will search for an element in a sorted array, using a binary search algorithm.

```
int [] array = {5, 2, 11, 7, 3};
Array.Sort(a);               // sorts the array
for (int i = 0; i < a.Length; i++)
    Console.Write("{0} ", a[i]);
Console.WriteLine();
int target = 5;
int index = Array.BinarySearch(a, target);
if (index < 0)
    Console.WriteLine("{0} not found", target);
else
    Console.WriteLine("{0} found at {1}", target, index);
```

A complete program containing the code shown above can be found in **ArrayMethods**. Here is the output:

```
2 3 5 7 11
5 found at 2
```

Sample Program

The program **ArrayDemo** is an interactive test program for arrays. A small array is created initially, and you can create new arrays. You can populate an array either with a sequence of square numbers or with random numbers. You can sort the array, reverse the array, and perform a binary search (which assumes that the array is sorted in ascending order). You can destroy the array by assigning the array reference to **null**.

Interfaces for System.Array

If you look at the documentation for methods of **System.Array**, you will see many references to various *interfaces,* such as **IComparable**. By using such interfaces you can control the behavior of methods of **System.Array**. For example, if you want to sort an array of objects of a class that you define, you must implement the interface **IComparable** in your class so that the **Sort** method knows how to compare elements to carry out the sort. The .NET Framework provides an implementation of **IComparable** for all the primitive types. We will come back to this point after we discuss interfaces in Chapter 17.

RANDOM NUMBER GENERATION

The **ArrayDemo** program contains the following code for populating an array with random integers between 0 and 100.

```
Random rand = new Random();
for (int i = 0; i < size; i++)
{
        array[i] = rand.Next(100);
}
```

The .NET Framework provides a useful class, **Random**, in the **System** namespace that can be used for generating pseudo-random numbers for simulations.

Constructors

There are two constructors:

```
Random();                    // uses default seed
Random(int seed);            // seed is specified
```

The default seed is based on date and time, resulting in a different stream of random numbers each time. By specifying a seed, you can produce a deterministic stream.

Next Methods

There are three overloaded **Next** methods that return a random **int**.

```
int Next();
int Next(int maxValue);
int Next(int minValue, int maxValue);
```

The first method returns an integer greater than or equal to zero and less than **Int32.MaxValue**. The second method returns an integer greater than or equal to zero and less than **maxValue**. The third method returns an integer greater than or equal to **minValue** and less than or equal to **maxValue**.

NextDouble Method

The **NextDouble** method produces a random double between 0 and 1.

```
double NextDouble();
```

The return value **r** is in the range: $0 <= r < 1$.

JAGGED ARRAYS

You can declare an array of arrays, or a "jagged" array. Each row can have a different number of elements.

```
int [][] binomial;
```

You then create the array of rows, specifying how many rows there are (each row is itself an array).

```
binomial = new int [rows][];
```

Next you create the individual rows:

```
binomial[i] = new int [i+1];
```

Finally you can assign individual array elements:

```
binomial[0][0] = 1;
```

The example program **Pascal** creates and prints Pascal's triangle.

```
// Pascal.cs

using System;

public class Pascal
{
public static void Main(string[] args)
{
   int [][] binomial;
   int rows = 5;
   binomial = new int [rows][];
   binomial[0] = new int[1];
   binomial[0][0] = 1;
   if (rows > 1)
   {
      binomial[1] = new int[2];
      binomial[1][0] = 1;
      binomial[1][1] = 1;
   }
   for (int i = 2; i < rows; i++)
   {
      binomial[i] = new int [i+1];
      binomial[i][0] = 1;
      binomial[i][i] = 1;
      for (int j = 1; j < i; j++)
      {
         binomial[i][j] = binomial[i-1][j-1]
                     + binomial[i-1][j];
      }
```

```
    }
    Console.WriteLine(
        "Pascal triangle via nested for loops");
    for (int i = 0; i < rows; i++)
    {
        for (int j = 0; j <= i; j++)
        {
            Console.Write("{0} ", binomial[i][j]);
        }
        Console.WriteLine();
    }
    ...
    }
}
```

Here is the output:

```
Pascal triangle via nested for loops
1
1 1
1 2 1
1 3 3 1
1 4 6 4 1
```

Higher dimensional jagged arrays can be created following the same principles.

RECTANGULAR ARRAYS

C# also permits you to define rectangular arrays, where all rows have the same number of elements. First you declare the array:

```
int [,] MultTable;
```

Then you create all the array elements, specifying the number of rows and columns:

```
MultTable = new int[rows, columns];
```

Finally you can assign individual array elements:

```
MultTable[i,j] = i * j;
```

The example program **RectangularArray** creates and prints out a multiplication table.

```
// RectangularArray.cs

using System;
```

```
public class RectangularArray
{
    public static void Main(string[] args)
    {
      int rows = 5;
      Console.WriteLine("Multiplication Table");
      int [,]MultTable = new int[rows, rows];
      for (int i = 0; i < rows; i++)
      {
          for (int j = 0; j < rows; j++)
          {
              MultTable[i,j] = i * j;
              Console.Write("{0}    ", MultTable[i,j]);
          }
          Console.WriteLine();
      }
      ...
    }
}
```

Here is the output:

```
Multiplication Table
0      0      0      0      0
0      1      2      3      4
0      2      4      6      8
0      3      6      9      12
0      4      8      12      16
```

Note that the columns do not quite line up. We will discuss formatting in Chapter 15.

Higher dimensional rectangular arrays can be created following the same principles.

ARRAYS AS COLLECTIONS

The class **System.Array** supports the **IEnumerable** interface. Hence arrays can be treated as *collections*, a topic we will discuss in Chapter 18. This means that a **foreach** loop can be used to iterate through the elements of an array.

The **Pascal** example code contains nested **foreach** loops to display the jagged array. The outer loop iterates through all the rows, and the inner loop iterates through all the elements within a row.

```
// Pascal.cs
...
```

```
Console.WriteLine(
   "Pascal triangle via nested foreach loop");
foreach (int[] row in binomial)
{
   foreach (int x in row)
   {
      Console.Write("{0} ", x);
   }
   Console.WriteLine();
}
```

In the **RectangularArray** example there is only one collection. The **foreach** loop prints out all the array elements on one line, which represents the order in which the array elements are stored in memory. You can see that C# uses "row major" order for storing rectangular arrays: All the elements of the first row are stored, then all the elements of the next row, and so on. Here is the code:

```
// RectangularArray.cs
...

foreach (int x in MultTable)
{
      Console.Write("{0} ", x);
}
Console.WriteLine();
```

Here is the output:

```
0 0 0 0 0 1 2 3 4 0 2 4 6 8 0 3 6 9 12 0 4 8 12 16
```

BANK CASE STUDY: STEP 1

We have covered enough C# that we can begin implementing some interesting programs. Over the next several chapters, the bulk of our examples will be focused on a case study of a banking system. The code for the case study will be in the **CaseStudy** directory of each chapter.

The examples we have looked at so far in this chapter have all been arrays of integers. Arrays can be constructed using *any* data type, including user-defined classes. In this section we will extend our bank account sample program to implement a **Bank** class, which will contain an array of **Account** objects. Our case study at this point consists of five classes, each in its own file.

> ▪ **InputWrapper**. This class simplifies prompting for input and reading in the data. It is identical to the class by this name that we have used previously.

* **Account**. This class encapsulates a single bank account, consisting of an **Id**, an **Owner**, and a **Balance**. Operations are **Deposit** and **Withdraw**.

* **Bank**. This class represents a bank, which has several accounts. Methods are provided to add an account, delete an account, and get a list of accounts.

* **TestBank**. This class provides an interactive test program for exercising the **Bank** class. Commands are provided to open an account, close an account, show all the accounts, and start an ATM to perform transactions on a particular account.

* **Atm**. This class provides a user interface for the ATM, which allows a user to perform transactions on a particular account. The operations supported are deposit, withdraw, change owner name, and show account information.

Account

The **Account** class is based on the **Account** class in the **AccountProperty** program in Chapter 10. This version of **Account** adds a **Transactions** property, which keeps a count of the number of transactions (deposits and withdrawals) that have been performed. A new method, **GetStatement**, returns a string showing the owner, the ID, the number of transactions, and the balance. The class no longer assigns an ID internally; instead, an ID is assigned by the **Bank** class. Here is the code for the class:

```
// Account.cs

public class Account
{
    private int id;
    private decimal balance;
    private string owner;
    private int numXact = 0;   // number of transactions
    public Account(decimal balance, string owner, int id)
    {
        this.balance = balance;
        this.owner = owner;
        this.id = id;
    }
    public void Deposit(decimal amount)
    {
        balance += amount;
        numXact++;
    }
    public void Withdraw(decimal amount)
    {
        balance -= amount;
```

```
        numXact++;
    }
    public decimal Balance
    {
        get
        {
            return balance;
        }
    }
    public int Id
    {
        get
        {
            return id;
        }
    }
    public string Owner
    {
        get
        {
            return owner;
        }
        set
        {
            owner = value;
        }
    }
    public int Transactions
    {
        get
        {
            return numXact;
        }
    }
    public string GetStatement()
    {
        string s = "Statement for " + this.Owner + " id = " +
                Id + "\n" + this.Transactions +
                " transactions, balance = " + balance;
        return s;
    }
}
```

Bank

The class **Bank** maintains an array of **Account** objects. Separate counters are maintained for the next ID and for the number of open accounts. Methods are provided to add an account, delete an account, get a list of accounts (in the form of an array of strings), and find an account, given the account ID.

The constructor creates an array that can store up to 10 accounts and then adds three accounts as initial test data.

```
// Bank.cs

using System;

public class Bank
{
    private Account[] accounts;
    private int nextid = 1;
    private int count = 0;
    public Bank()
    {
        accounts = new Account[10];
        AddAccount(100, "Bob");
        AddAccount(200, "Mary");
        AddAccount(300, "Charlie");
    }
    public int AddAccount(decimal bal, string owner)
    {
        Account acc;
        int id = nextid++;
        acc = new Account(bal, owner, id);
        accounts[count++] = acc;
        return id;
    }
    public string[] GetAccounts()
    {
        string[] array = new string[count];
        for (int i = 0; i < count; i++)
        {
            string owner = accounts[i].Owner;
            string sid = accounts[i].Id.ToString();
            string sbal = accounts[i].Balance.ToString();
            string str = sid + "\t" + owner + "\t" + sbal;
            array[i] = str;
        }
        return array;
    }
    public void DeleteAccount(int id)
    {
        int index = FindIndex(id);
        if (index != -1)
        {
            // move accounts down
            for (int i = index; i < count; i++)
            {
                accounts[i] = accounts[i+1];
            }
```

```
            count--;
        }
    }
    private int FindIndex(int id)
    {
        for (int i = 0; i < count; i++)
        {
            if (accounts[i].Id == id)
                return i;
        }
        return -1;
    }
    public Account FindAccount(int id)
    {
        for (int i = 0; i < count; i++)
        {
            if (accounts[i].Id == id)
                return accounts[i];
        }
        return null;
    }
}
```

TestBank

The **TestBank** class provides a user interface in the **Main** method to open an account, close an account, and show all the accounts. The command "account" brings up an ATM user interface to allow the user to perform transactions on a particular account.

```
// TestBank.cs

using System;

public class TestBank
{
    public static void Main()
    {
        Bank bank = new Bank();
        InputWrapper iw = new InputWrapper();
        string cmd;
        Console.WriteLine("Enter command, quit to exit");
        cmd = iw.getString("> ");
        while (! cmd.Equals("quit"))
        {
            if (cmd.Equals("open"))
            {
                decimal bal = iw.getDecimal(
                                    "starting balance: ");
```

```
            string owner = iw.getString("owner: ");
            int id = bank.AddAccount(bal, owner);
            Console.WriteLine("Account opened, id = {0}",
                            id);
        }
        else if (cmd.Equals("close"))
        {
            int id = iw.getInt("account id: ");
            bank.DeleteAccount(id);
        }
        else if (cmd.Equals("show"))
            ShowArray(bank.GetAccounts());
        else if (cmd.Equals("account"))
        {
            int id = iw.getInt("account id: ");
            Account acc = bank.FindAccount(id);
            Atm.ProcessAccount(acc);
        }
        else
            help();
        cmd = iw.getString("> ");
    }
}
private static void ShowArray(string[] array)
{
    foreach (string str in array)
        Console.WriteLine(str);
}
private static void help()
{
    Console.WriteLine(
        "The following commands are available:");
    Console.WriteLine("\topen      -- open an account");
    Console.WriteLine("\tclose     -- close an account");
    Console.WriteLine("\tshow      -- show all accounts");
    Console.WriteLine(
      "\taccount  -- perform transactions on an account");
    Console.WriteLine("\tquit      -- exit the program");
}
}
```

Atm

The **Atm** class has a single static method, **ProcessAccount**, which provides
a user interface for performing transactions on an account. The operations
supported are deposit, withdraw, change the owner name, and obtain a current statement for the account.

```csharp
// Atm.cs
using System;

public class Atm
{
    public static void ProcessAccount(Account acc)
    {
        Console.WriteLine("balance = {0}", acc.Balance);
        string cmd;
        InputWrapper iw = new InputWrapper();
        Console.WriteLine("Enter command, quit to exit");
        cmd = iw.getString(">> ");
        while (! cmd.Equals("quit"))
        {
            if (cmd.Equals("deposit"))
            {
                decimal amount = iw.getDecimal("amount: ");
                acc.Deposit(amount);
                Console.WriteLine("balance = {0}", acc.Balance);
            }
            else if (cmd.Equals("withdraw"))
            {
                decimal amount = iw.getDecimal("amount: ");
                acc.Withdraw(amount);
                Console.WriteLine("balance = {0}", acc.Balance);
            }
            else if (cmd.Equals("owner"))
            {
                string owner = iw.getString("new owner name: ");
                acc.Owner = owner;
                show(acc);
            }
            else if (cmd.Equals("show"))
                show(acc);
            else
                accountHelp();
            cmd = iw.getString(">> ");
        }
    }
    private static void show(Account acc)
    {
        Console.WriteLine(acc.GetStatement());
    }
    private static void accountHelp()
    {
        Console.WriteLine(
            "The following commands are available:");
        Console.WriteLine("\tdeposit  -- make a deposit");
        Console.WriteLine("\twithdraw -- make a withdrawal");
        Console.WriteLine("\towner    -- change owner name");
        Console.WriteLine(
```

```
        "\tshow     -- show account information");
     Console.WriteLine("\tquit    -- exit the ATM");
   }
}
```

Running the Case Study

You should become thoroughly familiar with this case study, as we will use it extensively in the next several chapters. You should both study the code and run it. Again, the program is located in the **CaseStudy** directory for this chapter. The following is a transcript of a sample run, in which an account is added, the accounts are shown, a deposit is made to the new account, an account is deleted, and the accounts are shown again.

```
Enter command, quit to exit
> open
starting balance: 400
owner: David
Account opened, id = 4
> show
1         Bob        100
2         Mary       200
3         Charlie    300
4         David      400
> account
account id: 4
balance = 400
Enter command, quit to exit
>> deposit
amount: 25
balance = 425
>> quit
> close
account id: 1
> show
2         Mary       200
3         Charlie    300
4         David      425
>
```

INDEXERS

C# provides various ways to help the user of a class access encapsulated data. In Chapter 10 we saw how *properties* can provide access to a single piece of data associated with a class, making it appear like a public field. In this section we will see how *indexers* provide a similar capability for accessing a group of data items, using an array index notation. Indexers can be provided when there is a private array or other collection. But an indexer can also be provided even if there is nothing like an array within the class.

The program **ColorIndex** provides an illustration. There are three **byte** private variables, **red**, **green**, and **blue**, that hold a color intensity value between 0 and 255 for the three primary colors. We want to provide a way of accessing these values through a "color index" that will be 0 for red, 1 for green, and 2 for blue. The following code does the job:

```
// ColorIndex.cs

public class ColorIndex
{
private byte red = 255;
   private byte green = 127;
   private byte blue = 0;
   public byte this[int index]
   {
      get
      {
         if (index == 0)
            return red;
         else if (index == 1)
            return green;
         else
            return blue;
      }
      set
      {
         if (index == 0)
            red = value;
         else if (index == 1)
            green = value;
         else
            blue = value;
      }
   }
   public string Color
   {
      get
      {
         return red + ":" + green + ":" + blue;
      }
   }
}
```

The notation is somewhat similar to that used for properties, with **set** and **get** functions. But there is no "name" for the indexer, as the indexer is accessed through a variable of type **ColorIndex** and an index. So where a property name would be present, we use **this** for an indexer, and there is an index. In making an assignment, the keyword **value** is used, just as for properties. Here is the code for the test program, where we make use of the index notation.

```
// TestColorIndex.cs

using System;

public class TestColorIndex
{
    public static void Main(string[] args)
    {
        ColorIndex ci = new ColorIndex();
        Console.WriteLine(ci.Color);
        Console.WriteLine("red = {0}", ci[0]);
        Console.WriteLine("green = {0}", ci[1]);
        Console.WriteLine("blue = {0}", ci[2]);
        ci[0] = 77;
        ci[1] = 133;
        ci[2] = 199;
        Console.WriteLine(ci.Color);
    }
}
```

Here is the output:

```
255:127:0
red = 255
green = 127
blue = 0
77:133:199
```

SUMMARY

In this chapter we provided a systematic discussion of the array data type. In C# arrays are objects. They are a reference data type and are based on the class **System.Array**. Methods are available to perform operations such as sorting and searching. The **Random** class provides a convenient way to populate arrays with test data. After examining one-dimensional arrays, we looked at two varieties of higher dimensional arrays. A jagged array is an array of arrays, and each row can have a different number of elements. In rectangular arrays, all rows have the same number of elements. Arrays are a special kind of collection, which means that the **foreach** loop can be used in C# for iterating through array elements. We introduced Step 1 of our banking system case study, where a bank that holds an array of accounts is created. We concluded the chapter with a discussion of indexers, which provides a way to access encapsulated data in a class with an array notation.

Inheritance

*Inheritance is a fundamental part of object-oriented program-ming, and we will discuss this subject in depth in this chapter and the following chapter. We will see that C# supports single inheri-tance, and all classes in C# ultimately inherit, or derive, from a common base class, **object**. Inheritance supports code reuse by automatically making all code in a base class available to the derived classes. Inheritance gives rise to another option for access control, called **protected**. Methods in a derived class may hide the corresponding method in the base class, possibly making use of the base class method in their implementation. We explore initial-ization issues connected with inheritance, which involve proper initialization of the base class as well as the current class. We con-clude this chapter by extending the case study to support an inheritance hierarchy of accounts, including checking and sav-ings accounts. We will continue our study of inheritance in the next chapter, taking up polymorphism and related topics.*

INHERITANCE FUNDAMENTALS

Inheritance is a key feature of the object-oriented programming paradigm. You abstract out common features of your classes and put them in a high-level base class. You can add or change features in more specialized derived classes, which "inherit" the standard behavior from the base class.

Inheritance facilitates code reuse and extensibility.

Consider **Account** as a base class, with derived classes such as **CheckingAccount**. All accounts share some characteristics, such as a balance. Different kinds of accounts differ in other respects. For example, a checking account has a monthly fee. Figure 13–1 illustrates the relationship between **Account** and **CheckingAccount**.

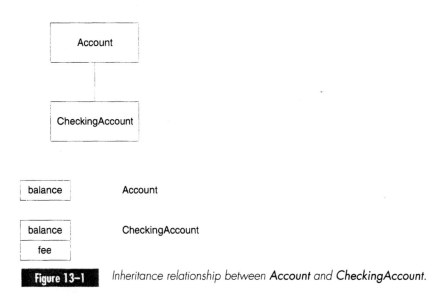

Figure 13–1   *Inheritance relationship between* Account *and* CheckingAccount.

Inheritance in C#

You implement inheritance in C# by specifying the derived class in the **class** statement with a colon followed by the base class. The program **SimpleAccount** illustrates deriving a new class **CheckingAccount** from the class **Account**.

```
// CheckingAccount.cs

public class CheckingAccount : Account
{
    private decimal fee = 5.00m;
    public void Post()
    {
        balance -= fee;
    }
}
```

The class **CheckingAccount** automatically has all the members that **Account** has, and in addition has the field **fee** and the method **Post**. Here is the code for the base class:

```
// Account.cs

public class Account
{
   protected decimal balance;
   public void Deposit(decimal amount)
   {
      balance += amount;
   }
   public void Withdraw(decimal amount)
   {
      balance -= amount;
   }
   public decimal Balance
   {
      get
      {
         return balance;
      }
   }
}
```

Here is code for a test program, which exercises both an **Account** object and a **CheckingAccount** object. Notice that the **CheckingAccount** object can use the **Deposit** and **Withdraw** methods and the **Balance** property of the base class. No code had to be provided in the derived class for these operations. The derived class can also make use of the new method **Post**.

```
// TestAccount.cs

using System;

public class TestAccount
{
   public static void Main(string[] args)
   {
      Account acc = new Account();
      Console.WriteLine("Account object");
      Console.WriteLine("balance = {0}", acc.Balance);
      acc.Deposit(100);
      acc.Withdraw(25);
      Console.WriteLine("balance = {0}", acc.Balance);
      CheckingAccount chk = new CheckingAccount();
      Console.WriteLine("CheckingAccount object");
      Console.WriteLine("balance = {0}", chk.Balance);
      chk.Deposit(200);
      chk.Withdraw(25);
      Console.WriteLine("balance = {0}", chk.Balance);
      chk.Post();
```

```
        Console.WriteLine("balance = {0}", chk.Balance);
    }
}
```

Here is the output:

```
Account object
balance = 0
balance = 75
CheckingAccount object
balance = 0
balance = 175
balance = 170
```

Single Inheritance

It is important to understand that C# supports only *single inheritance*. In C#
a class can derive from only *one* immediate base class. Some languages, such
as C++, support multiple inheritance, in which a class can derive from two or
more base classes. Multiple inheritance is a powerful feature, but it is also
difficult to use correctly. The single inheritance model of C# is simpler.

Although multiple inheritance is somewhat problematical, there is great
benefit in organizing class behavior into several independent *interfaces*. The
basic idea is to group related methods together into an interface and allow a
class to support multiple interfaces. We will discuss interfaces in detail in
Chapter 17.

Root Class

C# shares a characteristic with some other important object-oriented languages, such as Java and Smalltalk, that have a single inheritance model. C#
has a root class called **object** that is the ultimate base class of every class in
C#. You do not need to use the colon notation to show that your class
derives from **object**—the compiler does that for you automatically. If your
class is derived from another class, it will pick up the methods of its immediate base class plus the methods from classes further up the hierarchy. Figure
13–2 illustrates the three-level hierarchy of **CheckingAccount** derived from
Account, which in turn is derived from **object**.

Figure 13-2 *A three-level hierarchy ultimately deriving from **object**.*

The C# keyword **object** is an alias for **System.Object** in the .NET Framework class library. All classes in all .NET languages ultimately inherit from **System.Object**. We will study some of the important methods of this root class in Chapter 18.

ACCESS CONTROL

C# has two means for controlling accessibility of class members. Access can be controlled at both the class level and the member level.

Class Accessibility

An access modifier can be placed in front of the **class** keyword and controls who can get at the class at all. Access can be further restricted by member accessibility, discussed in the next subsection.

PUBLIC

The most common access modifier of a class is **public**, which makes the class available to everyone. All of our class examples so far have had **public** accessibility. Whenever we are implementing a class that anyone can use, we want to make it **public**.

INTERNAL

The **internal** modifier makes a class available within the current *assembly*, which can be thought of as a logical EXE or DLL. (Assemblies were introduced in Chapter 1 and will be discussed in more detail in Chapter 21.) All of our projects so far have built a single assembly, with both the client test program and the class(es) in this assembly. That means that if we had used **internal** for the class modifier, the programs would have still worked. But later, if we put our classes into a DLL and try to access them from a client program in a separate EXE, any **internal** classes would not be accessible. So using **public** for class accessibility is generally a good idea.

A common use of the **internal** modifier is for helper classes that are only intended to be used within the current assembly, and not generally.

Note that if you omit the access modifier in front of a class, **internal** will be the default used by the compiler.

Member Accessibility

Access to individual class members can be controlled by placing an access modifier such as **public** or **private** in front of the member. Member access can only further restrict access to a class, not widen it. Thus if you have a class with **internal** accessibility, making a member **public** will not make it accessible from outside the assembly.

PUBLIC

A **public** member can be accessed from outside the class.

PRIVATE

A **private** member can be accessed only from within the class.

PROTECTED

Inheritance introduces a third kind of accessibility, **protected**. A protected member can be accessed from within the class and from within any derived classes.

The **SimpleAccount** program that we have already examined illustrates use of **protected** accessibility. The field **balance** in the **Account** class is declared as **protected**, because the **Post** method of the **CheckingAccount** class needs access to **balance**. Note that read access is publicly available through the **Balance** method, but **Post** also updates **balance**. Here again is the definition of **Account**. Note use of the keyword **protected**.

```
// Account.cs

public class Account
{
    protected decimal balance;
    ...
```

And here is the **CheckingAccount** class that makes use of **balance**:

```
// CheckingAccount.cs

public class CheckingAccount : Account
```

```
{
   private decimal fee = 5.00m;
   public void Post()
   {
      balance -= fee;
   }
}
```

INTERNAL

An **internal** member can be accessed from within classes in the same assembly but not from classes outside the assembly.

INTERNAL PROTECTED

An **internal protected** member can be accessed either from within the assembly or from outside the assembly by a derived class.

METHOD HIDING

In our first example of inheritance we added a new method **Post** to our derived class **CheckingAccount**. The derived class inherited the methods **Deposit** and **Withdraw**, which are automatically available "as is." Sometimes we may want the derived class to do something a little different for some of the methods of the base class. In this case we will put code for these changed methods in the derived class, and we say the derived class "hides" the corresponding methods in the base class. Note that hiding a method requires that the signatures match exactly. (Methods have the same signature if they have the same number of parameters, and these parameters have the same types and modifiers, such as **ref** or **out**. The return type does not contribute to defining the signature of a method. We discussed signatures in Chapter 10.)

In C#, if you declare a method in a derived class that has the same signature as a method in the base class, you will get a compiler warning message. In such a circumstance, there are two things you may wish to do. The first is to *hide* the base class method, which is what we discuss in this section. The second is to *override* the base class method, which we will discuss in the next chapter.

To hide a base class method, place the keyword **new** in front of the method in the derived class. When you hide a method of the base class, you may want to call the base class method within your implementation of the new method. You can do this by using the keyword **base**, followed by a period, followed by the method name and actual parameters.

The example program **HideAccount** illustrates method hiding. This program has the same **Account** base class, as in our previous example **SimpleAccount**. But our derived class **CheckingAccount** is somewhat different. In place of calculating a flat fee, the fee instead is based on the number of transactions. Thus the methods **Deposit** and **Withdraw** now have to increment a count of the number of transactions besides performing the actual operation, which can be delegated to the base class by using the **base** keyword. Here is the code for the derived class:

```
// CheckingAccount.cs

public class CheckingAccount : Account
{
    private const decimal FEE = .25m;
    private int numXact = 0;    // number of transactions
    new public void Deposit(decimal amount)
    {
        base.Deposit(amount);
        numXact++;
    }
    new public void Withdraw(decimal amount)
    {
        base.Withdraw(amount);
        numXact++;
    }
    public void Post()
    {
        balance -= FEE * numXact;
        numXact = 0;
    }
}
```

INITIALIZATION

An important issue when working with inheritance is *initialization*. A common way to initialize a class instance is through a constructor. When the class is derived from a base class, we may want to invoke a base class constructor to perform further initialization. In this section we will see how to do implement such initializations. We will also review how initialization works without regard to inheritance.

Initialization Fundamentals

A classic problem in computer programming is uninitialized variables. In many programming languages you can get unpredictable results, based on what happens to be in memory when the program is run. C# addresses this issue by either requiring initialization or through assignment of default values.

Local variables *must* be initialized prior to use; you will get a fatal compiler error if you attempt to use a local variable which has not been initialized.

Member variables of a class are initialized to default values. Numeric data types are initialized to zero, and reference data types are initialized to **null**.

A member variable can be initialized right where it is defined. This code of both declaring and initializing a variable is called an *initializer*. An initializer applies to all class instances.

A member variable can be initialized in a constructor. The constructor code applies after the value has been set in the initializer, and can be used to initialize each instance individually.

The program **TestInitial** illustrates these fundamentals.

```
// TestInitial.cs

using System;

public class TestInitial
{
    private static int b;
    private int c = 1;
    private int d;
    public TestInitial()
    {
        Console.WriteLine("In TestInitial constructor");
        Console.WriteLine("c = {0}", c);
        Console.WriteLine("d = {0}", d);
        d = 2;
    }
    public static void Main(string[] args)
    {
        int a;
        //Console.WriteLine("a = {0}", a);
        Console.WriteLine("b = {0}", b);
        TestInitial ti = new TestInitial();
        Console.WriteLine(
            "In Main after TestInitial object constructed");
        Console.WriteLine("c = {0}", ti.c);
        Console.WriteLine("d = {0}", ti.d);
    }
}
```

If you build and run the program, you will get the following output:

```
b = 0
In TestInitial constructor
c = 1
d = 0
```

```
In Main after TestInitial object constructed
c = 1
d = 2
```

If you uncomment the line, writing out the local variable **a**, you will get a fatal error:

```
testinitial.cs(20,32): error CS0165: Use of unassigned local
variable 'a'
```

It is illegal to use a local variable without first initializing it. Fields of classes have a default value assigned, but you will get a warning if you do not assign a value in your own code.

Default Constructor

As discussed in Chapter 8, constructors can be used to assign values to fields and perform other initializations. If you do not explicitly code an instructor, a default constructor taking no parameters will be provided by the compiler. The default constructor initializes all fields to their default values. The program **InitialAccount\Step0** illustrates a very simple version of the **Account** class, with reliance on a default constructor.

```
// Account.cs

using System;

public class Account
{
    private int id;
    private decimal balance;
    private string owner;
    private int numXact; // number of transactions
    public string GetStatement()
    {
        string s = "owner = " + owner + ", id = " + id +
            ", transactions = " + numXact +", balance = " +
            balance;
        return s;
    }
}
```

The four fields of the class do not have initializers, and you will get warning messages when you compile, but the code is legal. The default constructor will assign these fields to their default values, which will be reported when the **GetStatement** method is called. Here is the test program:

```
// TestAccount.cs

using System;

public class TestAccount
{
    public static void Main(string[] args)
    {
        Account acc;
        acc = new Account();
        ShowAccount("Account", acc);
    }
    private static void ShowAccount(string caption,
                                        Account acc)
    {
        Console.Write("{0}: ", caption);
        Console.WriteLine(acc.GetStatement());
    }
}
```

An account object is constructed using **new**, which invokes the default constructor. **ShowAccount** calls the **GetStatement** method. Here is the output:

```
Account: owner = , id = 0, transactions = 0, balance = 0
```

Overloaded Constructors

You may overload a constructor just like you overload ordinary methods of a class. You provide code for several constructors, which must each have a unique signature. As part of one constructor you may invoke another constructor by using a special colon notation, followed by **this** and actual parameters. This code for the other constructor will then be invoked before entering the curly braces.

If you explicitly code one or more constructors, you can no longer have a default constructor provided automatically by the compiler. If you need to be able to create a new object instance without passing any parameters, you must define a constructor without parameters. You do not need to put any code in the curly braces.

The program **InitialAccount\Step1** illustrates several overloaded constructors. The class is designed so that the user of the class can invoke **new** with three parameters, two parameters, one parameter, or no parameters. Any parameters not explicitly assigned will be given their default values.

```
// Account.cs

using System;

public class Account
```

```
{
    private int id;
    private decimal balance;
    private string owner;
    private int numXact = 0;    // number of transactions
    public Account(decimal balance, string owner, int id)
        : this(balance, owner)
    {
        Console.WriteLine("Account(decimal, string, int)");
        this.id = id;
    }
    public Account(decimal balance, string owner)
        : this(balance)
    {
        Console.WriteLine("Account(decimal, string)");
        this.owner = owner;
    }
    public Account (decimal balance)
    {
        Console.WriteLine("Account(decimal)");
        this.balance = balance;
    }
    public Account()
    {
    }
    public string GetStatement()
    {
        string s = "owner = " + owner + ", id = " + id +
            ", transactions = " + numXact +", balance = " +
            balance;
        return s;
    }
}
```

Write statements are provided inside the various constructors so that you can see the order in which they are invoked. If you like, you may add a write statement to the constructor without parameters. Here is the test program:

```
// TestAccount.cs

using System;

public class TestAccount
{
    public static void Main(string[] args)
    {
        Account acc;
        acc = new Account(100, "Amy", 1);
        ShowAccount("Account", acc);
```

```
    acc = new Account(200, "Bob");
    ShowAccount("Account", acc);
    acc = new Account(300);
    ShowAccount("Account", acc);
    acc = new Account();
    ShowAccount("Account", acc);
  }
  private static void ShowAccount(string caption,
                                 Account acc)
  {
    Console.Write("{0}: ", caption);
    Console.WriteLine(acc.GetStatement());
  }
}
```

Before running the program, try to figure out the exact order in which the various constructors will be invoked and also what values will be assigned. Here is the output:

```
Account(decimal)
Account(decimal, string)
Account(decimal, string, int)
Account: owner = Amy, id = 1,transactions = 0, balance = 100
Account(decimal)
Account(decimal, string)
Account: owner = Bob, id = 0,transactions = 0, balance = 200
Account(decimal)
Account: owner = , id = 0, transactions = 0, balance = 300
Account: owner = , id = 0, transactions = 0, balance = 0
```

Invoking Base Class Constructors

If your derived class has a constructor with parameters, you may wish to pass some of these parameters along to a base class constructor. In C# you can conveniently invoke a base class constructor by using a colon, followed by the **base** keyword and a parameter list. This notation is similar to the notation applied for invoking another constructor in the derived class, only the **base** keyword is used in place of **this**.

Note that the syntax allows you to explicitly invoke a constructor only of an immediate base class. There is no notation that allows you to directly invoke a constructor higher up the inheritance hierarchy.

The program **InitialAccount\Step2** illustrates initialization in the **CheckingAccount** class. (The code for **Account** is the same as in Step 1.)

```
// CheckingAccount.cs

using System;
```

```
public class CheckingAccount : Account
{
        private const decimal FEE = 5.00m;
        public CheckingAccount(decimal balance, string owner,
                                int id): base(balance, owner, id)
        {
        }
        new public string GetStatement()
        {
                string s = base.GetStatement();
                s += ", fee = " + FEE;
                return s;
        }
}
```

Here is the code for the test program. An **Account** object is constructed, and then a **CheckingAccount** object is constructed. Again, you should figure out the order of the various constructors before running the program.

```
// TestAccount.cs

using System;

public class TestAccount
{
    public static void Main(string[] args)
    {
        Account acc;
        acc = new Account(100, "Amy", 1);
        ShowAccount("Account", acc);
        CheckingAccount chk;
        chk = new CheckingAccount(400, "David", 4);
        ShowAccount("CheckingAccount", chk);
    }
    private static void ShowAccount(string caption,
                                        Account acc)
    {
        Console.Write("{0}: ", caption);
        Console.WriteLine(acc.GetStatement());
    }
    private static void ShowAccount(string caption,
                                        CheckingAccount acc)
    {
        Console.Write("{0}: ", caption);
        Console.WriteLine(acc.GetStatement());
    }
}
```

Here is the output:

```
Account(decimal)
Account(decimal, string)
Account(decimal, string, int)
Account: owner = Amy, id = 1,transactions = 0, balance = 100
Account(decimal)
Account(decimal, string)
Account(decimal, string, int)
CheckingAccount: owner = David, id = 4, transactions = 0,
balance = 400, fee = 5
```

BANK CASE STUDY: STEP 2

We conclude this chapter by giving Step 2 of our case study. This step is not a direct extension of Step 1, as there is no bank consisting of many accounts. Also, there is no interactive test program. Instead, Step 2 illustrates an inheritance hierarchy consisting of an **Account** base class and derived classes **CheckingAccount** and **SavingsAccount**, with some simple hardcoded test data. Figure 13–3 illustrates this class hierarchy.

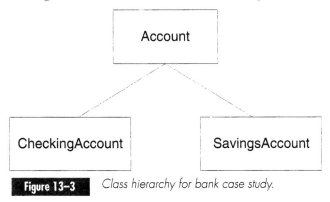

Figure 13–3   *Class hierarchy for bank case study.*

Our case study at this point consists of four classes, each in its own file.

* **Account**. This class encapsulates a single bank account consisting of an **Id**, an **Owner**, and a **Balance**. Operations are **Deposit** and **Withdraw**. There is also a field holding the number of transactions, and a **GetStatement** method is provided to show the current data for an account. The **Account** class counts the number of transactions.
* **CheckingAccount**. This derived class adds a monthly fee, which is assessed to checking accounts but not to other accounts.
* **SavingsAccount**. This derived class adds interest, which is paid to savings accounts but not to other accounts.

- **TestAccount**. This class provides a hardcoded test program, which instantiates some classes, performs some transactions, and obtains statements.

As usual, the case study code may be found in the **CaseStudy** directory for this chapter.

Account

The **Account** class for Step 2 is identical to the class for Step 1, except two of the fields are protected, because derived classes need to access them.

```
// Account.cs - Step 2

public class Account
{
    private int id;
    protected decimal balance;
    private string owner;
    protected int numXact = 0; // number of transactions
    ...
```

CheckingAccount

The **CheckingAccount** class is new to the case study in Step 2. It is similar to the **CheckingAccount** class in the standalone examples, but a somewhat different algorithm is used for calculating the fee. Some free transactions are allowed. Also, the base class already counts the number of transactions, so the **Deposit** and **Withdraw** methods can be used without change. The **GetStatement** method hides the corresponding method in the base class and adds the functionality of also showing the fee. The **Post** method subtracts the fee from the balance and resets the number of transactions to 0. Here is the code:

```
// CheckingAccount.cs - Step 2

using System;

public class CheckingAccount : Account
{
    private decimal fee = 5.00m;
    private const int FREEXACT = 2;
    public CheckingAccount(decimal balance, string owner,
                           int id) : base(balance, owner, id)
    {
    }
    public decimal Fee
    {
        get
```

```
         {
            if (numXact > FREEXACT)
               return fee;
            else
               return 0.00m;
         }
      }
      new public string GetStatement()
      {
         string s = base.GetStatement();
         s += ", fee = " + Fee;
         return s;
      }
      public void Post()
      {
         balance -= Fee;
         numXact = 0;
      }
}
```

SavingsAccount

The **SavingsAccount** class is new to the case study in Step 2. It adds the feature of interest, which is calculated monthly and based on an annual rate. Interest is paid on the minimum balance. The base class **Withdraw** method is hidden, so that the derived class can also update the minimum balance. The **GetStatement** method also hides the base class version, appending information about the interest paid to the statement string. The **Post** method adds the interest and resets the number of transactions and minimum balance.

Here is the code:

```
// SavingsAccount.cs - Step 2

using System;

public class SavingsAccount : Account
{
   private decimal minBalance;
   private decimal rate = 0.06m;
   public SavingsAccount(decimal balance, string owner,
                         int id) base(balance, owner, id)
   {
      minBalance = balance;
   }
   public decimal Interest
   {
      get
```

```
        {
            return minBalance * rate/12;
        }
    }
    new public void Withdraw(decimal amount)
    {
        base.Withdraw(amount);
        if (balance < minBalance)
        {
            minBalance = balance;
        }
    }
    public void Post()
    {
        balance += Interest;
        numXact = 0;
        minBalance = balance;
    }
    new public string GetStatement()
    {
        string s = base.GetStatement();
        s += ", interest = " + Interest;
        return s;
    }
    public decimal Rate
    {
        get
        {
            return rate;
        }
        set
        {
            rate = value;
        }
    }
}
```

TestAccount

The test program is hardcoded. It creates a few account objects, performs a few transactions, and obtains statements. It also shows the balance after posting. Here is the code:

```
// TestAccount.cs - Step 2

using System;

public class TestAccount
{
```

```
public static void Main(string[] args)
{
   Account acc;
   acc = new Account(100, "Bob", 1);
   ShowAccount("Account", acc);
   acc.Deposit(25);
   acc.Deposit(25);
   acc.Withdraw(50);
   ShowAccount("Account", acc);
   CheckingAccount chk = new CheckingAccount(200,
       "Charlie", 2);
   ShowAccount("CheckingAccount", chk);
   chk.Deposit(25);
   chk.Deposit(25);
   chk.Withdraw(100);
   ShowAccount("CheckingAccount", chk);
   chk.Post();
   Console.WriteLine("After posting, balance = {0}",
                     chk.Balance);
   SavingsAccount sav = new SavingsAccount(300,
       "David", 3);
   ShowAccount("SavingsAccount"v, sav);
   sav.Deposit(25);
   sav.Deposit(25);
   sav.Withdraw(100);
   ShowAccount("SavingsAccount", sav);
   sav.Post();
   Console.WriteLine("After posting, balance = {0}",
                     sav.Balance);   }
private static void ShowAccount(string caption,
                                   Account acc)
{
   Console.Write("{0}: ", caption);
   Console.WriteLine(acc.GetStatement());
}
private static void ShowAccount(string caption,
                                   CheckingAccount acc)
{
   Console.Write("{0}: ", caption);
   Console.WriteLine(acc.GetStatement());
}
private static void ShowAccount(string caption,
                                   SavingsAccount acc)
{
   Console.Write("{0}: ", caption);
   Console.WriteLine(acc.GetStatement());
}
}
```

Notice the three overloaded **ShowAccount** methods that do exactly the same thing! We will see in Chapter 14 that with virtual methods we can handle this kind of situation more simply, with a single method that applies to any **Account** object and does the proper thing, depending on the kind of account.

Running the Case Study

Again, you should both study the code and run the case study. In this case, running the case study is trivial, as the program is not interactive. Here is the output, which you should study to make sure you completely understand:

```
Account: Statement for Bob id = 1
0 transactions, balance = 100
Account: Statement for Bob id = 1
3 transactions, balance = 100
CheckingAccount: Statement for Charlie id = 2
0 transactions, balance = 200, fee = 0
CheckingAccount: Statement for Charlie id = 2
3 transactions, balance = 150, fee = 5
After posting, balance = 145
SavingsAccount: Statement for David id = 3
0 transactions, balance = 300, interest = 1.5
SavingsAccount: Statement for David id = 3
3 transactions, balance = 250, interest = 1.25
After posting, balance = 251.25
```

SUMMARY

In this chapter we began our study of inheritance, which is a fundamental part of object-oriented programming. C# supports single inheritance, and all classes in C# ultimately inherit, or derive, from a common base class, **object**. Inheritance supports code reuse by automatically making all code in a base class available to the derived classes. Inheritance gives rise to another option for access control, called **protected**. Methods in a derived class may hide the corresponding method in the base class, possibly making use of the base class method in their implementation. C# has a robust set of features for handling initialization issues, including a mechanism for the proper initialization of the base class as well as the current class. We extended the case study to support an inheritance hierarchy of accounts, including checking and savings accounts. We will continue our study of inheritance in the next chapter, taking up polymorphism and related topics.

Virtual Methods and Polymorphism

The fundamentals of inheritance we discussed in the last chapter are extremely important, but they constitute only part of the story of inheritance. The other part of the story involves the mechanism of virtual methods, *which are not bound to an object at compile time but are bound dynamically at runtime. This dynamic behavior enables* polymorphic code, *which is general code that applies to classes in a hierarchy, and the specific class that determines the behavior is determined at runtime. Polymorphic code can simplify program development and maintenance. In this chapter we examine how virtual methods and polymorphism work in C#. We will see that C# provides keywords* **virtual** *and* **override** *that precisely specify in base and derived classes, respectively, that the programmer is depending on runtime, dynamic binding. By providing a mechanism to specify polymorphic behavior in the language, C# helps programs deal with an issue known as the* "fragile base class problem," *which can result in unexpected behavior in a program when a base class in a library is modified, but the program itself is unchanged.*

We discuss several other related topics in this chapter. Sometimes in an inheritance hierarchy, the base class is never intended to be instantiated. Such a base class is said to be *abstract,* and *must* be derived from in order to be useful. At the opposite end of the spectrum, a class is said to be *sealed* if derivation is not allowed. A class hierarchy can be used to implement heterogeneous collections that can be treated polymorphically. We illustrate the topics of this chapter with the bank case study.

VIRTUAL METHODS AND DYNAMIC BINDING

In C# the normal way methods are tied to classes is through *static binding*. That means the type of an object reference is used at compile time to determine the class whose method is called. The program **StaticAccount** illustrates static binding, using a simplified version of our **Account** class and a derived **CheckingAccount** class. Note the use of the **new** keyword in the **Show** methods of the derived class to specify method hiding.

```
// StaticAccount.cs

using System;

public class Account
{
   public int balance = 100;
   public void Show()
   {
      Console.WriteLine("I am an Account");
   }
}

public class CheckingAccount : Account
{
   public int fee = 5;
   new public void Show()
   {
      Console.WriteLine("I am a CheckingAccount, fee = {0}",
                        fee);
   }
}
```

Here is a test program:

```
// TestStaticAccount.cs

using System;

public class TestAccount
{
   public static void Main(string[] args)
   {
      Account acc = new Account();
      CheckingAccount chk = new CheckingAccount();
      acc.Show();
      chk.Show();
      //chk = acc;         // illegal
      acc = chk;
      acc.Show();          // still Account.Show
   }
}
```

In this program **acc** is an object reference of type **Account**, and calling **Show** through this object reference will *always* result in **Account.Show** being called, no matter what kind of object **acc** may actually be referring to. Here is the output. Notice that the second time we call **Show** through **acc** we are still getting **Account**.

```
I am an Account
I am a CheckingAccount, fee = 5
I am an Account
```

Type Conversions in Inheritance

This program also illustrates another feature of inheritance, type conversions. After the objects **acc** and **chk** have been instantiated, the object references will be referring to different objects, one of type **Account** and the other of type **CheckingAccount**, as illustrated in Figure 14–1. Note that the **CheckingAccount** object has an additional field, **fee**.

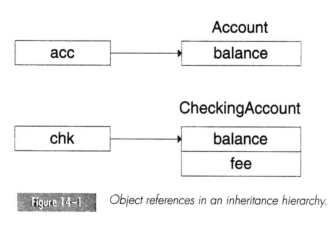

Figure 14–1   *Object references in an inheritance hierarchy.*

The test program tries two type conversions:

```
//chk = acc;        // illegal
acc = chk;
```

CONVERTING DOWN THE HIERARCHY

The first assignment is illegal (as you can verify by uncommenting and trying to compile). Suppose the assignment would be allowed. Then you would have an object reference of type **CheckingAccount** referring to an **Account** object, as illustrated in Figure 14–2.

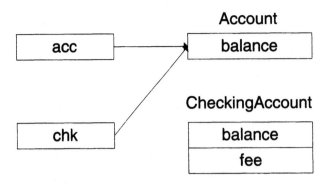

Figure 14-2 *Result of an illegal type conversion.*

If the conversion "down the hierarchy" (from a base class to a derived class) were allowed, the program would be open to a bad failure at runtime if code tried to access a nonexistent member, such as **chk** accessing the member **fee**.

The program **BadConversion** illustrates this behavior. The class definition is the same. In the test program an explicit cast operation is performed. There will then be no error messages at compile time, but there will be a runtime failure. Here is the code:

```
// BadConversion.cs

public class TestAccount
{
   public static void Main(string[] args)
   {
      Account acc = new Account();
      CheckingAccount chk = new CheckingAccount();
      acc.Show();
      chk.Show();
      chk = (CheckingAccount) acc;     // explicit cast
      decimal charge = chk.fee;        // this is bad
   }
}
```

Here is the output. Notice that an "exception" is thrown. We will discuss exceptions in Chapter 16.

```
I am an Account
I am a CheckingAccount, fee = 5

Exception occurred: System.InvalidCastException: An
exception of type System.InvalidCastException was thrown.
   at TestAccount.Main(String[] args) in
c:\oi\csharp\chap14\badconversion\badconversion.cs:line 11
```

CONVERTING UP THE HIERARCHY

The opposite assignment:

```
acc = chk;
```

is perfectly legal. We are converting "up the hierarchy." This is okay because of the IS-A relationship of inheritance. A checking account "is" an account. It is a special kind of account. Everything that applies to an account also applies to a checking account. There can be no "extra field" in the **Account** class that is not also present in the **CheckingAccount** class.

Virtual Methods

In C# you can make a small change to specify that a method in C# will be bound *dynamically*. That means it will be determined at runtime which class's method will be called. The program **VirtualAccount** illustrates this behavior. The file **VirtualAccount.cs** contains class definitions for a base class and a derived class, as before. But this time the **Show** method is declared as **virtual** in the base class. In the derived class the **Show** method is declared **override** (in place of **new** that we used before with method hiding). Now the **Show** method in the derived class does not hide the base class method, but *overrides* it.

```
// VirtualAccount.cs

using System;

public class Account
{
   public int balance = 100;
   virtual public void Show()
   {
      Console.WriteLine("I am an Account");
   }
}

public class CheckingAccount : Account
{
   public int fee = 5;
   override public void Show()
   {
      Console.WriteLine("I am a CheckingAccount, fee = {0}",
                        fee);
   }
}
```

We use the same test program (we just dropped the commented out illegal assignment and changed the comment on invoking the second

acc.Show):

```
// TestVirtualAccount.cs

public class TestAccount
{
    public static void Main(string[] args)
    {
        Account acc = new Account();
        CheckingAccount chk = new CheckingAccount();
        acc.Show();
        chk.Show();
        acc = chk;
        acc.Show();          // now CheckingAccount.Show
    }
}
```

Here is the output. This time, the second time we call **Show** through **acc**, we will be getting the **CheckingAccount** method.

```
I am an Account
I am a CheckingAccount, fee = 5
I am a CheckingAccount, fee = 5
```

Virtual Methods and Efficiency

Virtual method invocation is slightly less efficient than calling an ordinary nonvirtual method. With a virtual method call, there is some overhead at run-time associated with determining which class's method will be invoked. C# allows you to specify in a base class whether you want the flexibility of a virtual method or the slightly greater efficiency of a nonvirtual method. You simply decide whether or not to use the keyword **virtual**. (In some languages all methods are virtual, and you don't have this choice.)

METHOD OVERRIDING

The **override** keyword in C# is very useful for making programs clearer. In some languages, such as C++, there is no special notation for overriding a method in a derived class. You simply declare a method with the same signature as a method in the base class. If the base class method is virtual, the behavior is to override. If the base class method is not virtual, the behavior is to hide. In C# this behavior is made explicit.

The Fragile Base Class Problem

There is a subtle pitfall in object-oriented programming: "the fragile base class problem." Suppose there is no **override** keyword and you have a method in a class that does not hide or override any method in your base classes. But assume that you are using a third-party class library, and your class is ultimately derived from a class in this library. Now suppose a new version of the class library comes out, and the base class you are deriving from has a new virtual method whose signature happens to match one of the methods in your class. Now you can be in trouble! Code in the combined system that consists of your classes and the class library may now behave in unexpected ways. Code that was "expected" to call the new method in the class library—or in code in a derived class that deliberately overrides this method—may now call your method that has nothing whatever to do with the method in the class library.

This situation is rare, but if it occurs it can be extremely vicious. Fortunately, C# helps you avoid such situations by requiring you to use the **override** keyword if you are indeed going to perform an override. If you do not specify either **override** or **new**, you will get a compiler error or warning if a method in your derived class has the same signature as a method in a base class. Thus, if you build against a new version of the class library that introduces an accidental signature match with one of your methods, you will get warned by the compiler.

COM and the Fragile Base Class Problem

There is no inheritance in Microsoft's Component Object Model (COM). Microsoft used the fragile base class problem as a rationale for not providing inheritance. The issue is much more important for binary components, such as COM objects, than for traditional class libraries distributed in source code, because if the problem arises and you have no source for the library, your options are limited. The real killer is for the problem to crop up and not reveal itself in the development lab, but only in the field after the application has been deployed.

Microsoft .NET has similar aims to COM in providing binary components in multiple languages. The C# **override** concept uses a corresponding feature of .NET, so .NET is able to effectively utilize inheritance without the vulnerability that COM would have had.

POLYMORPHISM

The machinery of virtual functions makes it easy to write polymorphic code in C#. As an example of polymorphic code, consider our bank account case study. Imagine a large system with a great many different kinds of accounts. How will you write and maintain code that deals with all these different account types?

A traditional approach is to have a "type field" in an account structure. Then code that manipulates an account can key off this type field to determine the correct processing to perform, perhaps using a **switch** statement. Although straightforward, this approach can be quite tedious and error-prone. Introducing a new kind of account can require substantial maintenance.

Polymorphism can offer a cleaner solution. You organize the different kinds of accounts in a class hierarchy, and you structure your program so that you write general purpose methods that act upon an object reference whose type is that of the base class. Your code calls virtual methods of the base class. The call will be automatically dispatched to the appropriate class, depending on what kind of account is actually being referenced.

The program **PolyAccount** provides an illustration (a more full-blown illustration will be presented later in the chapter with Step 3 of the case study). This version of the **Account** hierarchy is similar to Step 2 of the case study presented in the previous chapter, only now there are virtual methods in the base class, and methods in the derived class override them. Here is the code for the base class:

```
// PolyAccount.cs

public class Account
{
    private int id;
    protected decimal balance;
    private string owner;
    protected int numXact = 0; // number of transactions
    public Account(decimal balance, string owner, int id)
    {
        this.balance = balance;
        this.owner = owner;
        this.id = id;
    }
    virtual public void Deposit(decimal amount)
    {
        balance += amount;
        numXact++;
    }
    virtual public void Withdraw(decimal amount)
    {
```

```
      balance -= amount;
      numXact++;
   }
   ...
   virtual public string GetStatement()
   {
      string s = "Statement for " + this.Owner + " id = " +
                 Id + "\n" + this.Transactions +
                 " transactions, balance = " + balance;
      return s;
   }
   virtual public void Post()
   {
   }
}
```

Methods in the derived classes override the virtual methods in the base class. Here is the code for **CheckingAccount** (which is similar to the code that will be used in Step 3 of the case study):

```
// PolyCheckingAccount.cs

using System;

public class CheckingAccount : Account
{
   private decimal fee = 5.00m;
   private const int FREEXACT = 2;
   public CheckingAccount(decimal balance, string owner,
                          int id) : base(balance, owner, id)
   {
   }
   public decimal Fee
   {
      get
      {
         if (numXact > FREEXACT)
            return fee;
         else
            return 0.00m;
      }
   }
   override public string GetStatement()
   {
      string s = base.GetStatement();
      s += ", fee = " + Fee;
      return s;
   }
   override public void Post()
   {
```

```
        balance -= Fee;
        numXact = 0;
    }
}
```

The payoff comes in the client program, which can now call the virtual methods polymorphically. Here is the code for the test program:

```
// TestPolyAccount.cs

using System;

public class TestAccount
{
    public static void Main(string[] args)
    {
        Account acc;
        acc = new Account(100, "Bob", 1);
        ShowAccount("Account", acc);
        acc.Deposit(25);
        acc.Deposit(25);
        acc.Withdraw(50);
        ShowAccount("Account", acc);
        acc = new CheckingAccount(200, "Charlie", 2);
        ShowAccount("CheckingAccount", acc);
        acc.Deposit(25);
        acc.Deposit(25);
        acc.Withdraw(100);
        ShowAccount("CheckingAccount", acc);
        acc.Post();
        Console.WriteLine("After posting, balance = {0}",
                            acc.Balance);
        acc = new SavingsAccount(300, "David", 3);
        ShowAccount("SavingsAccount", acc);
        acc.Deposit(25);
        acc.Deposit(25);
        acc.Withdraw(100);
        ShowAccount("SavingsAccount", acc);
        acc.Post();
        Console.WriteLine("After posting, balance = {0}",
                            acc.Balance);
    }
    private static void ShowAccount(string caption,
                                        Account acc)
    {
        Console.Write("{0}: ", caption);
        Console.WriteLine(acc.GetStatement());
    }
}
```

In this program there is a single **Account** object reference **acc**. At different places in the program, it is assigned to different kinds of account objects: **Account, CheckingAccount**, and **SavingsAccount**. The code that gets invoked is determined at runtime based upon the type of account being referenced. This is polymorphism. In particular, notice that we need only *one* helper method, **ShowAccount**.

The output is exactly the same as the case study Step 2 output from Chapter 13.

```
Account: Statement for Bob id = 1
0 transactions, balance = 100
Account: Statement for Bob id = 1
3 transactions, balance = 100
CheckingAccount: Statement for Charlie id = 2
0 transactions, balance = 200, fee = 0
CheckingAccount: Statement for Charlie id = 2
3 transactions, balance = 150, fee = 5
After posting, balance = 145
SavingsAccount: Statement for David id = 3
0 transactions, balance = 300, interest = 1.5
SavingsAccount: Statement for David id = 3
3 transactions, balance = 250, interest = 1.25
After posting, balance = 251.25
```

ABSTRACT CLASSES

Sometimes it does not make sense to instantiate a base class. Instead, the base class is used to define a standard template to be followed by the various derived classes. Such a base class is said to be *abstract*, and it cannot be instantiated. In C# you can designate a base class as abstract by using the keyword **abstract**. The compiler will then flag an error if you try to instantiate the class.

An abstract class may have abstract methods, which are not implemented in the class but only in derived classes. The purpose of an abstract method is to provide a template for polymorphism. The method is called through an object reference to the abstract class, but at runtime the object reference will actually be referring to one of the concrete derived classes. The keyword **abstract** is also used to declare abstract methods. In place of curly brackets and implementation code, you simply provide a semicolon after the declaration of the abstract method.

The **Account** class in Step 3 of the case study, which we will examine later in the chapter, provides an example of an abstract class.

```
// Account.cs - Step 3

abstract public class Account
{
   private int id;
   protected decimal balance;
   private string owner;
   protected int numXact = 0; // number of transactions
   ...
   abstract public void Post();
   abstract public string Prompt {get;}
}
```

SEALED CLASSES

At the opposite end of the spectrum from abstract classes are *sealed* classes. While you *must* derive from an abstract class, you *cannot* derive from a sealed class. A sealed class provides functionality that you can use as is, but you cannot derive from the class and hide or override some of the methods. An example in the .NET Framework class library of a sealed class is **System.String**.

Marking a class as sealed protects against unwarranted class derivations. It can also make the code a little more efficient, because any virtual functions in the sealed class are automatically treated by the compiler as nonvirtual.

In C# you use the **sealed** keyword to mark a class as sealed.

HETEROGENEOUS COLLECTIONS

A class hierarchy can be used to implement heterogeneous collections that can be treated polymorphically. For example, you can create an array whose type is that of a base class. Then you can store within this array object references whose type is the base class, but which actually may refer to instances of various derived classes in the hierarchy. You may then iterate through the array and call a virtual method. The appropriate method will be called for each object in the array.

The program **HeterogeneousAccount** illustrates a heterogeneous array of three accounts, which are a mixture of checking and savings accounts. The virtual property **Prompt** returns a prompt string, which is "C: " for a checking account and "S: " for a savings account. Listings for the classes will be provided in the next section, where we present Step 3 of the case study.

Here is the code for the test program that creates the heterogeneous array:

```
// HeterogeneousAccount.cs

using System;

public class TestAccount
{
   public static void Main(string[] args)
   {
      Account[] list = new Account[3];
      list[0] = new CheckingAccount(100, "Bob", 1);
      list[1] = new SavingsAccount(200, "Mary", 2);
      list[2] = new CheckingAccount(300, "Charlie", 3);
      foreach (Account acc in list)
         ShowAccount(acc.Prompt, acc);
   }
   private static void ShowAccount(string caption,
                                   Account acc)
   {
      Console.Write("{0}: ", caption);
      Console.WriteLine(acc.GetStatement());
   }
}
```

Here is the output:

```
C: : Statement for Bob id = 1
0 transactions, balance = 100, fee = 0
S: : Statement for Mary id = 2
0 transactions, balance = 200, interest = 1
C: : Statement for Charlie id = 3
0 transactions, balance = 300, fee = 0
```

CASE STUDY: STEP 3

Step 3 of the case study, as usual in the **CaseStudy** directory for this chapter, is an extension of Step 1 from Chapter 12. The big change is that now we support two kinds of accounts, **CheckingAccount** and **SavingsAccount**, which are derived from the abstract base class **Account**. Each kind of account has its own characteristics. There are now seven classes in all, each in its own file.

* **InputWrapper**. This class simplifies prompting for input and reading in the data. It is identical to the class by this name that we have used previously.
* **Account**. This abstract base class provides a template for accounts,

specifying an **Id**, an **Owner**, a **Balance**, and the number of **Transactions**. Operations are **Deposit, Withdraw,** and **GetStatement**. There is an abstract method **Post** and an abstract property **Prompt**. There is also a virtual method **MonthEnd**.

* **CheckingAccount**. This class provides a **Fee** property and overrides **GetStatement, Post,** and **Prompt**.
* **SavingsAccount**. This class provides an **Interest** property, which is based on a minimum balance. It overrides **Withdraw, GetStatement, Post, MonthEnd,** and **Prompt**.
* **Bank**. This class represents a bank, which has several accounts. Methods are provided to add an account, delete an account, and get a list of accounts.
* **TestBank**. This class provides an interactive test program for exercising the **Bank** class. Commands are provided to open an account, close an account, show all the accounts, and start an "ATM" to perform transactions on a particular account.
* **Atm**. This class provides a user interface for the ATM that allows a user to perform transactions on a particular account. The operations supported are deposit, withdraw, change owner name, and show account information. A special prompt of "C: " or "S: " is shown, depending on whether the account being operated upon is a checking or a savings account.

At this point you should try to understand in general terms how the case study works, especially the operation of the virtual functions. Do not be concerned about every nuance of the business rules of our little bank. The case study is elaborated in greater detail at Step 6 in Chapter 17, where we introduce interfaces. The use of interfaces will help us view the bank at a higher level of abstraction, and in that chapter we provide additional explanation of the case study and more sample runs.

Account

The **Account** class is similar to the version of the class used to illustrate polymorphism earlier in the chapter. The class is now abstract, with the abstract method **Post** and the abstract property **Prompt**. Notice the syntax used in specifying the signature of a property. In this case the property is read-only, so there is only a **get**. There is a nuance introduced here in the form of another virtual method, **MonthEnd**. This virtual method reinitializes an account for the next month. The basic initialization is to set the transaction count to zero. Additional initialization may be done in derived classes (such as the **SavingsAccount** class, discussed later in this chapter).

```
// Account.cs - Step 3

abstract public class Account
```

```
{
   private int id;
   protected decimal balance;
   private string owner;
   protected int numXact = 0; // number of transactions
   public Account(decimal balance, string owner, int id)
   {
      this.balance = balance;
      this.owner = owner;
      this.id = id;
   }
   virtual public void Deposit(decimal amount)
   {
      balance += amount;
      numXact++;
   }
   virtual public void Withdraw(decimal amount)
   {
      balance -= amount;
      numXact++;
   }
   public decimal Balance
   {
      get
      {
         return balance;
      }
   }
   public int Id
   {
      get
      {
         return id;
      }
   }
   public string Owner
   {
      get
      {
         return owner;
      }
      set
      {
         owner = value;
      }
   }
   public int Transactions
   {
      get
      {
```

```
            return numXact;
        }
    }
    virtual public string GetStatement()
    {
        string s = "Statement for " + this.Owner + " id = " +
                Id + "\n" + this.Transactions +
                " transactions, balance = " + balance;
        return s;
    }
    abstract public void Post();
    abstract public string Prompt {get;}
    virtual public void MonthEnd()
    {
        numXact = 0;
    }
}
```

CheckingAccount

Step 3 of the **CheckingAccount** class is similar to the class that was shown in the previous section on polymorphism. The difference is that **Post** method does not set the number of transactions to zero, as that is now the responsibility of the **MonthEnd** method, which is inherited from the **Account** class.

SavingsAccount

The **SavingsAccount** class has an interest rate, which is expressed as a property. The interest itself is the monthly interest, based on a minimum balance. To compute the minimum balance, the **Withdraw** method is overridden. The class also overrides **Post**, **GetStatement**, **Prompt**, and **MonthEnd**.

```
// SavingsAccount.cs - Step 3

using System;

public class SavingsAccount : Account
{
    private decimal minBalance;
    private decimal rate = 0.06m;
    public SavingsAccount(decimal balance, string owner,
                          int id) : base(balance, owner, id)
    {
        minBalance = balance;
    }
    public decimal Interest
    {
        get
        {
```

```
            return minBalance * rate/12;
        }
    }
    override public void Withdraw(decimal amount)
    {
        base.Withdraw(amount);
        if (balance < minBalance)
        {
            minBalance = balance;
        }
    }
    override public void Post()
    {
        balance += Interest;
    }
    override public string GetStatement()
    {
        string s = base.GetStatement();
        s += ", interest = " + Interest;
        return s;
    }
    public decimal Rate
    {
        get
        {
            return rate;
        }
        set
        {
            rate = value;
        }
    }
    override public string Prompt
    {
        get
        {
            return "S: ";
        }
    }
    override public void MonthEnd()
    {
        base.MonthEnd();
        minBalance = balance;
    }
}
```

Bank

The class **Bank** maintains an array of **Account** objects. The code is very similar for Step 1 provided in Chapter 12. The big change is that the

AddAccount method now takes an account type parameter, which is specified as an **enum** data type, **AccountType**. Based on the type, either a **CheckingAccount** or a **SavingsAccount** is instantiated. Also, the **GetAccounts** method is modified so that the prompt string for the particular kind of account is returned as part of the string describing the account.

```
// Bank.cs - Step 3

using System;

public enum AccountType
{
    Checking,
    Savings,
    Invalid
}

public class Bank
{
    private Account[] accounts;
    private int nextid = 1;
    private int count = 0;
    public Bank()
    {
        accounts = new Account[10];
        AddAccount(AccountType.Checking, 100, "Bob");
        AddAccount(AccountType.Savings, 200, "Mary");
        AddAccount(AccountType.Checking, 300, "Charlie");
    }
    public int AddAccount(AccountType type, decimal bal,
                          string owner)
    {
        Account acc;
        int id = nextid++;
        switch(type)
        {
            case AccountType.Checking:
                acc = new CheckingAccount(bal, owner, id);
                break;
            case AccountType.Savings:
                acc = new SavingsAccount(bal, owner, id);
                break;
            default:
                Console.WriteLine("Unexpected AccountType");
                return -1;
        }
        accounts[count++] = acc;
        return id;
    }
    public string[] GetAccounts()
```

```
{
    string[] array = new string[count];
    for (int i = 0; i < count; i++)
    {
        string owner = accounts[i].Owner;
        string stype = accounts[i].Prompt;
        string sid = accounts[i].Id.ToString();
        string sbal = accounts[i].Balance.ToString();
        string str = sid + "\t" + stype + owner + "\t" +
                     sbal;
        array[i] = str;
    }
    return array;
}
public void DeleteAccount(int id)
{
    int index = FindIndex(id);
    if (index != -1)
    {
        // move accounts down
        for (int i = index; i < count; i++)
        {
            accounts[i] = accounts[i+1];
        }
        count--;
    }
}
private int FindIndex(int id)
{
    for (int i = 0; i < count; i++)
    {
        if (accounts[i].Id == id)
            return i;
    }
    return -1;
}
public Account FindAccount(int id)
{
    for (int i = 0; i < count; i++)
    {
        if (accounts[i].Id == id)
            return accounts[i];
    }
    return null;
}
}
```

Atm

The **Atm** class is virtually identical to the Step 1 version. This is the beauty of polymorphism. The **ProcessAccount** method takes an object reference to the **Account** base class, and it calls virtual methods of this class, which get resolved properly at runtime to the appropriate methods of **CheckingAccount** or **SavingsAccount**. The only enhancement added to the Step 3 version is using the virtual **Prompt** property of **Account** to tailor the prompt according to the type of account being worked on.

```
// Atm.cs - Step 3

using System;

public class Atm
{
    public static void ProcessAccount(Account acc)
    {
        Console.WriteLine("balance = {0}", acc.Balance);
        string cmd;
        InputWrapper iw = new InputWrapper();
        Console.WriteLine("Enter command, quit to exit");
        cmd = iw.getString(acc.Prompt);
        while (! cmd.Equals("quit"))
        {
            if (cmd.Equals("deposit"))
            {
                decimal amount = iw.getDecimal("amount: ");
                acc.Deposit(amount);
                Console.WriteLine("balance = {0}", acc.Balance);
            }
            ...
            cmd = iw.getString(acc.Prompt);
        }
    }
    ...
```

TestBank

The **TestBank** class provides a user interface in the **Main** method to open an account, close an account, and show all the accounts. The command "account" brings up an ATM user interface to allow the user to perform transactions on a particular account. The only difference between Step 3 and Step 1 is in opening an account, where the user is queried for the type of account (checking or savings) to open.

```
// TestBank.cs - Step 3

using System;
```

```
public class TestBank
{
    public static void Main()
    {
        Bank bank = new Bank();
        InputWrapper iw = new InputWrapper();
        string cmd;
        Console.WriteLine("Enter command, quit to exit");
        cmd = iw.getString("> ");
        while (! cmd.Equals("quit"))
        {
            if (cmd.Equals("open"))
            {
                AccountType type;
                string stype = iw.getString("account type: ");
                switch(stype)
                {
                   case "checking":
                      type = AccountType.Checking;
                      break;
                   case "savings":
                      type = AccountType.Savings;
                      break;
                  default:
                      type = AccountType.Invalid;
                      break;
                }
                if (type == AccountType.Invalid)
                {
                   Console.WriteLine(
                     "Valid account types are checking/savings");
                   continue;
                }
                decimal bal = iw.getDecimal(
                    "starting balance: ");
                string owner = iw.getString("owner: ");
                int id = bank.AddAccount(type, bal, owner);
                Console.WriteLine("Account opened, id = {0}",
                                       id);
        }
...
```

Running the Case Study

When you run the case study, you should find similar behavior to Step 1. The difference, of course, is that when you open accounts, you specify checking or savings. The following transcript shows exercising the same commands used when running the Step 1 version at the end of Chapter 12.

We choose "savings" as the type of the new account that is added.

```
Enter command, quit to exit
> open
account type: savings
starting balance: 400
owner: David
Account opened, id = 4
> show
1        C: Bob        100
2        S: Mary       200
3        C: Charlie    300
4        S: David      400
> account
account id: 4
balance = 400
Enter command, quit to exit
S: deposit
amount: 25
balance = 425
S: quit
> close
account id: 1
> show
2        S: Mary       200
3        C: Charlie    300
4        S: David      425
>
```

SUMMARY

In this chapter we discussed the mechanism of *virtual methods*, which are not bound to an object at compile time but are bound dynamically at runtime. This dynamic behavior enables *polymorphic* code, which is general code that applies to classes in a hierarchy, and the specific class that determines the behavior is determined at runtime. Polymorphic code can simplify program development and maintenance. C# provides keywords **virtual** and **override** that precisely specify in base and derived classes, respectively, that the programmer is depending on runtime dynamic binding. By providing a mechanism to specify polymorphic behavior in the language, C# helps programs deal with an issue known as the fragile base class problem, which can result in unexpected behavior in a program when a base class in a library is modified, but the program itself is unchanged.

We discussed several other related topics in this chapter. Sometimes in an inheritance hierarchy, the base class is never intended to be instantiated.

Such a base class is said to be *abstract*, and *must* be derived from in order to be useful. At the opposite end of the spectrum, a class is said to be *sealed* if derivation is not allowed. A class hierarchy can be used to implement heterogeneous collections that can be treated polymorphically. Our bank case study provides a nice example of a heterogeneous collection of savings and checking accounts.

Formatting and Conversion

*A rather mundane but practical issue in programming is formatting, a topic that we have ignored so far. For simple programs where we are not concerned with appearance, the default formatting provided by .NET library classes may be quite adequate. When you do wish to control formatting, there are some simple facilities provided by the .NET library classes that you can use. Fundamentally, formatting is obtaining an appropriate string representation of an object. Every class in C# inherits the **ToString** method of the **object** base class, so there is always a string representation available. In many cases you will want to override the default. We will discuss how to control the format of numeric types and how to align strings. We will briefly revisit our bank case study to make our formatting look neater. In the rest of the chapter we will discuss conversions of various sorts. Many conversions among the standard types can be accomplished with the **System.Convert** class. Finally, we will see how you can define conversion operations in your own classes.*

TOSTRING

The fundamental issue in formatting is obtaining an appropriate string representation of an object. In C# every class ultimately derives from **object**, which has a method **ToString**, which returns a string representation of the object. Since primitive data types can be treated as classes, we can also apply the **ToString** method to data types like **int**, **decimal**, and **float**. If we use the object in a context where a string is expected, the **ToString** method will be called automatically to obtain its string representation.

Obtaining a string representation of a number should not be confused with *converting* a number to a string. A string and a number are fundamentally different data types, and in C# there is no implicit conversion from one to the other. Conversion is reserved for situations like converting an integer into a wider integer, or an integer to a floating point number, and so on. We will discuss conversions later in the chapter.

The program **NumberToString** illustrates obtaining a string representation in several simple scenarios.

```
// NumberToString.cs

using System;

public class NumberToString
{
    public static void Main()
    {
        int number = 444;
        Console.WriteLine(number);
        //string str = number;      // no implicit conversion
        string str = number.ToString();
        Console.WriteLine(str);
        Console.WriteLine("number = " + number);
        Console.WriteLine(444.ToString());
    }
}
```

Here is the output:

```
444
444
number = 444
444
```

ToString in Your Own Class

The **ToString** method is available in *every* class in C#, including classes you define yourself. As an example, consider the simple hotel class in **HotelToString\Step1**.

```
// Hotel.cs - Step 1

using System;

public class Hotel
{
   private string city;
   private string name;
   public Hotel(string city, string name)
   {
      this.city = city;
      this.name = name;
   }
}
```

In the test program we create two hotel objects and write them out with **WriteLine**, relying on **ToString** to implicitly obtain the string representation for us.

```
// HotelToString.cs

using System;

public class HotelToString
{
   public static void Main()
   {
      Hotel alpha = new Hotel("Atlanta", "Dixie");
      Hotel beta = new Hotel("Boston", "Yankee");
      Console.WriteLine(alpha);
      Console.WriteLine(beta);
   }
}
```

The program compiles and runs, but the output is a little disappointing:

```
Hotel
Hotel
```

The **ToString** method being used is the one defined in the base class **object** from which our **Hotel** class implicitly inherits. The base class knows nothing about the particulars of our class, so it does something very simple: It displays the name of the class. (You may wonder how the base class knows the name of our particular class. It obtains the name using a feature in .NET known as *reflection*, which we will touch upon in Chapter 20.)

The **ToString** method is virtual, which means we may override it in our own class to display a more meaningful representation. The new version of our class is implemented in the directory **HotelToString\Step2**.

```
// Hotel.cs - Step 2
```

```
using System;

public class Hotel
{
    private string city;
    private string name;
    public Hotel(string city, string name)
    {
        this.city = city;
        this.name = name;
    }
    override public string ToString()
    {
        return city + " " + name;
    }
}
```

The test program remains the same. The output is what we would expect:

```
Atlanta Dixie
Boston Yankee
```

Using Placeholders

When doing output with **WriteLine**, we usually use placeholders, {0}, {1}, and so on. This output mechanism uses **ToString** under the hood. **HotelToString\Step3** illustrates using placeholders in the test program.

```
// HotelToString.cs - Step 3

using System;

public class HotelToString
{
    public static void Main()
    {
        Hotel alpha = new Hotel("Atlanta", "Dixie");
        Hotel beta = new Hotel("Boston", "Yankee");
        Console.WriteLine("Hotel alpha is {0}", alpha);
        Console.WriteLine("Hotel beta is {0}", beta);
    }
}
```

Again the output is what we would expect.

```
Hotel alpha is Atlanta Dixie
Hotel beta is Boston Yankee
```

FORMAT STRINGS

C# has extensive formatting capabilities, which you can control through placeholders and format strings.

* Simple placeholders: {n}, where n is 0, 1, 2, and so on.
* Control width: {n,w}, where w is width (positive for right justified and negative for left justified).
* Format string: {n:S}, where S is a format string.
* Width and format string: {n,w:S}.

A format string consists of a format character followed by an optional precision specifier. Table 15–1 shows the available format characters.

Table 15–1	C# Format Characters

Format Character	Meaning
C	Currency (locale specific)
D	Decimal integer
E	Exponential (scientific)
F	Fixed point
G	General (E or F)
N	Number with embedded commas
X	Hexadecimal

We will illustrate a number of different format scenarios by a series of programs displaying powers of two in various formats, beginning with just using simple placeholders.

Simple Placeholders

The simplest way to perform output in C# is to use the **Console.WriteLine** method with placeholders {0}, {1}, and so on. Our first program is **PowerTwo\Step0**, which simply displays powers of two without any special formatting.

```
// PowerTwo.cs - Step 0

using System;

public class PowerTwo
{
   public static void Main()
   {
      long power = 1;
```

```
        for (int i = 0; i < 16; i++)
        {
           Console.WriteLine("{0} {1}", i, power);
           power *= 2;
        }
     }
}
```

Here is the output. You can see that the second column is not aligned.

```
0 1
1 2
2 4
3 8
4 16
5 32
6 64
7 128
8 256
9 512
10 1024
11 2048
12 4096
13 8192
14 16384
15 32768
```

Controlling Width

The simplest way to control format is through a width specifier. The place-holders now have the form {n,w}, where n = 0, 1, 2, and so on and w specifies the width (positive for right justified and negative for left justified). The program **PowerTwo\Step1** illustrates controlling width. The first column is printed left justified, and the second column is printed right justified.

```
// PowerTwo.cs - Step 1

using System;

public class PowerTwo
{
   public static void Main()
   {
      long power = 1;
      for (int i = 0; i < 16; i++)
      {
         // Negative value for left justification
         Console.WriteLine("{0,-3} {1,10}", i, power);
         power *= 2;
      }
```

```
      }
}
```

Here is the output. The columns are now nicely aligned.

```
0              1
1              2
2              4
3              8
4             16
5             32
6             64
7            128
8            256
9            512
10          1024
11          2048
12          4096
13          8192
14         16384
15         32768
```

Format String

The next step in formatting is to use a format string, usually in conjunction with a width specifier. The available format characters are shown in Table 15–1 earlier in the chapter. Here are some examples of placeholders with format strings. In each case the width is 36.

```
{0,36:D}       Decimal integer
{0,36:N0}      Number with commas, precision 0
{0,36:N4}      Number with commas, precision 4
{0,36:X}       Hexadecimal
{0,36:F}       Fixed point
{0,36:G}       General (E or F)
{0,36:F26}     Fixed point, precision 26
{0,36:E26}     Exponential, precision 26
```

The program **PowerFormat** illustrates use of these format strings in displaying 2^{60} or 2^{-60}.

```
// PowerFormat.cs

using System;

public class PowerFormat
{
    public static void Main()
    {
```

```
long bigint = 1;
decimal bigdecimal = 1;
decimal smalldecimal = 1;
double bigdouble = Math.Pow(2, 60);
double smalldouble = Math.Pow(2, -60);
for (int i = 1; i <= 60; i++)
{
   bigint *= 2;
   bigdecimal *= 2;
   smalldecimal /= 2;
}
Console.WriteLine("{0,36:D}", bigint);
Console.WriteLine("{0,36:N0}", bigint);
Console.WriteLine("{0,36:N4}", bigint);
Console.WriteLine("{0,36:X} (hex)", bigint);
Console.WriteLine("{0,36:N0}", bigdecimal);
Console.WriteLine("{0,36:F}", bigdouble);
Console.WriteLine("{0,36:G}", smalldouble);
Console.WriteLine("{0,36:F26}", smalldouble);
Console.WriteLine("{0,36:E26}", smalldouble);
   }
}
```

Here is the output:

```
              1152921504606846976
            1,152,921,504,606,846,976
        1,152,921,504,606,846,976.0000
                 1000000000000000 (hex)
            1,152,921,504,606,846,976
              1152921504606847000.00
                8.6736173798840355E-19
        0.00000000000000000086736174
8.6736173798840355000000000E-019
```

For some additional illustrations of numeric formatting you may look at the programs **PowerTwo\Step2** and **NegativePower**.

Currency

The "C" format character formats in a manner appropriate for currency, including using a currency symbol. Currency formatting is specific to a *locale*. The default locale is the United States, and the currency symbol is the dollar sign $. Working with other locales is beyond the scope of this book. If globalization issues are of interest to you, you may wish to study the documentation of the **System.Globalization** namespace.

The C format character is used in exactly the same manner as the other format characters discussed previously. The program **MoneyPower** provides an illustration. This program calculates the amount of money paid to a wise man who performed a service for an Eastern monarch. When asked for a reward, he replied that his wants were modest. All he wanted was the amount of money equal to a penny placed on the first square of a chessboard, two pennies on the second square, four pennies on the third square, eight pennies on the fourth square, and so. This program also illustrates using the **decimal** data type to obtain accurate representations of financial quantities, with many digits of precision. The program shows the total day by day.

```
// MoneyPower.cs

using System;

public class MoneyPower
{
   public static void Main()
   {
      decimal power = .01m;
      decimal total = 0m;
      for (int i = 1; i <= 64; i++)
      {
         total += power;
         Console.WriteLine("{0,-3} {1,30:C}", i, total);
         power *= 2;
      }
   }
}
```

Here is the output:

```
1                              $0.01
2                              $0.03
3                              $0.07
4                              $0.15
5                              $0.31
6                              $0.63
7                              $1.27
8                              $2.55
9                              $5.11
10                             $10.23
...
61         $23,058,430,092,136,939.51
62         $46,116,860,184,273,879.03
63         $92,233,720,368,547,758.07
64        $184,467,440,737,095,516.15
```

STRING FORMATTING METHODS

The **System.String** class has several useful methods to help you with formatting tasks. In this section we will discuss the methods **Format**, **PadLeft**, and **PadRight**.

Format

We have been discussing the use of format strings used in conjunction with placeholders and the **WriteLine** method of the **Console** class. Often we may wish to format numbers into a string. This task can be accomplished with the **Format** method of the **String** class.

```
public static string Format(
    string format,
    object[] args
);
```

The *format* has exactly the same syntax used in the **WriteLine** method. As an illustration, consider the **MoneyReport** program the wise man wrote to prepare a report for the king stating the amount owed him.

```
// MoneyReport.cs

using System;

public class MoneyReport
{
    public static void Main()
    {
        decimal amount = CalculateAmount();
        Console.WriteLine(CreateReport(amount));
    }
    public static decimal CalculateAmount()
    {
        decimal power = .01m;
        decimal total = 0m;
        for (int i = 1; i <= 64; i++)
        {
            total += power;
            power *= 2;
        }
        return power;
    }
    public static string CreateReport(decimal amount)
    {
        string str = "Dear Your Majesty,\n\t" +
            string.Format("You owe me {0,30:C}", amount) +
            "\nSincerely, Your Humble Servant";
```

```
      return str;
   }
}
```

Here is the output:

```
Dear Your Majesty,
         You owe me      $184,467,440,737,095,516.16
Sincerely, Your Humble Servant
```

PadLeft and PadRight

The **Format** method is useful for formatting numbers into a string. What if you want to control the formatting of just strings—i.e., make them align the way you want? An easy approach is to use the **PadLeft** and **PadRight** methods, which are quite self-explanatory. Each method has two overloaded forms. Consider **PadLeft**.

```
public string PadLeft(
   int totalWidth
);
public string PadLeft(
   int totalWidth,
   char paddingChar
);
```

The **totalWidth** is the total number of characters in the result string, equal to the original characters plus any padding characters. The default character used for padding is space, but you can change that by using the second form of the method.

The program **PowerTwo\Step2** illustrates use of **PadLeft** and **PadRight** to make headers line up properly with the columns of numbers underneath.

```
// PowerTwo.cs - Step 2

using System;

public class PowerTwo
{
   public static void Main()
   {
      decimal power = 1;
      string header1 = "Num";
      string header2 = "Power";
      string header = header1.PadRight(4) +
                  header2.PadLeft(30);
      Console.WriteLine(header);
      for (int i = 0; i < 64; i++)
```

```
        {
            Console.WriteLine("{0,-4}{1,30:N0}", i, power);
            power *= 2;
        }
    }
}
```

Here is the output:

```
Num                             Power
0                                   1
1                                   2
2                                   4
3                                   8
4                                  16
5                                  32
6                                  64
7                                 128
8                                 256
9                                 512
10                              1,024
...
61          2,305,843,009,213,693,952
62          4,611,686,018,427,387,904
63          9,223,372,036,854,775,808
```

BANK CASE STUDY: STEP 4

The Step 3 version of our bank case study from Chapter 14 does not do any special formatting, and the result is not very neat. As an example, try the top level "show" command:

```
> show
1       C: Bob      100
2       S: Mary     200
3       C: Charlie  300
```

The columns do not line up, and the balances are not shown as monetary amounts. If we examine the code for the "show" command, we see that it uses the **GetAccounts** method of the **Bank** class. In all we have to make minor code changes in three classes: **Bank**, **Account**, and **Atm**. Here are the new versions (**CaseStudy** directory for Chapter 15):

Bank

```
// Bank.cs - Step 4
...

public class Bank
{
...
    public string[] GetAccounts()
    {
        string[] array = new string[count];
        for (int i = 0; i < count; i++)
        {
            string owner = accounts[i].Owner.PadRight(12);
            string stype = accounts[i].Prompt;
            string sid = accounts[i].Id.ToString();
            string sbal =
            string.Format("{0:C}", accounts[i].Balance);
            string str =
                sid + "\t" + stype + owner + "\t" + sbal;
            array[i] = str;
        }
        return array;
    }
...
```

Here is a sample run, again using the "show" command. The result is much neater!

```
> show
1       C: Bob          $100.00
2       S: Mary         $200.00
3       C: Charlie      $300.00
```

Account

In the **Account** class, we add a **FormatBalance** method to return the balance as a string, showing the balance as a monetary amount with the currency symbol. We also update the virtual method **GetStatement** to use the **FormatBalance** method. Since the derived classes build upon the base class **GetStatement**, they will also correctly start to obtain a formatted balance.

```
// Account.cs - Step 4

using System;

abstract public class Account
{
...
```

```
public string FormatBalance()
{
   return string.Format("{0:C}", balance);
}
virtual public string GetStatement()
{
   string s = "Statement for " + this.Owner + " id = " +
      Id + "\n" + this.Transactions + " transactions,
      balance = " + FormatBalance();
   return s;
}
abstract public void Post();
abstract public string Prompt {get;}
virtual public void MonthEnd()
{
   numXact = 0;
}
}
```

Here is a sample run after this change has been implemented. Notice that we now get properly displayed currency for the balance. (This run also reflects small changes made in the **Atm** class and **CheckingAccount** classes, discussed in the next sections.)

```
> account
account id: 1
balance = $100.00
Enter command, quit to exit
C: show
Statement for Bob id = 1
0 transactions, balance = $100.00, fee = $0.00
```

Atm

Another formatting change is in the **Atm** class. The first display of the balance from the transcript above came from the **Atm** class. We must now use the **FormatBalance** method that was implemented in the **Account** class, in place of the **Balance** property. The balance is displayed in several other places in the **Atm** class, so we create a helper method **ShowBalance** to display the balance in the proper format, using the currency symbol.

```
// Atm.cs - Step 4

using System;

public class Atm
{
   public static void ProcessAccount(Account acc)
   {
```

```
            ShowBalance(acc);
            string cmd;
            InputWrapper iw = new InputWrapper();
            Console.WriteLine("Enter command, quit to exit");
            cmd = iw.getString(acc.Prompt);
            while (! cmd.Equals("quit"))
            {
                if (cmd.Equals("deposit"))
                {
                    decimal amount = iw.getDecimal("amount: ");
                    acc.Deposit(amount);
                    ShowBalance(acc);
                }
                else if (cmd.Equals("withdraw"))
                {
                    decimal amount = iw.getDecimal("amount: ");
                    acc.Withdraw(amount);
                    ShowBalance(acc);
                }
...
        private static void ShowBalance(Account acc)
        {
            Console.WriteLine("balance = {0}",
                            acc.FormatBalance());
        }
...
```

Checking Account and Savings Account

Finally, in the **CheckingAccount** class we must format the fee in
GetStatement.

```
override public string GetStatement()
{
    string s = base.GetStatement();
    s += ", fee = " + string.Format("{0:C}", Fee);
    return s;
}
```

And in **SavingsAccount** we must format the interest.

```
override public string GetStatement()
{
    string s = base.GetStatement();
    s += ", interest = " + string.Format("{0:C}", Interest);
    return s;
}
```

TYPE CONVERSIONS

Another important practical programming issue is converting among types. This is particularly important in C#, which is a strongly typed language. Where in some languages (such as Visual Basic 6) you can quite freely mix different data types and the compiler will usually sort things out in a reasonable manner, in C# you have to be quite precise in your use of types. We discussed this issue in Chapter 4.

While you are becoming oriented to the C# environment, you may find that having to make explicit type conversions is somewhat of a chore, but you should soon get used to it, and your programs can benefit from the increased robustness that type safety provides.

This section discusses type conversions, both for built-in types and for user-defined types.

Conversion of Built-In Types

The **Convert** class of the **System** namespace provides a comprehensive set of methods for converting among the built-in types. The conversion methods are static, with names of the form **ToXxxx**, where **Xxxx** is a type. Note that type names are those used in the **System** namespace, not C# type names. For example, to convert to an **int**, use the method **ToInt32**.

An illustration is provided by our **InputWrapper** class in **CaseStudy**.

```
// InputWrapper.cs
//
// Class to wrap simple stream input
// Datatype supported:
//      int
//      double
//      decimal
//      string

using System;

class InputWrapper
{
    public int getInt(string prompt)
    {
        Console.Write(prompt);
        string buf = Console.ReadLine();
        return Convert.ToInt32(buf);
    }
    public double getDouble(string prompt)
    {
        Console.Write(prompt);
        string buf = Console.ReadLine();
```

```
        return Convert.ToDouble(buf);
    }
    public decimal getDecimal(string prompt)
    {
        Console.Write(prompt);
        string buf = Console.ReadLine();
        return Convert.ToDecimal(buf);
    }
    public string getString(string prompt)
    {
        Console.Write(prompt);
        string buf = Console.ReadLine();
        return buf;
    }
}
```

Conversion of User-Defined Types

Recall from Chapter 4 that there are two kinds of conversions in C#: implicit and explicit. An *implicit* conversion can be performed transparently by the compiler when there is no loss of information, such as in widening an integer data type. Thus the following is legal:

```
int a = 718;
long b = a;
```

If there is a potential loss of information, the compiler will disallow a conversion, unless you explicitly tell the compiler to accept the conversion by performing a *cast* operation. Such a conversion is said to be *explicit*. Here is an example of an explicit conversion:

```
long c = 718;
c = c*c;
int d = (int) c;
```

To implement conversions in your own class you must define appropriate operators. Recall the discussion of operator overloading in Chapter 10. Operators are special static methods that contain the keyword **operator**. There are additional keywords, **implicit** and **explicit**, for defining implicit and explicit conversions.

We illustrate conversions through the class **Money**, which internally stores a money value as a **decimal**. Constructors are provided to create a money object from a **string**, a **double**, and a **decimal**. A property is provided that can return a string representation of a money object. We then provide three overloaded operators to explicitly convert to **Money** and three overloaded operators to implicitly convert to **string**, **double**, and **decimal**, respectively.

Our example program is in the **MoneyConvert** directory. Here is the code for defining the class. Note also that the code illustrates using the **System.Convert** class.

```
// Money.cs

using System;

public class Money
{
    private decimal amount;
    public Money(string str)
    {
        amount = Convert.ToDecimal(str);
    }
    public Money(double num)
    {
        amount = Convert.ToDecimal(num);
    }
    public Money(decimal num)
    {
        amount = num;
    }
    public Money()
    {
    }
    public string MoneyStr
    {
        get
        {
            return string.Format("{0:C}", amount);
        }
    }
    public static explicit operator Money(string str)
    {
        Money mon = new Money(str);
        return mon;
    }
    public static explicit operator Money(double num)
    {
        Money mon = new Money(num);
        return mon;
    }
    public static explicit operator Money(decimal num)
    {
        Money mon = new Money(num);
        return mon;
    }
    public static implicit operator string(Money mon)
    {
```

```
        return string.Format("{0:C}", mon.amount);
    }
    public static implicit operator double(Money mon)
    {
        return Convert.ToDouble(mon.amount);
    }
    public static implicit operator decimal(Money mon)
    {
        return mon.amount;
    }
}
```

Here is the code for the test program:

```
// MoneyConvert.cs

using System;

public class MoneyConvert
{
    public static void Main()
    {
        Money x = new Money("30.33");
        Console.WriteLine(x.MoneyStr);
        Money a = new Money();
        a = (Money) "40.44";
        Console.WriteLine((string) a);
        a = (Money) 50.55;
        Console.WriteLine((string) a);
        a = (Money) 60.66m;
        Console.WriteLine((string) a);
        string s = a;
        Console.WriteLine("a = (string) {0}", s);
        double b = a;
        Console.WriteLine("a (double) = {0}", b);
        decimal c = a;
        Console.WriteLine("a (decimal) = {0:C}", c);
    }
}
```

The conversion to **string** is implicit, as illustrated by the line of code

```
string s = a;
```

The only reason we do an explicit cast to **string** in the **WriteLine** statements is that without the cast, the call to **WriteLine** would be ambiguous, since **WriteLine** can also accept **decimal** and **double** parameters, and we define implicit conversions for these data types as well as to **string**. Thus to call **WriteLine** we must choose one of the data types for which we provide a conversion, and we pick **string**. Here is the output:

```
$30.33
$40.44
$50.55
$60.66
a = (string) $60.66
a (double) = 60.66
a (decimal) = $60.66
```

SUMMARY

In this chapter we discussed formatting and conversion. Fundamentally, formatting is obtaining an appropriate string representation of an object. Every class in C# inherits the **ToString** method of the **object** base class, so there is always a string representation available. This default simply returns the name of the class, so normally you will want to override the default. We discussed how to control the format of numeric types and how to align strings. We enhanced our bank case study to make the formatting look neater. We concluded the chapter with a discussion of conversions of various sorts. Many conversions among the standard types can be accomplished with the **System.Convert** class. You can define both explicit and implicit conversions in your own classes by providing the appropriate operators.

Exceptions

*A*n *inevitable part of programming is dealing with error conditions of various sorts. This chapter introduces the exception handling mechanism of C#, beginning with a discussion of the fundamentals of error processing and various alternatives that are available. We then carefully go through the C# exception mechanism, which includes a **try** block, **catch** handlers, and a **finally** block. You can raise exceptions by means of a **throw** statement. The .NET class library provides an **Exception** class, which you can use to pass information about an exception that occurred. To further specify your exception and to pass additional information, you can derive your own class from **Exception**. When handling an exception you may want to throw a new exception. In such a case you can use the "inner exception" feature of the **Exception** class to pass the original exception on with your new exception. We will illustrate these features with a simplified version of our case study example, and then provide an update to the case study itself, incorporating basic exception handling. We also provide an example of handling arithmetic exceptions.*

EXCEPTION FUNDAMENTALS

The traditional way to deal with errors when programming is to have the functions you call return a status code. The status code may have a particular value for a good return and other values to denote various error conditions. The calling function checks this status code, and if an error was encountered, it performs appropriate error handling. This function in return may pass an error code to its calling function, and so on up the call stack.

Although straightforward, this mechanism has a number of drawbacks. The basic disadvantage is lack of robustness. The called function may have impeccable error checking code and return appropriate error information, but all this information is useless if the calling function does not make use of it. The program may continue operation as if nothing were amiss, and sometime later crash for some mysterious reason.

Another disadvantage is that every function in the call stack must participate in the process, or the chain of error information will be broken. Also, unusual flow control can leave memory hanging without being deallocated.

In languages such as C# that have constructors and overloaded operators, there is not even a return value for some operations.

.NET Exception Handling

C# provides an *exception* mechanism that can be used for reporting and handling errors. An error is reported by "throwing" an exception. The error is handled by "catching" the exception. This mechanism is similar in concept to exceptions in C++ and Java.

Exceptions are implemented in .NET by the Common Language Runtime, so exceptions can be thrown in one .NET language and caught in another. The exception mechanism involves the following elements:

* Code that might encounter an exception should be enclosed in a **try** block.
* Exceptions are caught in a **catch** block.
* An Exception object is passed as a parameter to **catch**. The data type is **System.Exception** or a derived type.
* You may have multiple **catch** blocks. A match is made based on the data type of the Exception object.
* An optional **finally** clause contains code that will be executed whether or not an exception is encountered.
* In the called method, an exception is raised through a **throw** statement.

Exception Flow of Control

The general structure of code which might encounter an exception is shown below:

```
try
{
        // code that might cause an exception to be thrown
}
catch (ExceptionClass1 e)
{
        // code to handle this type of exception
}
catch (ExceptionClass2 e)
{
        // code to handle this other type of exception
}
// possibly more catch handlers
// optional finally clause (discussed later)
// statements after try ... catch
```

Each catch handler has a parameter specifying the data type of exception that it can handle. The exception data type can be **System.Exception** or a class ultimately derived from it. If an exception is thrown, the *first* catch handler that matches the exception data type is executed, and then control passes to the statement just after the catch block(s). If no handler is found, the exception is thrown to the next higher "context" (e.g., the function that called the current one). If no exception is thrown inside the **try** block, all the catch handlers are skipped.

Context and Stack Unwinding

As the flow of control of a program passes into nested blocks, local variables are pushed onto the stack and a new "context" is entered. Likewise, a new context is entered on a method call, which also pushes a return address onto the stack.

If an exception is not handled in the current context, the exception is passed to successively higher contexts until it is finally handled (or else is "uncaught" and is handled by a default system handler).

When the higher context is entered, C++ adjusts the stack properly, a process known as *stack unwinding*. In C# exception handling, stack unwinding involves both setting the program counter and cleaning up variables (popping stack variables and marking heap variables as free, so that the garbage collector can deallocate them).

Example Program

Now let's look at some code that illustrates the principles we have discussed so far. We will use a simplified version of our **Account** class, which has only methods **Deposit** and **Withdraw**, and the property **Balance**. Both methods will throw an exception if the amount passed as a parameter is negative. In addition, the **Withdraw** method will throw an exception if the new balance would be negative—overdrafts are not allowed. Our example program is in the directory **AccountExceptionDemo\Step1**.

```
// Account.cs

using System;

public class Account
{
    protected decimal balance;
    public Account(decimal balance)
    {
        this.balance = balance;
    }
    public void Deposit(decimal amount)
    {
        if (amount < 0.00m)
            throw new Exception(
                "The transaction amount cannot be negative.");
        balance += amount;
    }
    public void Withdraw(decimal amount)
    {
        if (amount < 0.00m)
            throw new Exception(
                "The transaction amount cannot be negative.");
        decimal newbal = balance - amount;
        if (newbal < 0.00m)
            throw new Exception(
                "The balance cannot be negative.");
        balance = newbal;
    }
    public decimal Balance
    {
        get
        {
            return balance;
        }
    }
}
```

Here is the test program. Notice that we place the entire body of the command processing loop inside a **try** block. The catch handler prints an error message that is passed within the exception object. Then after either normal processing or displaying an error message, a new command is read in. This simple scheme provides reasonable error processing, as a bad command will not be acted upon, and the user will have an opportunity to enter a new command.

```
// AccountExceptionDemo.cs

using System;

public class AccountExceptionDemo
{
    public static void Main(string[] args)
    {
        Account acc = new Account(100);
        ShowBalance(acc);
        string cmd;
        InputWrapper iw = new InputWrapper();
        Console.WriteLine("Enter command, quit to exit");
        cmd = iw.getString("> ");
        while (! cmd.Equals("quit"))
        {
            try
            {
                if (cmd.Equals("deposit"))
                {
                    decimal amount = iw.getDecimal("amount: ");
                    acc.Deposit(amount);
                    ShowBalance(acc);
                }
                else if (cmd.Equals("withdraw"))
                {
                    decimal amount = iw.getDecimal("amount: ");
                    acc.Withdraw(amount);
                    ShowBalance(acc);
                }
                else if (cmd.Equals("show"))
                    ShowBalance(acc);
                else
                    help();
            }
            catch (Exception e)
            {
                Console.WriteLine(e.Message);
            }
            cmd = iw.getString("> ");
        }
    }
...
```

Here is a transcript of a sample run. We try several kinds of bad input, and then a good one.

```
balance = $100.00
Enter command, quit to exit
> deposit
```

```
amount: -5
The transaction amount cannot be negative.
> withdraw
amount: 150
The balance cannot be negative.
> withdraw
amount: xxx
The input string was not in a correct format.
> withdraw
amount: 50
balance = $50.00
```

Notice that two of the exceptions were ones we threw ourselves, but one (when we entered "xxx" as the amount) was thrown by the .NET library code. Our catch handler deals with all these different exceptions in a simple, uniform manner.

System.Exception

The **System.Exception** class provides a number of useful methods and properties for obtaining information about an exception.

- **Message** returns a text string providing information about the exception. This message is set when the exception object is constructed. If no message is specified, a generic message will be provided, indicating the type of the exception. The **Message** property is read-only. (Hence, if you want to specify your own message, you must construct a new exception object, as done in the example above.)
- **StackTrace** returns a text string providing a stack trace at the place where the exception arose.
- **InnerException** holds a reference to another exception. When you throw a new exception, it is desirable not to lose the information about the original exception. The original exception can be passed as a parameter when constructing the new exception. The original exception object is then available through the **InnerException** property of the new exception. (We will provide an example of using inner exceptions later in this chapter.)

USER-DEFINED EXCEPTION CLASSES

You can do basic exception handling using only the base **Exception** class, as illustrated previously. In order to obtain more fine-grained control over exceptions, it is frequently useful to define your own exception class, derived from **Exception**. You can then have a more specific catch handler that looks specifically for your exception type. You can also define other members in your derived exception class, so that you can pass additional information to the catch handler.

We will illustrate by enhancing the **Withdraw** method of our **Account** class. We want to distinguish between the two types of exceptions we throw. The one type is essentially bad input data (a negative value). We will continue to handle this exception in the same manner as before (which is the same as bad input data that gives rise to a format exception, thrown by .NET library code). We will define a new exception class **BalanceException** to cover the case when the balance would become negative. In this case we want to allow the user an opportunity to correct the situation (in this case simply by making a deposit to cover the shortage). Our example program is **AccountExceptionDemo\Step2**. Here is the definition of our new exception class:

```
// BalanceException.cs

using System;

public class BalanceException : Exception
{
    private decimal shortage;
    public BalanceException(string message, decimal shortage)
        : base(message)
    {
        this.shortage = shortage;
    }
    public decimal Shortage
    {
        get
        {
            return shortage;
        }
    }
}
```

Note that we define a property **Shortage** that can be used to store the information about how short the balance is. The constructor of our exception class takes two parameters. The first parameter is an error message string, and the second parameter is the amount of the shortage. We pass the message string to the constructor of the base class. We must also modify the code of the **Account** class to throw our new type of exception when an illegal negative balance would be created.

```
// Account.cs

using System;
```

```
public class Account
{
   ...
   public void Withdraw(decimal amount)
   {
      if (amount < 0.00m)
         throw new Exception(
            "The transaction amount cannot be negative.");
      decimal newbal = balance - amount;
      if (newbal < 0.00m)
         throw new BalanceException(
            "The balance cannot be negative.", -newbal);
      balance = newbal;
   }
   ...
```

Finally we modify the code in our test program that processes the "withdraw" command. We place the call to **Withdraw** inside another **try** block, and we provide a catch handler for a **BalanceException**. In this catch handler we allow the user an opportunity to make a supplemental deposit. Here is the code:

```
// AccountExceptionDemo.cs
...
   else if (cmd.Equals("withdraw"))
   {
      decimal amount = iw.getDecimal("amount: ");
      try
      {
         acc.Withdraw(amount);
      }
      catch (BalanceException e)
      {
         Console.WriteLine(
            "You are short {0:C}", e.Shortage);
         Console.WriteLine("Please make a deposit");
         decimal supplemental = iw.getDecimal("amount: ");
         acc.Deposit(supplemental);
         acc.Withdraw(amount);    // try again
      }
   }
```

Here is a transcript of a sample run of our program:

```
balance = $100.00
Enter command, quit to exit
> withdraw
amount: 150
You are short $50.00
```

```
Please make a deposit
amount: 90
> show
balance = $40.00
```

STRUCTURED EXCEPTION HANDLING

One of the principles of structured programming is that a block of code should have a single entry point and a single exit point. The single exit point is convenient, because you can consolidate cleanup code in one place. The **goto** statement is bad, because it facilitates breaking this principle. But there are other ways to violate the principle of a single exit point, such as multiple **return** statements from a method.

Multiple return statements may not be too bad, because these may be encountered during normal, anticipated flow of control. But exceptions can cause a particular difficulty, since they interrupt the normal flow of control. In a common scenario you can have at least *three* ways of exiting a method:

- No exception is encountered, and any catch handlers are skipped.
- An exception is caught, and control passes to the code after the catch handlers.
- An exception is caught, and the catch handler itself throws another exception. Then code after the catch handler will be bypassed.

The first two cases do not present a problem, as in both cases control passes to the code after the catch handlers. But the third case is a source of difficulty.

Finally Block

The structured exception handling mechanism in C# resolves this problem with a **finally** block. The **finally** block is optional, but if present must appear immediately after the **catch** handlers. It is guaranteed that the code in the **finally** block will *always* execute before the method is exited, in all three cases described.

We illustrate use of **finally** in the **Withdraw** command of our **Account** example. See the directory **AccountExceptionDemo\Step3**. There are several ways to exit this block of code, and the user might become confused about her balance upon exiting. We insert a **finally** block, which will display the balance. Here is the code:

```
// AccountExceptionDemo.cs

    ...
    else if (cmd.Equals("withdraw"))
```

```
    {
       decimal amount = iw.getDecimal("amount: ");
       try
       {
          acc.Withdraw(amount);
       }
       catch (BalanceException e)
       {
          Console.WriteLine(
             "You are short {0:C}", e.Shortage);
          Console.WriteLine("Please make a deposit");
          decimal supplemental = iw.getDecimal("amount: ");
          acc.Deposit(supplemental);
          acc.Withdraw(amount);    // try again
       }
       finally
       {
          ShowBalance(acc);
       }
    }
    ...
```

Here is a transcript of a sample run. The first time, the user enters incorrect data for the supplemental deposit ("xxx"). The .NET library throws an exception, but before exiting, the code in the **finally** block is executed, showing the current (unchanged) balance. The user tries again, and this succeeds in making a supplemental deposit. Again the code in **finally** executes, this time showing a changed balance reflecting both a deposit and a withdrawal.

```
balance = $100.00
Enter command, quit to exit
> withdraw
amount: 150
You are short $50.00
Please make a deposit
amount: xxx
balance = $100.00
The input string was not in a correct format.
> withdraw
amount: 150
You are short $50.00
Please make a deposit
amount: 90
balance = $40.00
```

BANK CASE STUDY: STEP 5

The **CaseStudy** directory shows Step 5 of our bank case study. In the **Account** class we handle the same exception conditions that we illustrated previously, namely a negative amount in making either a deposit or withdrawal, and a negative balance in making a withdrawal. We have **try** blocks in both the **TestBank** and **Atm** classes. The catch handlers will display an error message for an exception thrown either by the **Account** class or by the .NET library.

The code does not illustrate any new features of exception handling, so we will not provide any listings here. However, it would be a good idea to look over the code and to run the program, and try to break it by inducing various error conditions. Here is an example run, where we try out some good and some bad inputs.

```
Enter command, quit to exit
> account
account id: xxx
The input string was not in a correct format.
> account
account id: 1
balance = $100.00
Enter command, quit to exit
C: deposit
amount: -5
The transaction amount cannot be negative.
C: deposit
amount: 5
balance = $105.00
C: withdraw
amount: 200
The balance cannot be negative.
C: show
Statement for Bob id = 1
1 transactions, balance = $105.00, fee = $0.00
C: withdraw
amount: xxx
The input string was not in a correct format.
C: withdraw
amount: 50
balance = $55.00
C: quit
> show
1       C: Bob          $55.00
2       S: Mary         $200.00
3       C: Charlie      $300.00
>
```

INNER EXCEPTIONS

In general, it is wise to handle exceptions, at least at some level, near their source, because you have the most information available about the context in which the exception occurred. A common pattern is to create a new exception object that captures more detailed information and throw this on to the calling program. In the following example, by catching the exception here, we are able to capture information about *which* parameter caused the problem.

```
private static int CheckedMultiply(object a, object b)
{
    int first, second;
    try
    {
        first = (int) a;
    }
    catch (InvalidCastException e)
    {
        throw new Exception("First operand is not an int", e);
    }
    try
    {
        second = (int) a;
    }
    catch (InvalidCastException e)
    {
        throw new Exception("Second operand is not an int",
                            e);
    }
    try
    {
        int product = checked(first * second);
        return product;
    }
    catch (OverflowException e)
    {
        throw new Exception("Integer overflow", e);
    }
}
```

When you throw a new exception, it is desirable not to lose the information about the original exception. The original exception can be passed as a parameter when constructing the new exception. The original exception is then available through the **InnerException** property of the new exception. Notice that in the code above we pass the exception object **e** as a parameter to the constructor of the new **Exception** object that we throw.

We will illustrate with the **ArithmeticExceptionDemo** program. First we review checked integer arithmetic (you may wish to refer to the last section of Chapter 5), and then we present the entire example program.

Checked Integer Arithmetic

By default in C#, integer overflow does not raise an exception. Instead the result is truncated. The **checked** operator will cause the integer calculation to check for overflow and throw an exception if an overflow condition arises. You can cause all integer arithmetic to be checked via the /**checked** compiler command line switch. You can turn off checking by the **unchecked** operator. Unchecked arithmetic is faster but less safe.

Example Program

The **ArithmeticExceptionDemo** program demonstrates a number of scenarios of arithmetic exceptions. You can experiment by commenting and uncommenting different sections of code. You can also try building with the /**checked** compiler option.

```
// ArithmeticExceptionDemo.cs
//
// This program demonstrates exceptions
// It handles exceptions within the CheckedMultiply method
// A more meaningful error message is written
//
// You can experiment with the different exceptions by
// commenting and uncommenting different statements in the
// main program

using System;

public class ArithmeticExceptionDemo
{
    private static long LongMultiply(object a, object b)
    {
        long product = (long) a * (long) b;
        return product;
    }
    private static int Multiply(object a, object b)
    {
        int product = (int) a * (int) b;
        return product;
    }
    private static int CheckedMultiply(object a, object b)
    {
        int first, second;
        try
        {
            first = (int) a;
```

```
      }
      catch (InvalidCastException e)
      {
         throw new Exception("First operand is not an int",
                             e);
      }
      try
      {
         second = (int) a;
      }
      catch (InvalidCastException e)
      {
         throw new Exception("Second operand is not an int",
                             e);
      }
      try
      {
         int product = checked(first * second);
         return product;
      }
      catch (OverflowException e)
      {
         throw new Exception("Integer overflow", e);
      }
   }
   public static int Main(string[] args)
   {
      int prod;
      long lprod;
      try
      {
         lprod = LongMultiply(56666L, 57777L);
         Console.WriteLine("product = {0}", lprod);
         prod = Multiply(56666, 57777);
         Console.WriteLine("product = {0}", prod);
         //Console.WriteLine("Operands: 56666, 57777");
         //prod = CheckedMultiply(56666, 57777);
         //Console.WriteLine("product = {0}", prod);
         Console.WriteLine("Operands: 56666L, 57777");
         prod = CheckedMultiply(56666L, 57777);
         Console.WriteLine("product = {0}", prod);
         //Console.WriteLine("Operands: 56666L, 57777");
         //prod = CheckedMultiply(56666, 57777L);
         //Console.WriteLine("product = {0}", prod);
      }
      catch (Exception e)
      {
         Console.WriteLine("Exception: {0}", e.Message);
         if (e.InnerException != null)
            Console.WriteLine("Inner Exception: {0}",
```

```
                              e.InnerException.Message);
        }
        return 0;
    }
}
```

Notice how in the main program we display the inner exception, if any. (If there is no inner exception, the **InnerException** property will be **null**.) Here is the output:

```
product = 3273991482
product = -1020975814
Operands: 56666L, 57777
Exception: First operand is not an int
Inner Exception: An exception of type
System.InvalidCastException was thrown.
```

SUMMARY

The traditional way to deal with errors in programs is to check an error return code. This approach has a number of defects, the most important of which is that the calling program may simply ignore error returns. C# provides an exception mechanism, which includes a **try** block, **catch** handlers, and a **finally** block. You can raise exceptions by means of a **throw** statement. The .NET class library provides an **Exception** class, which you can use to pass information about an exception that occurred. To further specify your exception and to pass additional information, you can derive your own class from **Exception**. When handling an exception, you may want to throw a new exception. In such a case you can use the "inner exception" feature of the **Exception** class to pass the original exception on with your new exception. We illustrated these features with a simplified version of our case study example, and we also provided an update to the case study itself, which incorporated basic exception handling. A final example of "checked multiply" demonstrated inner exceptions.

SEVENTEEN

Interfaces

The concept of interface *is very fundamental to computer programming. A large system is inevitably decomposed into parts, and it is critical to precisely specify the interfaces between these parts. Interfaces should be quite stable, as changing an interface affects multiple parts of the system. In C#* **interface** *is a keyword and has a very precise meaning. An interface is a reference type, similar to an abstract class, that* specifies *behavior. An interface can be thought of as a contract. A class or struct can "implement" an interface, and must adhere to the contract. Interfaces are a useful way to partition functionality. The methods of a class can be grouped into related interfaces. While a class in C# can inherit from only one other class, it can implement multiple interfaces. Another benefit of interfaces is that they facilitate very dynamic programs. C# provides convenient facilities to query a class at runtime to see whether it supports a particular interface. We will see that interfaces in C# and .NET are conceptually very similar to interfaces in Microsoft's Component Object Model, but are* much *easier to work with.*

In this chapter we will study interfaces in detail, and we will restructure our bank case study to take advantage of interfaces. In the following chapter we will examine several important generic interfaces in the .NET library, which will help us gain an understanding of how C# and the .NET library interact with each other to enable accomplishing useful programming tasks.

INTERFACE FUNDAMENTALS

Object-oriented programming is a powerful paradigm for helping to design and implement large systems. Using classes helps us to achieve abstraction and encapsulation. Classes are a natural decomposition of a large system into manageable parts. Inheritance adds another tool for structuring our system, enabling us to factor out common parts into base classes, helping us to accomplish greater code reuse. Interfaces provide yet another weapon for our arsenal.

The main purpose of an interface is to specify a contract independently of implementation. An interface has associated methods. Each method has a signature, which specifies the parameters with their data types, and the data type of the return value.

Interfaces in C#

In C# **interface** is a keyword, and you define an interface in a manner similar to defining a class. Like classes, interfaces are reference types. The big difference is that there is no implementation code in an interface; it is pure specification. Also note that an interface can have properties as well as methods (it could also have other members, such as indexers). The **IAccount** interface shown below has read-only properties **Balance** and **Id** and the read-write property **Owner**. Note the syntax, with a semicolon where the body of a method would be in a class. There is also a semicolon after **set** and **get** in a property. As a naming convention, interface names normally begin with a capital I.

```
interface IAccount
{
    void Deposit(decimal amount);
    void Withdraw(decimal amount);
    decimal Balance {get;}
    string Owner {get; set;}
    int Id {get;}
}

interface IStatement
{
    string FormatBalance();
    string GetStatement();
    int Transactions {get;}
    void Post();
    void MonthEnd();
    string Prompt {get;}
}
```

Interface Inheritance

Interfaces can inherit from other interfaces. Unlike classes in C#, for which there is only single inheritance, there can be multiple inheritance of interfaces. For example, the interface **IAccount** could be declared by inheriting from the two smaller interfaces, **IBasicAccount** and **IAccountInfo**. When declaring a new interface in this way, you can also introduce additional methods, as illustrated for **IAccount2**:

```
interface IBasicAccount
{
    void Deposit(decimal amount);
    void Withdraw(decimal amount);
    decimal Balance {get;}
}

interface IAccountInfo
{
    string Owner {get; set;}
    int Id {get;}
}

interface IAccount : IBasicAccount, IAccountInfo
{
}

interface IAccount2 : IAccount
{
    void NewMethod();
}
```

PROGRAMMING WITH INTERFACES

It is very easy to program with interfaces in C#. You implement interfaces through classes, and you can cast a class reference to obtain an interface reference. You can call an interface method through either a class reference or an interface reference.

Implementing Interfaces

In C# you specify that a class implements one or more interfaces by using the colon notation that is employed for class inheritance. A class can also inherit both from a class and from one or more interfaces. In this case the base class should appear first in the derivation list after the colon.

```
class CheckingAccount : Account, IAccount, IChecking
{
...
```

In this example the class **CheckingAccount** inherits from the class **Account**, and it implements the interfaces **IAccount** and **IChecking**. The methods of the interfaces must all be implemented by **CheckingAccount**, either directly or by way of inheritance.

We will examine a full-blown example of interfaces with the account inheritance hierarchy later in the chapter, when we implement Step 6 of the case study.

As a small example, consider the program **SmallInterface**. The class **Account** implements the interface **IBasicAccount**.

```
// Account.cs

interface IBasicAccount
{
   void Deposit(decimal amount);
   void Withdraw(decimal amount);
   decimal Balance {get;}
}

public class Account : IBasicAccount
{
   private decimal balance;
   public Account(decimal balance)
   {
      this.balance = balance;
   }
   public void Deposit(decimal amount)
   {
      balance += amount;
   }
   public void Withdraw(decimal amount)
   {
      balance -= amount;
   }
   public decimal Balance
   {
      get
      {
         return balance;
      }
   }
}
```

Using an Interface

If you know your class supports an interface, you may simply call methods through a reference to a class instance. If you don't know whether your class implements the interface, you may try casting the class reference to the interface reference. If the class does not support the interface, you will get an **InvalidCastException**.

```
try
{
   IBasicAccount ifc2 = (IBasicAccount) acc2;
   ifc2.Deposit(25);
   Console.WriteLine("balance = {0}", ifc2.Balance);
}
catch (InvalidCastException e)
{
   Console.WriteLine("IBasicAccount is not supported");
   Console.WriteLine(e.Message);
}
```

In our example, we have two classes. **Account** supports the interface **IBasicAccount**, and the other class **NoAccount** does not support the interface. Both classes have the same set of methods and properties. Continuing in the directory **SmallInterface**, here is the code for the test program **SmallInterface.cs**:

```
// SmallInterface.cs

using System;

public class SmallInterface
{
   public static void Main()
   {
      Account acc = new Account(100);
      // Use a class reference
      Console.WriteLine("balance = {0}", acc.Balance);
      acc.Deposit(25);
      Console.WriteLine("balance = {0}", acc.Balance);
      // Use an interface reference
      IBasicAccount ifc = (IBasicAccount) acc;
      ifc.Deposit(25);
      Console.WriteLine("balance = {0}", ifc.Balance);

      // Now try same things with class not implementing
      // IBasicAccount
      NoAccount acc2 = new NoAccount(500);
      // Use a class reference
      Console.WriteLine("balance = {0}", acc2.Balance);
      acc2.Deposit(25);
```

```
        Console.WriteLine("balance = {0}", acc2.Balance);
        // Try an interface pointer
        try
        {
            IBasicAccount ifc2 = (IBasicAccount) acc2;
            ifc2.Deposit(25);
            Console.WriteLine("balance = {0}", ifc2.Balance);
        }
        catch (InvalidCastException e)
        {
            Console.WriteLine(
                "IBasicAccount is not supported");
            Console.WriteLine(e.Message);
        }
    }
}
```

We first work with the class **Account**, which does support the interface **IBasicAccount**. We are successful in calling the methods both through a class reference and through an interface reference. Next we work with the class **NoAccount**. Although this class has the same methods as **Account**, in its declaration it does not indicate that it is implementing the interface **IBasicAccount**.

```
// NoAccount.cs

public class NoAccount
{
...
```

When we run the test program, we encounter an **InvalidCastException** when we attempt to cast the class reference to an interface reference.

```
balance = 100
balance = 125
balance = 150
balance = 500
balance = 525
IBasicAccount is not supported
An exception of type System.InvalidCastException was thrown.
```

DYNAMIC USE OF INTERFACES

A powerful feature of interfaces is their use in dynamic scenarios, allowing us to write general code that can test whether an interface is supported by a class. If the interface is supported, our code can take advantage of it; otherwise our program can ignore the interface. We could in fact implement such dynamic behavior through exception handling, as illustrated previously. Although entirely feasible, this approach is not very elegant. C# provides two operators, **is** and **as**, that facilitate working with interfaces at runtime.

We will illustrate with some code snippets from a more full-blown account example, which is a continuation of our bank account case study (discussed in detail later in the chapter). See the directory **TryInterfaces**.

We have two kinds of accounts, checking and savings. These accounts are implemented, respectively, in classes which inherit from **Account**. The class **CheckingAccount** implements the interface **IChecking** in addition to **IAccount** and **IStatement**. (The interfaces are defined in the file **AccountDefinitions.cs**.)

```
interface IChecking
{
    decimal Fee {get;}
}
```

The class **SavingsAccount** implements the additional interface **ISavings**.

```
interface ISavings
{
    decimal Interest {get;}
    decimal Rate {get; set;}
}
```

Our test program creates two checking account instances and one savings account instance, having IDs of 0, 1, and 2. The object references are stored in an array and can be selected by using an index, which coincides with the ID. Our command loop is generic and does not know which kind of account it is working on.

This kind of dynamic behavior is an extension of polymorphism, which we discussed in Chapter 14. With polymorphism you can call methods, which will behave differently depending upon the type of the object making the call. But the only methods you can call in this way are ones defined in the base class. Using the concept of interfaces, you can call other methods, depending on whether additional interfaces are supported. Thus if the interface **IChecking** is supported, you can call the **Fee** property. If the method **ISavings** is supported, you can call the **Interest** and **Rate** properties.

Here is the test program:

```
// TryInterfaces.cs

using System;
```

```
public class TryInterfaces
{
    public static void Main()
    {
        Account acc;
        IChecking ichk;
        ISavings isav;
        // Initialize accounts and show starting state
        Account[] accounts = new Account[3];
        accounts[0] = new CheckingAccount(100, "Bob", 0);
        accounts[1] = new SavingsAccount(200, "Mary", 1);
        accounts[2] = new CheckingAccount(300, "Charlie", 2);
        ShowAccounts(accounts);
        acc = accounts[0];
        Console.WriteLine(acc.GetStatement());
        // Command processing loop
        InputWrapper iw = new InputWrapper();
        string cmd;
        Console.WriteLine("Enter command, quit to exit");
        cmd = iw.getString("> ");
        while (! cmd.Equals("quit"))
        {
            try
            {
                if (cmd.Equals("show"))
                    ShowAccounts(accounts);
                else if (cmd.Equals("account"))
                {
                    int id = iw.getInt("account id: ");
                    acc = accounts[id];
                    Console.WriteLine(acc.GetStatement());
                }
                else if (cmd.Equals("deposit"))
                {
                    decimal amount = iw.getDecimal("amount: ");
                    acc.Deposit(amount);
                    ShowBalance(acc);
                }
                else if (cmd.Equals("withdraw"))
                {
                    decimal amount = iw.getDecimal("amount: ");
                    acc.Withdraw(amount);
                    ShowBalance(acc);
                }
                else if (cmd.Equals("statement"))
                {
                    Console.WriteLine(acc.GetStatement());
                }
                else if (cmd.Equals("fee"))
                {
```

```csharp
            // cast to interface and check for exception
            try
            {
                ichk = (IChecking) acc;
                Console.WriteLine("fee = {0:C}",
                                ichk.Fee);
            }
            catch (InvalidCastException e)
            {
                Console.WriteLine(
                    "IChecking is not supported");
                Console.WriteLine(e.Message);
            }
        }
        else if (cmd.Equals("interest"))
        {
            // use C# "is" operator
            if (acc is ISavings)
            {
                isav = (ISavings) acc;
                Console.WriteLine("interest = {0:C}",
                                isav.Interest);
            }
            else
                Console.WriteLine(
                    "ISavings is not supported");
        }
        else if (cmd.Equals("rate"))
        {
            // use C# "as" operator
            isav = acc as ISavings;
            if (isav != null)
            {
                isav = (ISavings) acc;
                Console.WriteLine("rate = {0}",
                                isav.Rate);
            }
            else
                Console.WriteLine(
                    "ISavings is not supported");
        }
        else
            help();
    }
    catch (Exception e)
    {
        Console.WriteLine(e.Message);
        if (e.InnerException != null)
        {
            Console.WriteLine(e.InnerException.Message);
```

```
                }
            }
            cmd = iw.getString("> ");
        }
    }
...
```

Here is a transcript of a sample run. We start with account #0. We can find the fee, but not the interest or the rate. We then switch to account #1, where we can find the interest and the rate, but not the fee. The program uses different mechanisms for determining whether an interface is supported.

```
0         C: Bob           $100.00
1         S: Mary          $200.00
2         C: Charlie       $300.00
Statement for Bob id = 0
0 transactions, balance = $100.00, fee = $0.00
Enter command, quit to exit
> fee
fee = $0.00
> interest
ISavings is not supported
> account
account id: 1
Statement for Mary id = 1
0 transactions, balance = $200.00, interest = $1.00
> interest
interest = $1.00
> rate
rate = 0.06
> fee
IChecking is not supported
An exception of type System.InvalidCastException was thrown.
```

is Operator

The processing of the "fee" command illustrates doing a cast and catching an exception. A neater solution is to test for the interface *before* you do the cast. For this purpose you may use the C# **is** operator. The "interest" command illustrates:

```
// use C# "is" operator
if (acc is ISavings)
{
   isav = (ISavings) acc;
   Console.WriteLine("interest = {0:C}", isav.Interest);
}
else
   Console.WriteLine("ISavings is not supported");
```

The **is** operator is not the most efficient solution, as a check of the type is made *twice*:

* When the is operator is invoked
* When the actual type conversion is performed

as Operator

When you use the **as** operator, you obtain an interface reference directly. The interface reference is **null** if the class does not support the interface. The type is checked only once in this scenario.

```
// use C# "as" operator
isav = acc as ISavings;
if (isav != null)
{
    isav = (ISavings) acc;
    Console.WriteLine("rate = {0}", isav.Rate);
}
else
    Console.WriteLine("ISavings is not supported");
```

If you are experienced with COM (Component Object Model), the operation of finding out if an interface is supported should be very familiar to you.

Interfaces in C# and COM

There are many similarities between .NET and COM. In both, the concept of interface plays a fundamental role. Interfaces are useful for specifying contracts. Interfaces support a very dynamic style of programming.

In COM you must yourself provide a very elaborate infrastructure in order to implement a COM component. You must implement a class factory for the creation of COM objects. You must implement the **QueryInterface** method of **IUnknown** for the dynamic checking of interfaces. You must implement **AddRef** and **Release** for proper memory management.

With C# (and other .NET languages) the Common Language Runtime does all this for you automatically. You create an object via **new**. You check for an interface via **is** or **as** and obtain the interface by a cast. The garbage collector takes care of memory management for you.

BANK CASE STUDY: STEP 6

We will now apply our knowledge of interfaces to do a little restructuring of the bank case study. Actually, comparatively little rewriting is needed, as C# interfaces integrate quite seamlessly into traditional class inheritance. One of the big benefits of using interfaces is that they raise the level of abstraction somewhat, helping you to understand the system by way of the interface contacts, without worrying about how the system is implemented. It turns out that the implementation we have already constructed, using an abstract base class and two concrete derived classes, works perfectly for the interfaces. But we now have a nice abstract contract, which could be implemented many different ways.

As usual, our case study code is in the **CaseStudy** directory for this chapter.

The Contract

COMMON INTERFACES

We begin by examining the functionality of our base class **Account**. The methods and properties divide fairly naturally into two groups. The first group is concerned with operations on an account object (deposit or withdraw) and getting and setting fields. This group of methods and properties constitutes the **IAccount** interface. These interfaces are defined in **AccountDefinitions.cs**.

```
interface IAccount
{
   void Deposit(decimal amount);
   void Withdraw(decimal amount);
   decimal Balance {get;}
   string Owner {get; set;}
   int Id {get;}
}
```

You may wonder why the **Balance, Owner,** and **Id** properties are in the **IAccount** interface when they are already in the abstract base class **Account**. Is there a redundancy here? Their functions in the interface and in the abstract base class are totally different. In the interface, they are part of the *contract*. Every class which implements the **IAccount** interface *must* support these properties. The abstract base class *implements* these properties.

You may also wonder about properties in the **IAccount** interface. Does this mean that somehow an interface can contain data? Not at all. The properties specify *behavior* — how you can read and write a property value using a convenient notation. The implementation of a property, where the data is stored, is in a class that implements the interface.

The second group is concerned with getting a statement of an account and constitutes the **IStatement** interface.

```
interface IStatement
{
    string FormatBalance();
    string GetStatement();
    int Transactions {get;}
    void Post();
    void MonthEnd();
    string Prompt {get;}
}
```

We will go through the methods of **IStatement**.

1. **FormatBalance** returns a string representation of the balance in proper currency format.

2. **GetStatement** returns a string giving a complete statement for the account, including items such as the owner, id, balance, and number of transactions. Specific kinds of accounts will append supplementary information.

3. **Transactions** returns a count of the number of transactions so far in the current month.

4. **Post** will apply credits or debits for the current month. A checking account may have a debit of a fee, and a savings account a credit of interest.

5. **MonthEnd** will initialize the account for the next month. The transactions count will be set to 0. For a savings account, the minimum balance (used for calculating interest) will be set to the current balance.

6. **Prompt** returns a string indicating the type of account. The prompt string can be an aid to a user interface, giving a cue to the user about which kind of account is being worked on.

ICHECKING

The **IChecking** interface is an additional interface supported only by checking accounts.

```
interface IChecking
{
    decimal Fee {get;}
}
```

There is a single property, **Fee**, which is computed as the monthly fee owed for this account. (Note that the fee will not actually be debited from the balance until the **Post** method is invoked.)

ISAVINGS

The **ISavings** interface is an additional interface supported only by savings accounts.

```
interface ISavings
{
    decimal Interest {get;}
    decimal Rate {get; set;}
}
```

There are two properties. **Rate** is an annual interest rate. **Interest** is computed by multiplying **Rate/12** by the minimum balance.

The Implementation

There are no changes required to the **Account** class. This class is abstract, so it is not required to implement any interfaces. This class contains common code that does not have to be provided separately by derived classes.

Abstract Classes and Interfaces

You should now be able to understand clearly the differences between interfaces and abstract classes. At the beginning we pointed out an analogy, but they are actually quite different. Although it cannot be instantiated, an abstract class can contain implementation code that derived classes can take advantage of. An interface never contains any implementation. Since C# does not support multiple inheritance of classes, a concrete class can only inherit from a single abstract class. But it can implement many interfaces.

CHECKINGACCOUNT

The **CheckingAccount** class now derives from one class, **Account**, and three interfaces, the two common interfaces **IAccount** and **IStatement**, and the special interface **IChecking**. *None* of the implementation code has to change. We simply used the interfaces to codify the existing methods.

```
// CheckingAccount.cs - Step 6

using System;

public class CheckingAccount : Account, IAccount,
                              IStatement, IChecking
{
...
```

SAVINGSACCOUNT

The **SavingsAccount** class also derives from one class, **Account**, and three interfaces, the two common interfaces **IAccount** and **IStatement**, and the special interface **ISavings**. Again, none of the implementation code has to change.

```
// SavingsAccount.cs - Step 6

using System;

public class SavingsAccount : Account, IAccount,
                             IStatement, ISavings
{
...
```

The Client

The client code, which uses the account classes, is where things get interesting. We can now write very general, dynamic code, which can tailor itself to the particular type of account it is working on, based on which interfaces are supported.

To keep things simple, in Step 6 we do not include the **Bank** class, but instead provide a special class **TestInterfaces**, which can be used to test the methods and properties of the various interfaces. The operations are performed on a set of three hardcoded accounts: two checking and one savings. The structure of this class is similar to the **TryInterfaces** class we demonstrated earlier in the chapter, but the goals of the two classes are different. The **TryInterfaces** class was intended to demonstrate different ways of dynamically working with interfaces (catch exceptions, use the **is** operator, and use the **as** operator). The class **TestInterfaces** is intended to exercise the account classes fairly thoroughly (though not exhaustively; we do not provide test for every single method). We pick the **as** operator as the generally most useful operator for working with interfaces dynamically, and use it throughout.

Rather than give the entire listing in one piece (it is rather long), we break it into sections that we discuss individually.

INITIALIZATION AND SETUP

```
// TestInterfaces.cs

using System;

public class TestInterfaces
{
```

```
static Account acc;
static IAccount iacc;
static IStatement istat;
static IChecking ichk;
static ISavings isav;
public static void Main()
{
    // Initialize accounts and show starting state
    Account[] accounts = new Account[3];
    accounts[0] = new CheckingAccount(100, "Bob", 0);
    accounts[1] = new SavingsAccount(200, "Mary", 1);
    accounts[2] = new CheckingAccount(300, "Charlie", 2);
    ShowAccounts(accounts);
    acc = accounts[0];
    SetInterfaces();
    Console.WriteLine(istat.GetStatement());
    ...
```

We declare references for an **Account** object and for the various interfaces. Since we want to access these variables from static helper methods, we make them static fields of our class.

In **Main** we create an array of three accounts and initialize them with some test data, two checking accounts and one savings account. We show the starting accounts. The **Account** reference **acc** is used to refer to the current account we are working on, and that is set to be an account with id/index of 0. Next we initialize the interface references (discussed below). Finally, we obtain a statement of the initial account, going through an **IStatement** interface reference. Here is the output that will be generated from the statements we have looked at so far:

```
0       C: Bob          $100.00
1       S: Mary         $200.00
2       C: Charlie      $300.00
IAccount is supported
IStatement is supported
IChecking is supported
Statement for Bob id = 0
0 transactions, balance = $100.00, fee = $0.00
```

Part of what **SetInterfaces** does is to display which interfaces are supported by the current account. Since account #0 is a checking account, the interfaces shown above are the proper ones. Here is the code for **SetInterfaces**.

```
private static void SetInterfaces()
{
    iacc = acc as IAccount;
    if (iacc != null)
        Console.WriteLine("IAccount is supported");
```

```
    istat = acc as IStatement;
    if (istat != null)
        Console.WriteLine("IStatement is supported");
    ichk = acc as IChecking;
    if (ichk != null)
        Console.WriteLine("IChecking is supported");
    isav = acc as ISavings;
    if (isav != null)
        Console.WriteLine("ISavings is supported");
}
```

COMMAND PROCESSING LOOP

Next the program enters into a command processing loop of identical structure to command loops from previous versions of our case study. If a non-supported command is entered, a help message is displayed that gives a brief summary of each command:

```
The following commands are available:
        show      -- show all accounts
        account   -- set account to work on
        deposit   -- deposit to account
        withdraw  -- withdraw from account
        statement-- display account statement
        post      -- post to account
        month     -- initialize for new month
        fee       -- show fee (checking only)
        interest  -- show interest (savings only)
        rate      -- show rate (savings only)
        quit      -- exit the program
```

SHOW ALL ACCOUNTS

The "show" command shows all the accounts by calling the helper method **ShowAccounts**, which we previously implemented. It is perfectly legal to use a class reference such as **acc**, and so there was no need to change this code to use an interface pointer.

```
private static void ShowAccounts(Account[] array)
{
    foreach (Account acc in array)
    {
        string owner = acc.Owner.PadRight(12);
        string stype = acc.Prompt;
        string sid = acc.Id.ToString();
        string sbal = acc.FormatBalance();
        string str = sid + "\t" + stype + owner + "\t" + sbal;
        Console.WriteLine(str);
```

```
    }
}
```

ShowAccount is called as part of the initialization code discussed previously. In this version of the case study we work with three hardcoded accounts, and no commands are available to open and close accounts. Here is the output from **ShowAccount**:

```
0       C: Bob          $100.00
1       S: Mary         $200.00
2       C: Charlie      $300.00
```

CHOOSING AN ACCOUNT

The "account" command lets the user choose a particular account to work on. The user is prompted for an account id, and then both the class instance reference **acc**, and the interface references **iacc**, **istat**, **ichk**, and **isav** are initialized for this account. A statement is then displayed for the selected account. If an illegal account number is selected, normal exception code processing will kick in.

```
else if (cmd.Equals("account"))
{
    int id = iw.getInt("account id: ");
    acc = accounts[id];
    SetInterfaces();
    Console.WriteLine(istat.GetStatement());
}
...
catch (Exception e)
{
    Console.WriteLine(e.Message);
    if (e.InnerException != null)
    {
        Console.WriteLine(e.InnerException.Message);
    }
}
```

Here is an illustration of running the program and choosing first the legal account number 1 and then the illegal account number 7. Note the generic error message. We would have to write more code to display a more precise error message.

```
> account
account id: 1
IAccount is supported
IStatement is supported
ISavings is supported
Statement for Mary id = 1
```

```
0 transactions, balance = $200.00, interest = $1.00
> account
account id: 7
An exception of type System.IndexOutOfRangeException was
thrown.
```

METHODS OF IACCOUNT

The "deposit" and "withdraw" commands call the corresponding methods of
IAccount, and are always available for both checking and savings accounts.
Note that we use **iacc**, which is an interface reference to **IAccount**.

```
else if (cmd.Equals("deposit"))
{
   decimal amount = iw.getDecimal("amount: ");
   iacc.Deposit(amount);
   ShowBalance(istat);
}
else if (cmd.Equals("withdraw"))
{
   decimal amount = iw.getDecimal("amount: ");
   iacc.Withdraw(amount);
   ShowBalance(istat);
}
```

Here are two sample transactions applied to account #1 we previously
selected.

```
> deposit
amount: 125
balance = $325.00
> withdraw
amount: 25
balance = $300.00
```

METHODS OF ISTATEMENT

The commands "statement," "post," and "month" exercise the methods
GetStatement, **Post**, and **MonthEnd**, respectively, of the interface
IStatement. Our code uses **istat**, which is an interface reference to
IStatement.

```
else if (cmd.Equals("statement"))
{
   Console.WriteLine(istat.GetStatement());
}
else if (cmd.Equals("post"))
{
   istat.Post();
```

```
      Console.WriteLine(istat.GetStatement());
}
else if (cmd.Equals("month"))
{
   istat.MonthEnd();
      Console.WriteLine(istat.GetStatement());
}
```

Here is the result of trying these commands for our current account #1:

```
> statement
Statement for Mary id = 1
1 transactions, balance = $300.00, interest = $1.00
> post
Statement for Mary id = 1
1 transactions, balance = $301.00, interest = $1.00
> month
Statement for Mary id = 1
0 transactions, balance = $301.00, interest = $1.51
```

Note that after the "month" command, we have reinitialized for a new month, and the minimum balance is now $301, so the (projected) interest for the following month is higher.

METHODS OF ISAVINGS

Since our current account happens to be a savings account, we'll next examine the "interest" and "rate" commands, which call the **Interest** and **Rate** properties of **ISavings**. We use **isav**, an interface reference to **ISavings**. Note that our code explicitly checks if we have a valid interface reference. We will try out one of these commands again, after we have set the account to a checking account.

```
else if (cmd.Equals("interest"))
{
   if (isav == null)
      Console.WriteLine("ISavings is not supported");
   else
      Console.WriteLine("interest = {0:C}", isav.Interest);
}
else if (cmd.Equals("rate"))
{
   if (isav == null)
      Console.WriteLine("ISavings is not supported");
   else
      Console.WriteLine("rate = {0}", isav.Rate);
}
```

Here is the output as we continue working with account #1, which is a savings account. We will then attempt to apply the "fee" method.

```
> interest
interest = $1.51
> rate
rate = 0.06
> fee
IChecking is not supported
```

METHODS OF ICHECKING

Finally, let's look at the "fee" command, which calls the **Fee** property of
IChecking, going through **ichk**, an interface reference to **IChecking**. Our
code verifies that we have the proper interface reference and displays an
error message if we do not, as illustrated previously.

```
else if (cmd.Equals("fee"))
{
    if (ichk == null)
        Console.WriteLine("IChecking is not supported");
    else
        Console.WriteLine("fee = {0:C}", ichk.Fee);
}
```

The following output shows us setting the account to #2, finding the fee
(which is zero, since we have two free transactions allowed), performing
three transactions, and then finding the fee. Finally we obtain a statement
and then attempt to use the "interest" command.

```
> account
account id: 2
IAccount is supported
IStatement is supported
IChecking is supported
Statement for Charlie id = 2
0 transactions, balance = $300.00, fee = $0.00
> fee
fee = $0.00
> deposit
amount: 100
balance = $400.00
> deposit
amount: 100
balance = $500.00
> withdraw
amount: 50
balance = $450.00
> fee
fee = $5.00
> statement
Statement for Charlie id = 2
```

```
3 transactions, balance = $450.00, fee = $5.00
> interest
ISavings is not supported
```

At this point you should understand the case study quite thoroughly and be well acquainted with classes, inheritance, and interfaces.

RESOLVING AMBIGUITY

When working with interfaces, an ambiguity can arise if a class implements two interfaces and each has a method with same name and signature. As an example, consider the following versions of the interfaces **IAccount** and **IStatement**. Each interface contains the method **Show**.

```
interface IAccount
{
    void Deposit(decimal amount);
    void Withdraw(decimal amount);
    decimal Balance {get;}
    void Show();
}

interface IStatement
{
    int Transactions {get;}
    void Show();
}
```

How can the class specify implementations of these methods? The answer is to use the interface name to qualify the method, as illustrated in the program **Ambiguous**. The **IAccount** version **IAccount.Show** will display only the balance, and **IStatement.Show** will display both the number of transactions and the balance.

```
// Account.cs (project "Ambiguous")

...

public class Account : IAccount, IStatement
{
    private decimal balance;
    int numXact = 0;
    public Account(decimal balance)
    {
        this.balance = balance;
    }
    public void Deposit(decimal amount)
```

```
    {
        balance += amount;
        ++numXact;
    }
    public void Withdraw(decimal amount)
    {
        balance -= amount;
        ++numXact;
    }
    public decimal Balance
    {
        get
        {
            return balance;
        }
    }
    void IAccount.Show()
    {
        Console.WriteLine("balance = {0}", balance);
    }
    public int Transactions
    {
        get
        {
            return numXact;
        }
    }
    void IStatement.Show()
    {
        Console.WriteLine("{0} transactions, balance = {1}",
                            numXact, balance);
    }
}
```

Here is the test program:

```
// Ambiguous.cs

using System;

public class Ambiguous
{
    public static void Main()
    {
        Account acc = new Account(100);
        // acc.Show();
        // illegal - MUST go through an interface
        IAccount iacc = (IAccount) acc;
        IStatement istat = (IStatement) acc;
        iacc.Show();
        istat.Show();
```

```
        iacc.Deposit(25);
        iacc.Withdraw(10);
        iacc.Show();
        istat.Show();
    }
}
```

You will notice that in the definition of the class **Account**, the qualified methods **IAccount.Show** and **IStatement.Show** do not have an access modifier such as **public**. Such qualified methods *cannot be accessed* through a reference to a class instance. They can *only* be accessed through an interface reference of the type explicitly shown in the method definition. The test program attempted to use a class instance reference, but the program would not compile, so this attempt was commented out. In the test program we use interface references to make the calls to **Show**. Here is the output from the program:

```
balance = 100
0 transactions, balance = 100
balance = 115
2 transactions, balance = 115
```

SUMMARY

The term *interface* is widely used in computer programming to describe how parts of a large system fit together. In C# **interface** is a keyword and has a very precise meaning. An interface is a reference type, similar to an abstract class, that *specifies* behavior. An interface can be thought of as a contract. A class or struct can "implement" an interface, and must adhere to the contract. Interfaces are a useful way to partition functionality. The methods of a class can be grouped into related interfaces. While a class in C# can inherit from only one other class, it can implement multiple interfaces. Another benefit of interfaces is that they facilitate very dynamic programs. C# provides the operators **is** and **as** that can be used to query a class at runtime to see whether it supports a particular interface. Interfaces in C# and .NET are conceptually very similar to interfaces in Microsoft's Component Object Model, but are *much* easier to work with. We illustrated interfaces with our bank case study. Defining clear interfaces helps us specify the behavior of our system more precisely and succinctly. Finally we looked at how to resolve an ambiguity that can arise if two interfaces have the same method.

In the next chapter we will examine several important generic interfaces in the .NET library, which will help us gain an understanding of how C# and the .NET library interact with each other to enable accomplishing useful programming tasks.

PART FOUR

C # AND THE .NET FRAMEWORK

C # AND THE .NET FRAMEWORK

C# draws much of its power from the .NET Framework. In this final part of the book we explore thoroughly the relationships between C# and the .NET Framework, and we introduce some important .NET services. We introduce collections, which generalize arrays, and we examine fundamental operations such as copying and comparing objects. In .NET interfaces are provided for such basic operations, which makes for a very flexible architecture, as different classes can implement these interfaces in a manner appropriate for them. The .NET Framework provides a versatile callback mechanism, known as the delegate, which has many applications. Delegates are the foundation of events, and they are also used in starting threads. We look at directories and files, multiple thread programming, and attributes. Attributes are a powerful mechanism in .NET, enabling the programmer to accomplish tasks declaratively, writing little or no code. You can implement your own custom attributes in C#. You can read information about custom attributes, or any other metadata, by a mechanism known as reflection. C# permits you to code at a lower level by writing "unsafe" code, which can help you interoperate with legacy code. We conclude the book with introductions to components and to Windows programming.

Interfaces and the .NET Framework

*In the previous chapter we saw how useful interfaces can be in specifying contracts for our own classes. Interfaces can help us program at a higher level of abstraction, enabling us to see the essential features of our system without being bogged down in implementation details. In this chapter we will examine the role of interfaces in the .NET Framework, where they are ubiquitous. Many of the standard classes implement specific interfaces, and we can call into the methods of these interfaces to obtain useful services. Collections are an example of classes in the .NET Framework that support a well-defined set of interfaces that provide useful functionality. In order to work with collections effectively, you need to override certain methods of the **object** base class. We will provide a new implementation of our case study, using a collection of accounts in place of an array of accounts.*

Besides calling into interfaces that are implemented by library classes, many .NET classes call standard interfaces. If we provide our own implementation of such interfaces, we can have .NET library code call our own code in appropriate ways, customizing the behavior of library code. We will look at examples, including object cloning and comparison of objects. This behavior of your program being called into has traditionally been provided by "callback" functions. In C# there is a type-safe, object-oriented kind of callback known as a delegate, a topic we will examine in Chapter 19.

315

COLLECTIONS

The .NET Framework class library provides an extensive set of classes for working with collections of objects. These classes are all in the **System.Collections** namespace and implement a number of different kinds of collections, including lists, queues, stacks, arrays, and hashtables. The collections contain **object** instances. Since all types derive ultimately from **object**, any built-in or user-defined type may be stored in a collection.

In this section we will look at a representative class in this namespace, **ArrayList**. We will examine the interfaces implemented by this class and see how to use array lists in our programs. Part of our task in using arrays lists and similar collections is to properly implement our class whose instances are to be stored in the collection. In particular, our class must generally override certain methods of **object**.

ArrayList Example

To get our bearings, let's begin with a simple example of using the **ArrayList** class. An array list, as the name suggests, is a list of items stored like an array. An array list can be dynamically sized and will grow as necessary to accommodate new elements being added.

As mentioned, collection classes are made up of instances of type **object**. We will illustrate creating and manipulating a collection of **string**. We could also just as easily create a collection of any other built-in or user-defined type. If our type were a value type, such as **int**, the instance would be boxed before being stored in the collection. When the object is extracted from the collection, it will be unboxed back to **int**.

Our example program is **StringList**. It initializes a list of strings, and then lets the user display the list, add strings, and remove strings. A simple "help" method displays the commands that are available:

```
The following commands are available:
        show     -- show all strings
        array    -- show strings via array loop
        add      -- add a string
        remove   -- remove a string
        removeat -- remove a string at index
        count    -- show count and capacity
        quit     -- exit the program
```

Here is the code of our example program:

```
// StringList.cs

using System;
using System.Collections;
```

```csharp
public class StringList
{
    private static ArrayList list;
    public static void Main()
    {
        // Initialize strings and show starting state
        list = new ArrayList(4);
        ShowCount();
        AddString("Bob");
        AddString("Mary");
        AddString("Charlie");
        ShowList(list);
        ShowCount();
        // Command processing loop
        InputWrapper iw = new InputWrapper();
        string cmd;
        Console.WriteLine("Enter command, quit to exit");
        cmd = iw.getString("> ");
        while (! cmd.Equals("quit"))
        {
            try
            {
                if (cmd.Equals("show"))
                    ShowList(list);
                if (cmd.Equals("array"))
                    ShowArray(list);
                else if (cmd.Equals("add"))
                {
                    string str = iw.getString("string: ");
                    AddString(str);
                }
                else if (cmd.Equals("remove"))
                {
                    string str = iw.getString("string: ");
                    RemoveString(str);
                }
                else if (cmd.Equals("removeat"))
                {
                    int index = iw.getInt("index: ");
                    RemoveAt(index);
                }
                else if (cmd.Equals("count"))
                    ShowCount();
                else
                    help();
            }
            catch (Exception e)
            {
                Console.WriteLine(e.Message);
                if (e.InnerException != null)
```

```
                {
                    Console.WriteLine(e.InnerException.Message);
                }
            }
            cmd = iw.getString("> ");
        }
    }
    private static void ShowList(ArrayList array)
    {
        foreach (string str in array)
        {
            Console.WriteLine(str);
        }
    }
    private static void ShowArray(ArrayList array)
    {
        for (int i = 0; i < array.Count; i++)
        {
            Console.WriteLine("array[{0}] = {1}", i, array[i]);
        }
    }
    private static void ShowCount()
    {
        Console.WriteLine("list.Count = {0}", list.Count);
        Console.WriteLine("list.Capacity = {0}",
                        list.Capacity);
    }
    private static void AddString(string str)
    {
        if (list.Contains(str))
            throw new Exception("list contains " + str);
        list.Add(str);
    }
    private static void RemoveString(string str)
    {
        if (list.Contains(str))
            list.Remove(str);
        else
            throw new Exception(str + " not on list");
    }
    private static void RemoveAt(int index)
    {
        list.RemoveAt(index);
    }
    private static void help()
    {
    ...
    }
}
```

Here is a sample run of the program:

```
list.Count = 0
list.Capacity = 4
Bob
Mary
Charlie
list.Count = 3
list.Capacity = 4
Enter command, quit to exit
> add
string: David
> add
string: Ellen
> add
string: Bob
list contains Bob
> count
list.Count = 5
list.Capacity = 8
> array
array[0] = Bob
array[1] = Mary
array[2] = Charlie
array[3] = David
array[4] = Ellen
> remove
string: Charlie
> array
array[0] = Bob
array[1] = Mary
array[2] = David
array[3] = Ellen
> removeat
index: 2
> array
array[0] = Bob
array[1] = Mary
array[2] = Ellen
> remove
string: David
David not on list
> removeat
index: 3
Index was out of range.  Must be non-negative and less than
size. Parameter name: index
```

COUNT AND CAPACITY

An array list has properties **Count** and **Capacity**. The **Count** is the current number of elements in the list, and **Capacity** is the number of available "slots." If you add a new element when the capacity has been reached, the **Capacity** will be automatically increased. The default starting capacity is 16, but it can be adjusted by passing a starting size to the constructor. The **Capacity** will double when it is necessary to increase it. The "count" command in the sample program displays the current values of **Count** and **Capacity**, and you can observe how these change by adding new elements.

FOREACH LOOP

The **System.Collections.ArrayList** class implements the **IEnumerable** interface, as we will discuss later in the chapter, which means that you can use a **foreach** loop to iterate through it.

```
private static void ShowList(ArrayList array)
{
   foreach (string str in array)
   {
      Console.WriteLine(str);
   }
}
```

ARRAY NOTATION

ArrayList implements the **IList** interface, which has the property **Item**. In C# this property is an indexer, so you can use array notation to access elements of an array list. The "array" command demonstrates accessing the elements of the list using an index.

```
private static void ShowArray(ArrayList array)
{
   for (int i = 0; i < array.Count; i++)
   {
      Console.WriteLine("array[{0}] = {1}", i, array[i]);
   }
}
```

ADDING TO THE LIST

The **Add** method allows you to append an item to an array list. If you want to make sure you do not add a duplicate item, you can make use of the **Contains** method to check whether the proposed new item is already contained in the list.

```
private static void AddString(string str)
```

```
    {
        if (list.Contains(str))
            throw new Exception("list contains " + str);
        list.Add(str);
    }
```

REMOVE METHOD

The **Remove** method allows you to remove an item from an array list. Again you can make use of the **Contains** method to check whether the item to be deleted is on the list.

```
    private static void RemoveString(string str)
    {
        if (list.Contains(str))

            list.Remove(str);

        else

            throw new Exception(str + " not on list");

    }
```

REMOVEAT METHOD

The **RemoveAt** method allows you to remove an item at a specified integer index. If the item is not found, an exception of type **ArgumentOutOfRangeException** will be thrown. (In our program we just let our normal test program exception handling pick up the exception.)

```
    private static void RemoveAt(int index)
    {
        list.RemoveAt(index);
    }
```

Collection Interfaces

The classes **ArrayList**, **Array**, and many other collection classes implement a set of four fundamental interfaces.

```
public class ArrayList : IList, ICollection, IEnumerable,
                         ICloneable
```

In this section we will examine the first three interfaces. We will look at **ICloneable** later in the chapter.

IENUMERABLE AND IENUMERATOR

The most basic interface is **IEnumerable**, which has a single method, **GetEnumerator**.

```
interface IEnumerable
{
    IEnumerator GetEnumerator();
}
```

GetEnumerator returns an interface reference to **IEnumerator**, which is the interface used for iterating through a collection. This interface has the property **Current** and the methods **MoveNext** and **Reset**.

```
interface IEnumerator
{
    object Current {get;}
    bool MoveNext();
    void Reset();
}
```

The enumerator is initially positioned *before* the first element in the collection and it must be advanced before it is used. The program **AccountList\Step0**, which we will discuss in detail later, illustrates using an enumerator to iterate through a list.

```
private static void ShowEnum(ArrayList array)
{
    IEnumerator iter = array.GetEnumerator();
    bool more = iter.MoveNext();
    while (more)
    {
        Account acc = (Account) iter.Current;
        Console.WriteLine(acc.Info);
        more = iter.MoveNext();
    }
}
```

This pattern of using an enumerator to iterate through a list is so common that C# provides a special kind of loop, **foreach**, that can be used for iterating through the elements of *any* collection. Here is the comparable code using **foreach**.

```
private static void ShowAccounts(ArrayList array)
{
    foreach (Account acc in array)
    {
        Console.WriteLine(acc.Info);
    }
}
```

ICOLLECTION

The **ICollection** interface is derived from **IEnumerable** and adds a **Count** property and a **CopyTo** method. There are also synchronization properties that can help you deal with thread safety issues, a topic we will touch on in Chapter 20.

```
interface ICollection : IEnumerable
{
   int Count {get;}
   bool IsReadOnly {get;}
   bool IsSynchronized {get;}    bool Contains(object value);
   object SyncRoot {get;}
   void CopyTo(Array array, int index);
}
```

ILIST

The **IList** interface is derived from **ICollection** and provides methods for adding an item to a list, removing an item, and so on. There is an indexer provided that enables array notation to be used.

```
interface IList : ICollection
{
   object this[int index] {get; set;}
   int Add(object value);
   void Clear();
   bool Contains(object value);
   int IndexOf(object value);
   void Insert(int index, object value);
   void Remove(object value);
   void RemoveAt(int index);
}
```

Our sample code illustrated using the indexer and the **Add**, **Contains**, **Remove**, and **RemoveAt** methods.

A Collection of User-Defined Objects

We will now look at an example of a collection of user-defined objects. The mechanics of calling the various collection properties and methods is very straightforward and is essentially identical to the usage for collections of built-in types. What is different is that in your class you must override at least the **Equals** method in order to obtain proper behavior in your collection. For built-in types, you did not have to worry about this issue, because **Equals** is provided by the class library for you.

Our example program is **AccountList**, which comes in two steps. Step 0 illustrates a very simple **Account** class, with no methods of **object** overridden.

```
// Account.cs - Step 0

using System;

public class Account
{
   private decimal balance;
   private string owner;
   private int id;
   public Account(decimal balance, string owner, int id)
   {
      this.balance = balance;
      this.owner = owner;
      this.id = id;
   }
   public string Info
   {
      get
      {
         return id.ToString().PadRight(4)
                + owner.PadRight(12)
                + string.Format("{0:C}", balance);
      }
   }
}
```

The test program **AccountList.cs** contains code to initialize an array list of **Account** objects, show the initial accounts, and then perform a command loop. A simple **help** method gives a brief summary of the available commands:

```
The following commands are available:
        show      -- show all accounts
        enum      -- enumerate all accounts
        add       -- add an account (specify id)
```

The code is very straightforward, so we won't give a listing. You can examine the code online. We gave the implementation of the "enum" command as an example of explicitly using an enumerator. Here is a sample run of the program:

```
accounts.Count = 0
accounts.Capacity = 16
1    Bob         $100.00
2    Mary        $200.00
3    Charlie     $300.00
```

```
accounts.Count = 3
accounts.Capacity = 16
Enter command, quit to exit
> enum
1    Bob          $100.00
2    Mary         $200.00
3    Charlie      $300.00
> add
balance: 100
owner: Bob
id: 1
> show
1    Bob          $100.00
2    Mary         $200.00
3    Charlie      $300.00
1    Bob          $100.00
```

The salient point is that the "add" command is not protected against adding a duplicate element ("Bob"). Our code is similar to what we used before in the **StringList** program, but now the **Contains** method does not work properly. The default implementation of **Equals** in the **object** root class is to check for reference equality, and the two "Bob" elements have the same data but different references.

AccountList\Step1 contains corrected code for the **Account** class. In the test program we have code for both "add" and "remove," and everything behaves properly. Here is the code added to **Account.cs**.

```
// Account.cs - Step 1

using System;

public class Account
{
...
    public override bool Equals(object obj)
    {
        Account acc = (Account) obj;
        return (acc.id == this.id);
    }
}
```

Our test for equality involves just the account ID. For example, two people with the same name could have an account at the same bank, but their account IDs should be different.

Here is the code for implementing the "add" and "remove" commands.

```
private static void AddAccount(decimal bal, string owner,
                               int id)
{
```

```
{
      int AddAccount(AccountType type, decimal bal,
                  string owner);
      ArrayList GetAccounts();
      void DeleteAccount(int id);
      Account FindAccount(int id);
      ArrayList GetStatements();
}

public class Bank : IBank
{
   private ArrayList accounts;
   private int nextid = 1;
   public Bank()
   {
      accounts = new ArrayList();
      AddAccount(AccountType.Checking, 100, "Bob");
      AddAccount(AccountType.Savings, 200, "Mary");
      AddAccount(AccountType.Checking, 300, "Charlie");
   }
   public int AddAccount(AccountType type, decimal bal,
                     string owner)
   {
      Account acc;
      int id = nextid++;
      switch(type)
      {
         case AccountType.Checking:
            acc = new CheckingAccount(bal, owner, id);
            break;
         case AccountType.Savings:
            acc = new SavingsAccount(bal, owner, id);
            break;
         default:
            Console.WriteLine("Unexpected AccountType");
            return -1;
      }
      accounts.Add(acc);
      return id;
   }
   public ArrayList GetAccounts()
   {
      return accounts;
   }
   public void DeleteAccount(int id)
   {
      CheckingAccount acc = new CheckingAccount(0m, "", id);
      if (accounts.Contains(acc))
         accounts.Remove(acc);
      else
```

```
        throw new Exception(
            "Account " + id + " not on list");
public Account FindAccount(int id)
{
    foreach (Account acc in accounts)
    {
        if (acc.Id == id)
            return acc;
    }
    return null;
}
public ArrayList GetStatements()
{
    ArrayList array = new ArrayList(accounts.Count);
    foreach (Account acc in accounts)
    {
        acc.Post();
        string str = acc.GetStatement();
        acc.MonthEnd();
        array.Add(str);
        str = "-----------------------------------------";
        array.Add(str);
    }
    return array;
}
}
```

As discussed in the introduction to this section, we replace the array of accounts by an array list. This change simplifies the code, notably in the **DeleteAccount** method. We don't need the **FindIndex** helper method any longer, and we don't have to code moving elements around in the array. One little nuance is that when we construct an account object to use for matching when we call **Remove**, we cannot create an **Account** instance, because **Account** is an abstract class. So we just pick one kind of account, **CheckingAccount**.

The new **GetStatements** method uses **foreach** to iterate through all the accounts. We exploit polymorphism on the calls to **Post**, **GetStatement**, and **MonthEnd** to get the proper behavior for each account type. We call **Post** before **GetStatement**, so the balances will be updated to reflect fees and interest. We then call **MonthEnd** to initialize for the next month.

The **GetAccounts** method now returns a copy of the array list itself. The client program can now do what it needs to do, providing more flexibility than our previous approach, which returned strings. For example, a GUI client could provide a totally different user interface. We will introduce GUI programming in Chapter 22.

Account

```
// Account.cs - Step 7

using System;

abstract public class Account
{
...
   public override bool Equals(object obj)
   {
      Account acc = (Account) obj;
      return (acc.Id == this.Id);
   }
}
```

TestBank

```
// TestBank.cs - Step 7

using System;
using System.Collections;

public class TestBank
{
   public static void Main()
   {
      Bank bank = new Bank();
      InputWrapper iw = new InputWrapper();
      string cmd;
      Console.WriteLine("Enter command, quit to exit");
      cmd = iw.getString("> ");
      while (! cmd.Equals("quit"))
      {
         ...
         else if (cmd.Equals("show"))
               ShowAccounts(bank.GetAccounts());
         else if (cmd.Equals("account"))
         {
            int id = iw.getInt("account id: ");
            Account acc = bank.FindAccount(id);
            Atm.ProcessAccount(acc);
         }
         else if (cmd.Equals("month"))
               ShowStringList(bank.GetStatements());
         else
            help();
         cmd = iw.getString("> ");
      }
```

```
    }
    private static void ShowAccounts(ArrayList array)
    {
        foreach (Account acc in array)
        {
            string owner = acc.Owner.PadRight(12);
            string stype = acc.Prompt;
            string sid = acc.Id.ToString();
            string sbal = string.Format("{0:C}", acc.Balance);
            string str = owner + "\t" + stype + sid + "\t" +
                        sbal;
            Console.WriteLine(str);
        }
    }
    private static void ShowStringList(ArrayList array)
    {
        foreach (string str in array)
            Console.WriteLine(str);
    }
    ...
}
```

Here is a sample run:

```
Enter command, quit to exit
> show
Bob            C: 1    $100.00
Mary           S: 2    $200.00
Charlie        C: 3    $300.00
> account
account id: 1
balance = $100.00
Enter command, quit to exit
C: deposit
amount: 50
balance = $150.00
C: deposit
amount: 50
balance = $200.00
C: withdraw
amount: 95
balance = $105.00
C: show
Statement for Bob id = 1
3 transactions, balance = $105.00, fee = $5.00
C: quit
> show
Bob            C: 1    $105.00
Mary           S: 2    $200.00
Charlie        C: 3    $300.00
> month
```

```
Statement for Bob id = 1
3 transactions, balance = $100.00, fee = $5.00
------------------------------------------------
Statement for Mary id = 2
0 transactions, balance = $201.00, interest = $1.00
------------------------------------------------
Statement for Charlie id = 3
0 transactions, balance = $300.00, fee = $0.00
------------------------------------------------
> show
Bob             C: 1    $100.00
Mary            S: 2    $201.00
Charlie         C: 3    $300.00
```

COPY SEMANTICS AND ICLONEABLE

Many times in programming you have occasion to make a copy of a variable. When you program in C#, it is very important that you have a firm understanding of exactly what happens when you copy various kinds of data. In this section we will look carefully at the copy semantics of C#. We will compare reference copy, shallow memberwise copy, and deep copy. We will see that by implementing the **ICloneable** interface in your class, you can enable deep copy.

Copy Semantics in C#

Recall that C# has value types and reference types. A value type contains all its own data, while a reference type refers to data stored somewhere else. If a reference variable gets copied to another reference variable, both will refer to the same object. If the object referenced by the second variable is changed, the first variable will also reflect the new value.

As an example, consider what happens when you copy an array, which is a reference type. Consider the program **ArrayCopy**.

```
// ArrayCopy.cs

using System;

public class ArrayCopy
{
    public static int Main(string[] args)
    {
        int [] arr1 = {1, 4, 9};
        int [] arr2 = arr1;
        show(arr1, "first array");
```

```
        show(arr2, "second array");
        arr1[1] = 444;         // this will change BOTH arrays!
        show(arr1, "first array");
        show(arr2, "second array");
        return 0;
    }
    public static void show (int [] arr, string caption)
    {
        Console.WriteLine("----{0}----", caption);
        for (int i = 0; i < arr.Length; i++)
        {
            Console.Write("{0} ", arr[i]);
        }
        Console.WriteLine();
    }
}
```

When we make the assignment **arr2 = arr1**, we wind up not with two independent arrays, but rather two references to the same array. When we make a change to an element of the first array, both arrays will wind up changed. Here is the output:

```
----first array----
1 4 9
----second array----
1 4 9
----first array----
1 444 9
----second array----
1 444 9
```

Shallow Copy and Deep Copy

A struct in C# automatically implements a "memberwise" copy, sometimes known as a "shallow copy." The **object** root class has a protected method, **MemberwiseClone**, which will perform a memberwise copy of members of a class.

If one or more members of a class are of a reference type, this memberwise copy may not be good enough. The result will be two references to the same data, not two independent copies of the data. To actually copy the data itself and not merely the references, you will need to perform a "deep copy." Deep copy can be provided at either the language level or the library level. In C++ deep copy is provided at the language level through a *copy constructor*. In C# deep copy is provided by the .NET Framework through a special interface, **ICloneable**, which you can implement in your classes in order to enable them to perform deep copy.

Example Program

We will illustrate all these ideas in the program **CopyDemo**. This program makes a copy of a **Course**. The **Course** class consists of a title and a collection of students.

```
// Course.cs

using System;
using System.Collections;

public class Course : ICloneable
{
    public string Title;
    public ArrayList Roster;
    public Course(string title)
    {
        Title = title;
        Roster = new ArrayList();
    }
    public void AddStudent(string name)
    {
        Roster.Add(name);
    }
    public void Show(string caption)
    {
        Console.WriteLine("-----{0}-----", caption);
        Console.WriteLine("Course : {0} with {1} students",
            Title, Roster.Count);
        foreach (string name in Roster)
        {
            Console.WriteLine(name);
        }
    }
    public Course ShallowCopy()
    {
        return (Course) this.MemberwiseClone();
    }
    public object Clone()
    {
        Course course = new Course(Title);
        course.Roster = (ArrayList) Roster.Clone();
        return course;
    }
}
```

The test program constructs a **Course** instance **c1** and then makes a copy **c2** by various methods.

REFERENCE COPY

The first way the copy is performed is by the straight assignment **c2 = c1**. Now we get two references to the same object, and if we make any change through the first reference, we will see the same change through the second reference. The first part of the test program illustrates such an assignment.

```
// CopyDemo.cs

using System;
using System.Collections;

public class CopyDemo
{
   private static Course c1, c2;
   public static void Main()
   {
      Console.WriteLine("Copy is done via c2 = c1");
      InitializeCourse();
      c1.Show("original");
      c2 = c1;
      c2.Show("copy");
      c2.Title = ".NET Programming";
      c2.AddStudent("Charlie");
      c2.Show("copy with changed title and new student");
      c1.Show("original");

      ...
   }
   private static void InitializeCourse()
   {
      c1 = new Course("Intro to C#");
      c1.AddStudent("John");
      c1.AddStudent("Mary");
   }
}
```

We initialize with the title "Intro to C#" and two students. We make the assignment **c2 = c1**, and then change the title and add another student for **c2**. We then show both **c1** and **c2**, and we see that both reflect both of these changes. Here is the output from this first part of the program:

```
Copy is done via c2 = c1
-----original-----
Course : Intro to C# with 2 students
John
Mary
-----copy-----
Course : Intro to C# with 2 students
John
```

```
Mary
-----copy with changed title and new student-----
Course : .NET Programming with 3 students
John
Mary
Charlie
-----original-----
Course : .NET Programming with 3 students
John
Mary
Charlie
```

MEMBERWISE CLONE

The next way we will illustrate doing a copy is a memberwise copy, which can be accomplished using the **MemberwiseClone** method of **object**. Since this method is **protected**, we cannot call it directly from outside our **Course** class. Instead, in **Course** we define a method, **ShallowCopy**, which is implemented using **MemberwiseClone**.

```
// Course.cs

using System;
using System.Collections;

public class Course : ICloneable
{
   ...
   public Course ShallowCopy()
   {
      return (Course) this.MemberwiseClone();
   }
   ...
}
```

Here is the second part of the test program, which calls the **ShallowCopy** method. Again we change the title and a student in the second copy.

```
// CopyDemo.cs

using System;
using System.Collections;

public class CopyDemo
{
      ...
      Console.WriteLine(
         "\nCopy is done via c2 = c1.ShallowCopy()");
```

```
        InitializeCourse();
        c2 = c1.ShallowCopy();
        c2.Title = ".NET Programming";
        c2.AddStudent("Charlie");
        c2.Show("copy with changed title and new student");
        c1.Show("original");
        ...
```

Here is the output of this second part of the program. Now the **Title** field has its own independent copy, but the **Roster** collection is just copied by reference, so each copy refers to the same collection of students.

```
Copy is done via c2 = c1.ShallowCopy()
-----copy with changed title and new student-----
Course : .NET Programming with 3 students
John
Mary
Charlie
-----original-----
Course : Intro to C# with 3 students
John
Mary
Charlie
```

USING ICLONEABLE

The final version of copy relies on the fact that our **Course** class supports the **ICloneable** interface and implements the **Clone** method. To clone the **Roster** collection we use the fact that **ArrayList** implements the **ICloneable** interface, as discussed earlier in the chapter. Note that the **Clone** method returns an **object**, so we must cast to **ArrayList** before assigning to the **Roster** field.

```
// Course.cs

using System;
using System.Collections;

public class Course : ICloneable
{
    ...
    public object Clone()
    {
        Course course = new Course(Title);
        course.Roster = (ArrayList) Roster.Clone();
        return course;
    }
}
```

Here is the third part of the test program, which calls the **Clone** method. Again we change the title and a student in the second copy.

```
// CopyDemo.cs

using System;
using System.Collections;

public class CopyDemo
{
    ...
    Console.WriteLine(
        "\nCopy is done via c2 = c1.Clone()");
    InitializeCourse();
    c2 = (Course) c1.Clone();
    c2.Title = ".NET Programming";
    c2.AddStudent("Charlie");
    c2.Show("copy with changed title and new student");
    c1.Show("original");
    ...
```

Here is the output from the third part of the program. Now we have completely independent instances of **Course**. Each has its own title and set of students.

```
Copy is done via c2 = c1.Clone()
-----copy with changed title and new student-----
Course : .NET Programming with 3 students
John
Mary
Charlie
-----original-----
Course : Intro to C# with 2 students
John
Mary
```

COMPARING OBJECTS

We have quite exhaustively studied issues involved in *copying* objects. We will now examine the issues involved in *comparing* objects. In order to compare objects, the .NET Framework uses the interface **IComparable**. In this section we will examine the use of the interface **IComparable** through an example of sorting an array.

Sorting an Array

The **System.Array** class provides a static method, **Sort**, that can be used for sorting an array. The program **ArrayName\Step0** illustrates an attempt to apply this **Sort** method to an array of **Name** objects, where the **Name** class simply encapsulates a **string** through a read-only property **Text**.

```
// ArrayName.cs - Step 0

using System;

public class Name
{
    private string text;
    public Name(string text)
    {
        this.text = text;
    }
    public string Text
    {
        get
        {
            return text;
        }
    }
}
public class ArrayName
{
    public static int Main(string[] args)
    {
        Name[] array = new Name[10];
        array[0] = new Name("Michael");
        array[1] = new Name("Charlie");
        array[2] = new Name("Peter");
        array[3] = new Name("Dana");
        array[4] = new Name("Bob");
        Array.Sort(array);
        return 0;
    }
}
```

ANATOMY OF ARRAY.SORT

What do you suppose will happen when you run this program? Here is the result:

```
Exception occurred: System.ArgumentException: At least one
object must implement IComparable.
```

The static method **Sort** of the **Array** class relies on some functionality of the objects in the array. The array objects must implement **IComparable**.

Suppose we don't know whether the objects in our array support **IComparable**. Is there a way we can find out programmatically at runtime?

USING THE IS OPERATOR

There are in fact three ways we have seen so far to dynamically check if an interface is supported:

* Use exceptions.
* Use the **as** operator.
* Use the **is** operator.

In this case the most direct solution is to use the **is** operator (which is applied to an object, not to a class). See **ArrayName\Step1**.

```
// ArrayName.cs - Step 1

...
public class ArrayName
{
    public static int Main(string[] args)
    {
        Name[] array = new Name[10];
        array[0] = new Name("Michael");
        array[1] = new Name("Charlie");
        array[2] = new Name("Peter");
        array[3] = new Name("Dana");
        array[4] = new Name("Bob");
        if (array[0] is IComparable)
            Array.Sort(array);
        else
            Console.WriteLine(
                "Name does not implement IComparable");
        return 0;
    }
}
```

Here is the output from running the program. We're still not sorting the array, but at least we fail more gracefully.

```
Name does not implement IComparable
```

THE USE OF DYNAMIC TYPE CHECKING

We can use dynamic type checking of object references to make our programs more robust. We can degrade gracefully rather than fail completely.

For example, in our array program the desired outcome is to print the array elements in sorted order. We could check whether the objects in the array support **IComparable**, and if not, we could go ahead and print out the array elements in unsorted order, obtaining at least some functionality.

Implementing IComparable

Consulting the documentation for **System**, we find the following specification for **IComparable**:

```
public interface IComparable
{
      int CompareTo(object object);
}
```

We will implement **IComparable** in the class **Name**. See **ArrayName\Step2**. We also add a simple loop in **Main** to display the array elements after sorting.

```
// ArrayName.cs - Step 2

using System;

public class Name : IComparable
{
   private string text;
   public Name(string text)
   {
      this.text = text;
   }
   public string Text
   {
      get
      {
         return text;
      }
   }
   public int CompareTo(object obj)
   {
      string s1 = this.Text;
      string s2 = ((Name) obj).Text;
      return String.Compare(s1, s2);
   }
}
public class ArrayName
{
   public static int Main(string[] args)
   {
      ...
      foreach (Name name in array)
        Console.WriteLine(name);
      return 0;
```

```
        }
    }
```

AN INCOMPLETE SOLUTION

If we run the above program, we do not exactly get the desired output:

```
Name
Name
Name
Name
Name
```

The first five lines of output are blank, and in place of the string in **Name**, we get the class name **Name** displayed. The unassigned elements of the array are **null**, and they compare successfully with real elements, always being less than a real element.

COMPLETE SOLUTION

We should test for **null** before displaying. The most straightforward way to correct the issue of the strings in **Name** not displaying is to use the **Text** property. A more interesting solution is to override the **ToString** method in our **Name** class. Here is the complete solution, in the directory **ArrayName\Step3**.

```
// ArrayName.cs - Step 3

using System;

public class Name : IComparable
{
    private string text;
    public Name(string text)
    {
        this.text = text;
    }
    public string Text
    {
        get
        {
            return text;
        }
    }
    public int CompareTo(object obj)
    {
```

```
        string s1 = this.Text;
        string s2 = ((Name) obj).Text;
        return String.Compare(s1, s2);
    }
    override public string ToString()
    {
        return text;
    }
}

public class ArrayName
{
    public static int Main(string[] args)
    {
        Name[] array = new Name[10];
        array[0] = new Name("Michael");
        array[1] = new Name("Charlie");
        array[2] = new Name("Peter");
        array[3] = new Name("Dana");
        array[4] = new Name("Bob");
        if (array[0] is IComparable)
            Array.Sort(array);
        else
            Console.WriteLine(
                "Name does not implement IComparable");
        foreach (Name name in array)
        {
            if (name != null)
                Console.WriteLine(name);
        }
        return 0;
    }
}
```

Here is the output:

```
Bob
Charlie
Dana
Michael
Peter
```

UNDERSTANDING FRAMEWORKS

Our example offers some insight into the workings of frameworks. A framework is *more* than a library. In a typical library, you are concerned with your code calling library functions. In a framework, you call into the framework *and the framework calls you.* Your program can be viewed as the middle layer of a sandwich.

* Your code calls the bottom layer.
* The top layer calls your code.

The .NET Framework is an excellent example of such an architecture. There is rich functionality that you can call directly. There are many interfaces, which you can optionally implement to make your program behave appropriately when called by the framework.

SUMMARY

In this chapter we examined the ubiquitous role of interfaces in the .NET Framework. Many of the standard classes implement specific interfaces, and we can call into the methods of these interfaces to obtain useful services. Collections are an example of classes in the .NET Framework that support a well-defined set of interfaces that provide useful functionality. Collections support the interfaces **IEnumerable**, **ICollection**, **IList**, and **ICloneable**. The first three interfaces provide the standard methods for iterating the elements of a list, obtaining a count of the number of elements, adding and removing elements, and so on. The **ICloneable** interface is used to implement a deep copy of a class. In order to work with collections effectively, you need to override certain methods of the **object** base class, such as **Equals**. We also looked at comparison of objects, which are implemented through the **IComparable** interface.

The .NET Framework class library is an excellent example of a rich framework, in which your code can be viewed as the middle layer of a sandwich. There is rich functionality that you can call, and there are many interfaces that you can optionally implement to make your program behave properly when called by the framework.

In the next chapter we will look at another variety of another program calling into your code. We will look at *delegates,* which can be viewed as object-oriented, type-safe callback functions. We will also look at *events,* which are a higher level construct built on top of delegates.

Delegates and Events

In the previous two chapters we examined interfaces in some detail. One feature of interfaces is that they facilitate writing code in such a way that your program is called into *by some other code. This style of programming has been available for a long time, under the guise of "callback" functions. In this chapter we examine* delegates *in C#, which can be thought of as type-safe and object-oriented callback functions. Delegates are the foundation for a more elaborate callback protocol, known as* events. *Events are a cornerstone of COM, the predecessor of .NET, and are widely used in Windows programming. We will study events and look at several example programs that illustrate delegates and events.*

DELEGATES

A *callback function* is one which your program specifies and "registers" in some way, and then gets called by another program. In C and C++ callback functions are implemented by function pointers.

In C# you can encapsulate a reference to a method inside a delegate object. While a function pointer can reference only a static function, a delegate can refer to either a static method or an instance method. When a delegate refers to an instance method, it stores both an object instance and an entry point to the instance method. The instance method can then be called through this object instance. When a delegate object refers to a static method, it stores just the entry point of this static method.

You can then pass this delegate object to other code, which can then call your method. The code that calls your delegate method does not have to know at compile time which method is being called.

In C# a delegate is considered a reference type that is similar to a class type. A new delegate instance is created just like any other class instance, using the **new** operator. In fact, C# delegates are implemented by the .NET Framework class library as a class, derived ultimately from **System.Delegate**.

Delegates are object-oriented and type-safe, and they enjoy the safety of the managed code execution environment.

Declaring a Delegate

You declare a delegate in C# using a special notation with the keyword **delegate** and the signature of the encapsulated method. A naming convention suggests your name should end with "Callback." Here is an example of a delegate declaration:

```
public delegate void NotifyCallback(decimal balance);
```

Defining a Method

When you instantiate a delegate, you will need to specify a method, which must match the signature in the delegate declaration. The method may be either a static method or an instance method. Here are some examples of methods that can be hooked to the **NotifyCallback** delegate:

```
private static void NotifyCustomer(decimal balance)
{
   Console.WriteLine("Dear customer,");
   Console.WriteLine(
      "   Account overdrawn, balance = {0}", balance);
}
private static void NotifyBank(decimal balance)
{
   Console.WriteLine("Dear bank,");
   Console.WriteLine(
      "   Account overdrawn, balance = {0}", balance);
}
private void NotifyInstance(decimal balance)
{
   Console.WriteLine("Dear instance,");
   Console.WriteLine(
      "   Account overdrawn, balance = {0}", balance);
}
```

Creating a Delegate Object

You instantiate a delegate object with the **new** operator, just as you would with any other class. The following code illustrates creating two delegate objects. The first one is hooked to a static method, and the second to an instance method. The second delegate object internally will store both a method entry point and an object instance that is used for invoking the method.

```
NotifyCallback custDlg = new NotifyCallback(NotifyCustomer);
...
DelegateAccount da = new DelegateAccount();
NotifyCallback instDlg =
   new NotifyCallback(da.NotifyInstance);
```

Calling a Delegate

You "call" a delegate just as you would a method. The delegate object is not a method, but it has an encapsulated method. The delegate object "delegates" the call to this encapsulated method, hence the name "delegate." In the following code the delegate object **notifyDlg** is called whenever a negative balance occurs on a withdrawal. In this example the **notifyDlg** delegate object is initialized in the method **SetDelegate**.

```
private NotifyCallback notifyDlg;
...
public void SetDelegate(NotifyCallback dlg)
{
   notifyDlg = dlg;
}
...
public void Withdraw(decimal amount)
{
   balance -= amount;
   if (balance < 0)
      notifyDlg(balance);
}
```

Combining Delegate Objects

A powerful feature of delegates is that you can combine them. Delegates can be "multicast," in which they have an invocation list of methods. When such a delegate is called, all the methods on the invocation list will be called in turn. The **+** operator can be used to combine the invocation methods of two delegate objects. The **−** operator can be used to remove methods.

```
NotifyCallback custDlg = new NotifyCallback(NotifyCustomer);
```

```
NotifyCallback bankDlg = new NotifyCallback(NotifyBank);
NotifyCallback currDlg = custDlg + bankDlg;
```

In this example we construct two delegate objects, each with an associated method. We then create a new delegate object whose invocation list will consist of both the methods **NotifyCustomer** and **NotifyBank**. When **currDlg** is called, these two methods will be invoked. Later on in the code we may remove a method.

```
currDlg -= bankDlg;
```

Now **NotifyBank** has been removed from the delegate, and the next time **currDlg** is called, only **NotifyCustomer** will be invoked.

Complete Example

The program **DelegateAccount** illustrates using delegates in our bank account scenario. The file **DelegateAccount.cs** declares the delegate **NotifyCallback**. The class **DelegateAccount** contains methods matching the signature of the delegate. The **Main** method instantiates delegate objects and combines them in various ways. The delegate objects are passed to the **Account** class, which uses its encapsulated delegate object to invoke suitable notifications when the account is overdrawn.

Observe how dynamic and loosely coupled is this structure. The **Account** class does not know or care which notification methods will be invoked in the case of an overdraft. It simply calls the delegate, which in turn calls all the methods on its invocation list. These methods can be adjusted at runtime.

Here is the code for the **Account** class:

```
// Account.cs

public class Account
{
    private decimal balance;
    private NotifyCallback notifyDlg;
    public Account(decimal bal, NotifyCallback dlg)
    {
        balance = bal;
        notifyDlg = dlg;
    }
    public void SetDelegate(NotifyCallback dlg)
    {
        notifyDlg = dlg;
    }
    public void Deposit(decimal amount)
    {
        balance += amount;
    }
```

```csharp
   public void Withdraw(decimal amount)
   {
      balance -= amount;
      if (balance < 0)
         notifyDlg(balance);
   }
   public decimal Balance
   {
      get
      {
         return balance;
      }
   }
}
```

Here is the code declaring and testing the delegate:

```csharp
// DelegateAccount.cs

using System;

public delegate void NotifyCallback(decimal balance);

public class DelegateAccount
{
   public static void Main(string[] args)
   {
      NotifyCallback custDlg =
         new NotifyCallback(NotifyCustomer);
      NotifyCallback bankDlg =
         new NotifyCallback(NotifyBank);
      NotifyCallback currDlg = custDlg + bankDlg;
      Account acc = new Account(100, currDlg);
      Console.WriteLine("balance = {0}", acc.Balance);
      acc.Withdraw(125);
      Console.WriteLine("balance = {0}", acc.Balance);
      acc.Deposit(200);
      acc.Withdraw(125);
      Console.WriteLine("balance = {0}", acc.Balance);
      currDlg -= bankDlg;
      acc.SetDelegate(currDlg);
      acc.Withdraw(125);
      DelegateAccount da = new DelegateAccount();
      NotifyCallback instDlg =
         new NotifyCallback(da.NotifyInstance);
      currDlg += instDlg;
      acc.SetDelegate(currDlg);
      acc.Withdraw(125);
   }
   private static void NotifyCustomer(decimal balance)
   {
```

```
            Console.WriteLine("Dear customer,");
            Console.WriteLine(
                "    Account overdrawn, balance = {0}", balance);
        }
        private static void NotifyBank(decimal balance)
        {
            Console.WriteLine("Dear bank,");
            Console.WriteLine(
                "    Account overdrawn, balance = {0}", balance);
        }
        private void NotifyInstance(decimal balance)
        {
            Console.WriteLine("Dear instance,");
            Console.WriteLine(
                "    Account overdrawn, balance = {0}", balance);
        }
    }
```

Here is the output from running the program. Notice which notification methods get invoked, depending upon the operations that have been performed on the current delegate object.

```
balance = 100
Dear customer,
    Account overdrawn, balance = -25
Dear bank,
    Account overdrawn, balance = -25
balance = -25
balance = 50
Dear customer,
    Account overdrawn, balance = -75
Dear customer,
    Account overdrawn, balance = -200
Dear instance,
    Account overdrawn, balance = -200
```

STOCK MARKET SIMULATION

As a further illustration of the use of delegates, consider the simple stock market simulation, implemented in the directory **StockMarket**. The simulation consists of two modules:

* The **Admin** module provides a user interface for configuring and running the simulation. It also implements operations called by the simulation engine.

* The **Engine** module is the simulation engine. It maintains an internal clock and invokes randomly generated operations, based on the configuration parameters passed to it.

Figure 19–1 shows the high level architecture of the simulation.

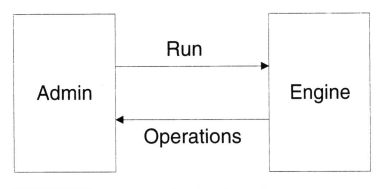

Architecture of stock market simulation.

The following operations are available:

* PrintTick: shows each clock tick.
* PrintTrade: shows each trade.

The following configuration parameters can be specified:

* Ticks on/off
* Trades on/off
* Count of how many ticks to run the simulation

Running the Simulation

Build and run the example program in **StockMarket**. Start with the default configuration: Ticks are OFF, Trades are ON, Run count is 100. (Note that the results are random and will be different each time you run the program.)

```
Ticks are OFF
Trades are ON
Run count = 100
Enter command, quit to exit
: run
    2   ACME    23   600
   27   MSFT    63   400
   27   IBM    114   600
   38   MSFT    69   400
   53   MSFT    75   900
   62   INTC    27   800
```

```
64   MSFT    82   200
68   MSFT    90   300
81   MSFT    81   600
83   INTC    30   800
91   MSFT    73   700
99   IBM    119   400
:
```

The available commands are listed when you type "help" at the colon prompt. The commands are:

```
count     set run count
ticks     toggle ticks
trades    toggle trades
config    show configuration
run       run the simulation
quit      exit the program
```

The output shows clock tick, stock, price, volume.

Delegate Code

Two delegates are declared in the **Admin.cs** file.

```
public delegate void TickCallback(int ticks);
public delegate void TradeCallback(int ticks, string stock,
                                   int price, int volume);
```

As we saw in the previous section, a delegate is similar to a class, and a delegate object is instantiated by **new**.

```
TickCallback tickDlg = new TickCallback(PrintTick);
TradeCallback tradeDlg = new TradeCallback(PrintTrade);
```

A method is passed as the parameter to the delegate constructor. The method signature must match that of the delegate.

```
public static void PrintTick(int ticks)
{
   Console.Write("{0} ", ticks);
   if (++printcount == LINECOUNT)
   {
      Console.WriteLine();
      printcount = 0;
   }
}
```

Passing the Delegates to the Engine

The **Admin** class passes the delegates to the **Engine** class in the constructor of the **Engine** class.

```
Engine engine = new Engine(tickDlg, tradeDlg);
```

Random Number Generation

The heart of the simulation is the **Run** method of the **Engine** class. At the core of the **Run** method is assigning simulated data based on random numbers. We use the **System.Random** class, which we discussed in Chapter 12.

```
double r = rangen.NextDouble();
if (r < tradeProb[i])
{
   int delta = (int) (price[i] * volatility[i]);
   if (rangen.NextDouble() < .5)
   {
      delta = -delta;
   }
   price[i] += delta;
   int volume = rangen.Next(minVolume, maxVolume) * 100;
   tradeOp(tick, stocks[i], price[i], volume);
```

Using the Delegates

In the **Engine** class, delegate references are declared:

```
TickCallback tickOp;
TradeCallback tradeOp;
```

The delegate references are initialized in the **Engine** constructor:

```
public Engine(TickCallback tickOp, TradeCallback tradeOp)
{
   this.tickOp = tickOp;
   this.tradeOp = tradeOp;
}
```

The method that is wrapped by the delegate object can then be called through the delegate reference:

```
if (showTicks)
   tickOp(tick);
```

EVENTS

Delegates are the foundation for a more elaborate callback protocol known as *events*. Conceptually, servers implement *incoming* interfaces, which are called by clients. In a diagram, such an interface may be shown with a small bubble (a notation used in COM). Sometimes a client may wish to receive notifications from a server when certain "events" occur. In such a case the server will specify an *outgoing* interface. The server defines the interface and the client implements it. In a diagram, such an interface may be shown with an arrow (again, a notation used in COM). Figure 19–2 illustrates a server

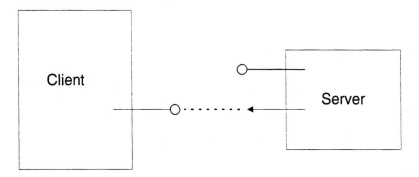

Figure 19–2   *A server with an incoming interface and an outgoing interface.*

with one incoming interface and one outgoing interface. In the case of the outgoing interface, the client will implement an incoming interface, which the server will call.

Events in C# and .NET

The .NET Framework provides an easy-to-use implementation of the event paradigm built on delegates. C# simplifies working with .NET events by providing the keyword **event** and operators to hook up event handlers to events and to remove them. We will examine this event architecture through salient code from the example program **EventDemo**, which illustrates a chat room.

Server-Side Event Code

We begin with server-side code, in **ChatServer.cs**. The .NET event architecture uses delegates of a specific signature:

```
public delegate void JoinHandler(object sender,
                                 ChatEventArg e);
```

The first parameter specifies the object that sent the event notification.

The second parameter is used to pass data along with the notification. Typically, you will derive a class from **EventArg** to hold your specific data.

```
public class ChatEventArg : EventArgs
{
   public string Name;
   public ChatEventArg(string name)
   {
      Name = name;
   }
}
```

A delegate object reference is declared using the keyword **event**.

```
public event JoinHandler Join;
```

A helper method is typically provided to facilitate calling the delegate object(s) that have been hooked up to the event.

```
protected void OnJoin(ChatEventArg e)
{
   if (Join != null)
   {
      Join(this, e);
   }
}
```

A test for **null** is made in case no delegate objects have been hooked up to the event. Typically, access is specified as **protected** so that a derived class has access to this helper method. You can then "fire" the event by calling the helper method.

```
public void JoinChat(string name)
{
   members.Add(name);
   OnJoin(new ChatEventArg(name));
}
```

Client-Side Event Code

The client provides event handler functions.

```
public static void OnJoinChat(object sender, ChatEventArg e)
{
   Console.WriteLine(
      "sender = {0}, {1} has joined the chat",
      sender, e.Name);
}
```

The client hooks the handler to the event, using the **+=** operator.

```
ChatServer chat = new ChatServer("OI Chat Room");
```

```
// Register to receive event notifications from the server
chat.Join += new JoinHandler(OnJoinChat);
```

The event starts out as **null**, and event handlers get added through **+=**. All of the registered handlers will get invoked when the event delegate is called. You may unregister a handler through **-=**.

Chat Room Example

The chat room example in **EventDemo** illustrates the complete architecture on both the server and client side. The server provides the following methods:

- JoinChat
- QuitChat
- ShowMembers

Whenever a new member joins or quits, the server sends a notification to the client. The event handlers print out an appropriate message. Here is the output from running the program:

```
sender = OI Chat Room, Michael has joined the chat
sender = OI Chat Room, Bob has joined the chat
sender = OI Chat Room, Sam has joined the chat
--- After 3 have joined---
Michael
Bob
Sam
sender = OI Chat Room, Bob has quit the chat
--- After 1 has quit---
Michael
Sam
```

CLIENT CODE

The client program provides event handlers. It instantiates a server object and then hooks up its event handlers to the events. The client then calls methods on the server. These calls will trigger the server firing events back to the client, which get handled by the event handlers.

```
// ChatClient.cs

using System;

class ChatClient
{
   public static void OnJoinChat(object sender,
                                 ChatEventArg e)
   {
      Console.WriteLine(
```

```
            "sender = {0}, {1} has joined the chat",
            sender, e.Name);
   }
   public static void OnQuitChat(object sender,
                                    ChatEventArg e)
   {
      Console.WriteLine(
         "sender = {0}, {1} has quit the chat",
         sender, e.Name);
   }
   public static void Main()
   {
      ChatServer chat = new ChatServer("OI Chat Room");
      // Register to receive event notifications from the
      // server
      chat.Join += new JoinHandler(OnJoinChat);
      chat.Quit += new QuitHandler(OnQuitChat);
      // Call methods on the server
      chat.JoinChat("Michael");
      chat.JoinChat("Bob");
      chat.JoinChat("Sam");
      chat.ShowMembers("After 3 have joined");
      chat.QuitChat("Bob");
      chat.ShowMembers("After 1 has quit");
   }
}
```

SERVER CODE

The server provides code to store in a collection the names of people who have joined the chat. When a person quits the chat, the name is removed from the collection. Joining and quitting the chat triggers firing an event back to the client. The server also contains the "plumbing" code for setting up the events, including declaration of the delegates, the events, and the event arguments. There are also helper methods for firing the events.

```
// ChatServer.cs

using System;
using System.Collections;

public class ChatEventArg : EventArgs
{
   public string Name;
   public ChatEventArg(string name)
   {
      Name = name;
   }
}
```

```csharp
public delegate void JoinHandler(object sender,
                            ChatEventArg e);
public delegate void QuitHandler(object sender,
                            ChatEventArg e);

public class ChatServer
{
    private ArrayList members = new ArrayList();
    private string chatName;
    public event JoinHandler Join;
    public event QuitHandler Quit;
    public ChatServer(string chatName)
    {
        this.chatName = chatName;
    }
    override public string ToString()
    {
        return chatName;
    }
    protected void OnJoin(ChatEventArg e)
    {
        if (Join != null)
        {
            Join(this, e);
        }
    }
    protected void OnQuit(ChatEventArg e)
    {
        if (Quit != null)
        {
            Quit(this, e);
        }
    }
    public void JoinChat(string name)
    {
        members.Add(name);
        OnJoin(new ChatEventArg(name));
    }
    public void QuitChat(string name)
    {
        members.Remove(name);
        OnQuit(new ChatEventArg(name));
    }
    public void ShowMembers(string msg)
    {
        Console.WriteLine("--- " + msg + "---");
        foreach (string member in members)
        {
            Console.WriteLine(member);
        }
    }
}
```

It may appear that there is a fair amount of such "plumbing" code, but it is *much* simpler than the previous connection point mechanism used by COM for events. Also, in practice various wizards and other tools will generate the infrastructure for you automatically. We will see how easy it is to work with events in Windows programming in Chapter 22.

SUMMARY

In this chapter we examined delegates, which can be thought of as type-safe and object-oriented callback functions. In C# you can encapsulate a reference to a method inside a delegate object. You can then pass this delegate object to other code, which can then call your method. The code that calls your delegate method does not have to know at compile time which method is being called. Delegates are the foundation for a more elaborate callback protocol, known as events. We looked at several example programs that illustrate delegates and events.

Advanced Features

*I*n this chapter we discuss a number of advanced features of C# programming using the .NET Framework. These topics are important in their own right, and they provide further examples of important C# concepts that we have been studying. The first topic is directories and files, which we will use later in the chapter in a number of examples. We then study programming with multiple threads. The .NET Framework provides a clean threading model based on delegates, and there is a flexible set of classes to support thread lifetime management and synchronization. The C# language makes it easy to program support of critical sections through a **lock** keyword. The .NET Framework makes it even easier to create thread-safe classes without any programming whatever, through use of a synchronization attribute. We examine another important built-in attribute, Serializable, which makes it easy to save complex data structures to persistent storage with minimal coding. We then see how to implement custom attributes. Next we introduce the powerful reflection API, which gives programmatic access to metadata. We conclude the chapter with a discussion of unsafe code, which enables you to program C# at a lower level, when necessary, using constructs such as pointers.

DIRECTORIES AND FILES

Our first topic, directories and files, is not particularly advanced but is quite fundamental. In this section we will first examine the **System.IO.Directory** class in the .NET Framework that allows us to work with directories. We will then look at file input and output, which makes use of an intermediary called a *stream*.

Directories

The classes supporting input and output are in the namespace **System.IO**. The classes **Directory** and **DirectoryInfo** contain routines for working with directories. All the methods of **Directory** are static, and so you can call them without having a directory instance. The **DirectoryInfo** class contains instance methods. In many cases you can accomplish the same objective using methods of either class. The methods of **Directory** always perform a security check. If you are going to reuse a method several times, it may be better to obtain an instance of **DirectoryInfo** and use its instance methods, because a security check may not always be necessary. (We do not discuss security in this book. For a discussion of security in .NET you may wish to refer to the book *Application Development Using C# and .NET*, another book in the Prentice Hall/Object Innovations series on .NET technology.)

We illustrate both classes with a simple program **DirectoryDemo**, which contains DOS-like commands to show the contents of the current directory ("dir") and to change the current directory ("cd"). A directory can contain both files and other directories. The method **GetFiles** returns an array of **FileInfo** objects, and the method **GetDirectories** returns an array of. **DirectoryInfo** objects. In this program we only use the **Name** property of **FileInfo**. In the following section we will see how to read and write files using streams.

```
// DirectoryDemo.cs

using System;
using System.IO;

public class DirectoryDemo
{
    private static string path;
    private static DirectoryInfo dir;
    public static void Main()
    {
        path = Directory.GetCurrentDirectory();
        Console.WriteLine("path = {0}", path);
        dir = new DirectoryInfo(path);
        InputWrapper iw = new InputWrapper();
```

```
    string cmd;
    Console.WriteLine("Enter command, quit to exit");
    cmd = iw.getString("> ");
    while (! cmd.Equals("quit"))
    {
        try
        {
            if (cmd.Equals("cd"))
            {
                path = iw.getString("path: ");
                dir = new DirectoryInfo(path);
                Directory.SetCurrentDirectory(path);
            }
            else if (cmd.Equals("dir"))
            {
                FileInfo[] files = dir.GetFiles();
                Console.WriteLine("Files:");
                foreach (FileInfo f in files)
                    Console.WriteLine("   {0}", f.Name);
                DirectoryInfo[] dirs = dir.GetDirectories();
                Console.WriteLine("Directories:");
                foreach (DirectoryInfo d in dirs)
                    Console.WriteLine("   {0}", d.Name);
            }
            else
                help();
        }
        ...
```

Here is a sample run of the program. Notice that the current directory
starts out as the directory containing the program's executable.

```
path = C:\OI\CSharp\Chap20\DirectoryDemo\bin\Debug
Enter command, quit to exit
> dir
Files:
   DirectoryDemo.exe
   DirectoryDemo.pdb
Directories:
> cd
path: c:\oi\csharp\chap20
> dir
Files:
Directories:
   Assemblies
   AttributeDemo
   DirectoryDemo
   FileDemo
   ReflectionDemo
   SerializeAccount
```

```
ThreadAccount
ThreadDemo
UnsafeAccount
UnsafeBlock
UnsafePointer
```

Files and Streams

Programming languages have undergone an evolution in how they deal with the important topic of input/output (I/O). Early languages, such as FORTRAN, COBOL, and the original BASIC, had I/O statements built into the language. Later languages have tended not to have I/O built into the language, but instead rely on a standard library for performing I/O, such as the **<stdio.h>** library in C. The library in languages like C works directly with files.

Still later languages, such as C++ and Java, introduced a further abstraction called a *stream*. A stream serves as an intermediary between the program and the file. Read and write operations are done to the stream, which is tied to a file. This architecture is very flexible, because the same kind of read and write operations can apply not only to a file, but to other kinds of I/O, such as network sockets. This added flexibility introduces a slight additional complexity in writing programs, because you have to deal not only with files but also with streams, and there exists a considerable variety of stream classes. But the added complexity is well worth the effort, and C# strikes a nice balance, with classes that make performing common operations quite simple.

As with directories, the **System.IO** namespace contains two classes for working with files. The **File** class has all static methods, and the **FileInfo** class has instance methods. The program **FileDemo** extends the **DirectoryDemo** example program to illustrate reading and writing text files. We will illustrate binary file I/O later in this chapter, when we discuss serialization. The directory commands are retained so that you can easily exercise the program on different directories. The two new commands are "read" and "write." The "read" command illustrates using the **File** class. The "dir" command, already present in the **DirectoryDemo** program, illustrates using the **FileInfo** class.

Here is the code for the "read" command. The user is prompted for a file name. The static **OpenText** method returns a **StreamReader** object, which is used for the actual reading. There is a **ReadLine** method for reading a line of text, similar to the **ReadLine** method of the **Console** class. A **null** reference is returned by **ReadLine** when at end of file. Our program simply displays the contents of the file at the console. When done, we close the **StreamReader**.

```
...
else if (cmd.Equals("read"))
{
   string fileName = iw.getString("file name: ");
   StreamReader reader = File.OpenText(fileName);
   string str;
   str = reader.ReadLine();
   while (str != null)
   {
      Console.WriteLine(str);
      str = reader.ReadLine();
   }
   reader.Close();
}
...
```

Here is the code for the "write" command. Again we prompt for a file name. This time we also prompt for whether or not to append to the file. There is a special constructor for the **StreamWriter** class that will directly return a **StreamWriter** without first getting a file object. The first parameter is the name of the file, and the second a **bool** flag specifying the append mode. If **true**, the writes will append to the end of an already existing file. If **false**, the writes will overwrite an existing file. In both cases, if a file of the specified name does not exist, a new file will be created.

```
...
else if (cmd.Equals("write"))
{
   fileName = iw.getString("file name: ");
   string strAppend = iw.getString("append (yes/no): ");
   bool append = (strAppend == "yes" ? true : false);
   StreamWriter writer = new StreamWriter(fileName, append);
   Console.WriteLine("Enter text, blank line to terminate");
   string str = iw.getString(">>");
   while (str != "")
   {
      writer.WriteLine(str);
      str = iw.getString(">>");
   }
   writer.Close();
}
...
```

Here is a sample run of the program. We first obtain a listing of existing files in the current directory. We then create a new text file, **one.txt**, and enter a couple of lines of text data. We again do "dir", and our new file shows up. We try out the "read" command. You could also open up the file in a text editor to verify that it has been created and has the desired data. Next we write out another line of text to this same file, this time saying "yes" for append mode. We conclude by reading the contents of the file.

```
path = C:\OI\CSharp\Chap20\FileDemo\bin\Debug
Enter command, quit to exit
> dir
Files:
    FileDemo.exe
    FileDemo.pdb
Directories:
> write
file name: one.txt
append (yes/no): no
Enter text, blank line to terminate
>>hello, world
>>this is second line
>>
> dir
Files:
    FileDemo.exe
    FileDemo.pdb
    one.txt
Directories:
> read
file name: one.txt
hello, world
this is second line
> write
file name: one.txt
append (yes/no): yes
Enter text, blank line to terminate
>>and a third line
>>
> read
file name: one.txt
hello, world
this is second line
and a third line
```

MULTIPLE THREAD PROGRAMMING

Modern programming environments allow you to program with multiple threads. Threads run inside of processes and allow multiple concurrent execution paths. If there are multiple CPUs, you can achieve parallel processing through the use of threads. On a single processor machine, you can often achieve greater efficiency by using multiple threads, because when one thread is blocked, for example, waiting on an I/O completion, another thread can continue execution. Also, the use of multiple threads can make a program more responsive to shorter tasks, such as tasks requiring user responses.

Along with the potential benefit of programming with multiple threads, there is greater program complexity, because you have to manage the issues of starting up threads, controlling their lifetimes, and synchronizing among threads. Since threads are within a common process and share an address space, it is possible for two threads to concurrently access the same data. Such concurrent access, known as a "race condition," can lead to erroneous results when non-atomic operations are performed, a topic we will discuss in detail later in this section.

.NET Threading Model

The .NET Framework provides extensive support for multiple thread programming in the **System.Threading** namespace. The core class is **Thread**, which encapsulates a thread of execution. This class provides methods to start and suspend threads, to sleep, and to perform other thread management functions. The method that will execute for a thread is encapsulated inside a delegate of type **ThreadStart**. As we saw in Chapter 19, a delegate can wrap either a static or an instance method. When starting a thread, it is frequently useful to define an associated class, which will contain instance data for the thread, including initialization information. A designated method of this class can be used as the **ThreadStart** delegate method.

CONSOLE LOG DEMONSTRATION

The **ThreadDemo** program provides an illustration of this architecture. The **ConsoleLog** class encapsulates a thread ID and parameters specifying a sleep interval and a count of how many lines of output will be written to the console. It provides the method **ConsoleLog** that writes out logging information to the console, showing the thread ID and number of elapsed (millisecond) ticks. Here is the program code:

```
// ThreadDemo.cs

using System;
using System.Threading;

class ConsoleLog
{
    private int delta;
    private int count;
    private int ticks = 0;
    private static int nextThreadId = 1;
    private int threadId;
    public ConsoleLog(int delta, int count)
```

```
    {
        this.delta = delta;
        this.count = count;
        this.threadId = nextThreadId++;
    }
    public void ConsoleThread()
    {
        for (int i = 0; i < count; i++)
        {
            Console.WriteLine("Thread {0}: ticks = {1}",
                                threadId, ticks);
            Thread.Sleep(delta);
            ticks += delta;
        }
    }
}

public class ThreadDemo
{
    public static void Main()
    {
        ConsoleLog slowLog = new ConsoleLog(1000, 5);
        ConsoleLog fastLog = new ConsoleLog(400, 5);
        ThreadStart slowStart =
            new ThreadStart(slowLog.ConsoleThread);
        ThreadStart fastStart =
            new ThreadStart(fastLog.ConsoleThread);
        Thread slowThread = new Thread(slowStart);
        Thread fastThread = new Thread(fastStart);
        Console.WriteLine("Starting threads ...");
        slowThread.Start();
        fastThread.Start();
        Console.WriteLine("Threads have started");
    }
}
```

The program is configured with a "slow" thread and a "fast" thread. The slow thread will sleep for 1 second between outputs, and the fast thread will sleep for only 400 milliseconds. A **ConsoleLog** object is created for each of these threads, initialized with appropriate parameters. Both will do five lines of output.

Next, appropriate delegates are created of type **ThreadStart**. Notice that we use an instance method, **ConsoleThread**, as the delegate method. Use of an instance method rather than a static method is appropriate in this case, because we want to associate parameter values (sleep interval and output count) with each delegate instance.

We then create and start the threads. We write a message to the console just before and just after starting the threads. When do you think the message "Threads have started" will be displayed, relative to the output from the threads themselves? Here is the output from running the program. You will notice a slight delay as the program executes, reflecting the sleep periods.

```
Starting threads ...
Threads have started
Thread 1: ticks = 0
Thread 2: ticks = 0
Thread 2: ticks = 400
Thread 2: ticks = 800
Thread 1: ticks = 1000
Thread 2: ticks = 1200
Thread 2: ticks = 1600
Thread 1: ticks = 2000
Thread 2 is terminating
Thread 1: ticks = 3000
Thread 1: ticks = 4000
Thread 1 is terminating
```

The "Threads have started" message is displayed immediately, reflecting the asynchronous nature of the two additional threads. The **Start** calls return immediately, and the second message prints. Meanwhile, the other threads get started by the system, which takes a little bit of time, and then they each start producing output.

RACE CONDITIONS

A major issue in concurrency is shared data. If two computations access the same data, different results can be obtained depending on the timing of the different accesses, a situation known as a race condition. Race conditions present a programming challenge because they can occur unpredictably. Careful programming is required to ensure they do not occur.

Race conditions can easily arise in multithreaded applications, because threads belonging to the same process share the same address space and thus can share data. Consider two threads making deposits to a bank account, where the deposit operation is not atomic:

* Get balance.
* Add amount to balance.
* Store balance.

The following sequence of actions will then produce a race condition, with invalid results.

1. Balance starts at $100.
2. Thread 1 makes deposit of $25 and is interrupted after getting balance and adding amount to balance, but before storing balance.
3. Thread 2 makes deposit of $5000 and goes to completion, storing $5100.

4. Thread 1 now finishes, storing $125, overwriting the result of thread 2. The $5000 deposit has been lost!

The program **ThreadAccount\Race** illustrates this race condition. The **Account** class has a method **DelayDeposit**, which updates the balance non-atomically. The thread sleeps for 5 seconds in the middle of the update operation, leaving open a window of vulnerability for another thread to come in.

```
// Account.cs

using System.Threading;

public class Account
{
   protected decimal balance;
   public Account (decimal balance)
   {
      this.balance = balance;
   }
   public void Deposit(decimal amount)
   {
      balance += amount;
   }
   public void DelayDeposit(decimal amount)
   {
      decimal newbal = balance + amount;
      Thread.Sleep(5000);
      balance = newbal;
   }
   public decimal Balance
   {
      get
      {
         return balance;
      }
   }
}
```

The test program launches threads in a manner similar to that used in the **ThreadDemo** program. The **AsynchAccount** class contains the thread methods that will be used by thread 1 (to call **DelayDeposit**) and thread 2 (to call **Deposit**).

```
// ThreadAccount.cs

using System;
using System.Threading;

class AsynchAccount
{
```

```
    private decimal amount;
    public AsynchAccount(decimal amount)
    {
        this.amount = amount;
    }
    public void AsynchDelayDeposit()
    {
        ThreadAccount.account.DelayDeposit(amount);
    }
    public void AsynchDeposit()
    {
        ThreadAccount.account.Deposit(amount);
    }
}

public class ThreadAccount
{
    public static Account account;
    public static void Main()
    {
        account = new Account(100);
        AsynchAccount asynch1 = new AsynchAccount(25);
        AsynchAccount asynch2 = new AsynchAccount(5000);
        ThreadStart start1 =
            new ThreadStart(asynch1.AsynchDelayDeposit);
        ThreadStart start2 =
            new ThreadStart(asynch2.AsynchDeposit);
        Console.WriteLine("balance = {0:C}", account.Balance);
        Console.WriteLine(
            "delay deposit of {0:C} on thread 1", 25);
        Thread t1 = new Thread(start1);
        Thread t2 = new Thread(start2);
        t1.Start();
        Console.WriteLine(
            "deposit of {0:C} on thread 2", 5000);
        t2.Start();
        t2.Join();
        Console.WriteLine(
        "balance = {0:C} (thread 2 done)", account.Balance);
        t1.Join();
        Console.WriteLine("balance = {0:C} (thread 1 done)",
                          account.Balance);
    }
}
```

The call **t2.Join** blocks the current thread until thread **t2** finishes. This technique enables us to show the balance after a thread has definitely completed. Here is the output. As you can see, we have exactly replicated the race condition scenario outlined at the beginning of this section.

```
balance = $100.00
delay deposit of $25.00 on thread 1
deposit of $5,000.00 on thread 2
balance = $5,100.00 (thread 2 done)
balance = $125.00 (thread 1 done)
```

Thread Synchronization Programming

Such race conditions can be avoided by serializing access to the shared data. Suppose only one thread at a time is allowed to access the bank account. Then the first thread that starts to access the balance will complete the operation before another thread begins to access the balance (the second thread will be blocked). In this case threads synchronize based on accessing data.

Another way threads can synchronize is for one thread to block until another thread has completed. The **Join** method is a means for accomplishing this kind of thread synchronization, as illustrated above.

The **System.Threading** namespace provides a number of thread synchronization facilities. In this section we will illustrate use of the **Monitor** class. We will also look at use of the C# keyword **lock**, which uses monitors under the hood.

MONITOR

You can serialize access to shared data using the **Enter** and **Exit** methods of the **Monitor** class.

* **Monitor.Enter** obtains the monitor lock for an object. An object is passed as a parameter. This call will block if another thread has entered the monitor of the same object. It will not block if the current thread has previously entered the monitor.
* **Monitor.Exit** releases the monitor lock. If one or more threads are waiting to acquire the lock, and the current thread has executed **Exit** as many times as it has executed **Enter**, one of the threads will be unblocked and allowed to proceed.

An object reference is passed as the parameter to **Monitor.Enter** and **Monitor.Exit**. This is the object on which the monitor lock is acquired or released. To acquire a lock on the current object, pass **this**.

The program **ThreadAccount\Monitor** illustrates the use of monitors to protect the critical section where the balance is updated. In this program we also place the calls to **ShowBalance** just before exiting the monitor. This technique will ensure that we see the balance as soon as it has been updated.

```
// Account.cs

using System;
using System.Threading;
```

```
public class Account
{
    protected decimal balance;
    public Account (decimal balance)
    {
        this.balance = balance;
    }
    public void Deposit(decimal amount)
    {
        Monitor.Enter(this);
        balance += amount;
        ShowBalance();
        Monitor.Exit(this);
    }
    public void DelayDeposit(decimal amount)
    {
        Monitor.Enter(this);
        decimal newbal = balance + amount;
        Thread.Sleep(5000);
        balance = newbal;
        ShowBalance();
        Monitor.Exit(this);
    }
    public decimal Balance
    {
        get
        {
            return balance;
        }
    }
    private void ShowBalance()
    {
        Console.WriteLine("balance = {0:C} ({1})",
                          balance,
                          Thread.CurrentThread.Name);
    }
}
```

The test program is the same as in the previous example, except we are now doing the display of the new balance immediately after the thread has updated the balance. Here is the output. Notice that the synchronization is successful—we did not have the $5000 deposit wiped out!

```
balance = $100.00
delay deposit of $25.00 on thread 1
deposit of $5,000.00 on thread 2
balance = $125.00 (Thread 1)
balance = $5,125.00 (Thread 2)
```

LOCK

C# provides the **lock** statement as a convenient way to obtain a mutual exclusion lock implemented by the **Monitor** class. The program **ThreadAccount\Lock** illustrates use of the **lock** statement. Besides using **lock**, this example introduces a property **Owner**. The owner is completely independent of the balance, and so we do not need any lock around the code to get the owner. Here is the relevant code for the modified **Account** class.

```
// Account.cs

using System;
using System.Threading;

public class Account
{
    protected decimal balance;
    protected string owner;
    public Account (decimal balance)
    {
        this.balance = balance;
        this.owner = "Tom Thread";
    }
    public void Deposit(decimal amount)
    {
        lock(this)
        {
            balance += amount;
            ShowBalance();
        }
    }
    public void DelayDeposit(decimal amount)
    {
        lock(this)
        {
            decimal newbal = balance + amount;
            Thread.Sleep(5000);
            balance = newbal;
            ShowBalance();
        }
    }
    public string Owner
    {
        get
        {
            return owner;
        }
    }
```

The test program is similar to the program for testing monitors, but it adds code at the end of **Main** to get the owner name, after sleeping briefly to make sure the threads have started and have hit the locks.

```
// ThreadAccount.cs

...

public class ThreadAccount
{
    public static Account account;
    public static void Main()
    {
        account = new Account(100);
        AsynchAccount asynch1 =
            new AsynchAccount(25);
        AsynchAccount asynch2 =
            new AsynchAccount(5000);
        ThreadStart start1 =
            new ThreadStart(asynch1.AsynchDelayDeposit);
        ThreadStart start2 =
            new ThreadStart(asynch2.AsynchDeposit);
        Console.WriteLine("balance = {0:C}", account.Balance);
        Console.WriteLine(
            "delay deposit of {0:C} on thread 1", 25);
        Thread t1 = new Thread(start1);
        t1.Name = "Thread 1";
        Thread t2 = new Thread(start2);
        t2.Name = "Thread 2";
        t1.Start();
        Console.WriteLine(
            "deposit of {0:C} on thread 2", 5000);
        t2.Start();
        Thread.Sleep(100);   // allow time for threads to start
        Console.WriteLine("owner = {0}", account.Owner);
    }
}
```

Here is the output. It is the same as for the previous example, with an additional line of output showing the owner. This extra line of output is displayed almost immediately, with very little pause. The output from the threads comes afterwards.

```
balance = $100.00
delay deposit of $25.00 on thread 1
deposit of $5,000.00 on thread 2
owner = Tom Thread
balance = $125.00 (Thread 1)
balance = $5,125.00 (Thread 2)
```

```
          {
              return owner;
          }
      }
      public decimal Balance
      {
          get
          {
              return balance;
          }
      }
      private void ShowBalance()
      {
          Console.WriteLine("balance = {0:C} ({1})",
                            balance,
                            Thread.CurrentThread.Name);
      }
}
```

Here is the output:

```
balance = $100.00
delay deposit of $25.00 on thread 1
deposit of $5,000.00 on thread 2
balance = $125.00 (Thread 1)
balance = $5,125.00 (Thread 2)
owner = Tom Thread
```

As you can see, the race condition has been avoided, and there is no explicit thread synchronization code using monitors, the **lock** statement, or a similar construct. However, the behavior is somewhat different from our previous program, **ThreadAccount\Lock**. Now *all* method calls into **Account** are serialized, including calling the property to obtain the owner. When you ran the program, you should have noticed a pronounced delay before the owner was displayed, whereas this happened almost immediately in the **Lock** example. This automatic synchronization is coarse grained, so we obtained greater concurrency, in this example, by implementing the synchronization ourselves.

Serializable Attribute

A second example of a useful attribute provided by the .NET Framework is **Serializable**. When this attribute is applied to a class, the Framework provides code to *serialize* object instances of the class. "Serialize" means convert a graph of objects into a linear sequence of bytes. This sequence of bytes can then be written to a stream or otherwise used to transmit all the data associated with the object instance. Objects can be serialized without writing special code, because the metadata knows the object's memory layout.

The program **SerializeAccount** illustrates serialization of the **Account** class by means of an attribute. The code for the **Account** class is shown below, and only one line of code is involved: The attribute **[System.Serializable]** is placed before the class. In this case, *all* the data members of the class will be serialized. If you want to exclude a data member from being serialized, for example, because it contained some kind of temporary cache of data, you can place the attribute **[System.NonSerialized]** in front of the member you want excluded.

```
// Account.cs

using System;

[System.Serializable]
public class Account
{
    private decimal balance;
    private string owner;
    private int id;
    ...
```

The **SerializeAccount** class illustrates serializing and deserializing a collection of **Account** objects. What is powerful about the serialization mechanism is that you can serialize complex graphs of objects simply by making each object serializable, which in turn can be done in the .NET Framework by using an attribute. A composite object is serialized by serializing each of its constituent objects. The .NET Framework collection classes, such as **ArrayList**, have serialization support built in.

While making a class serializable is simply a matter of using an attribute, you must write a little code to cause an object graph to serialize itself. If you are using serialization to implement persistence, you need to perform the following four basic steps to save the data.

1. Instantiate a **FileInfo** object where the data will be saved.
2. Open up a **Stream** object for writing to the file.
3. Instantiate a formatter object for laying out the objects in a suitable format.
4. Apply the formatter's **Serialize** method to the root object and the stream.

There is similar code for deserializing. There are two built-in formatters provided by the .NET Framework:

* **BinaryFormatter** lays out object data in a binary format.
* **SOAPFormatter** lays out object data in an XML format.

If you use a binary formatter, you will need the following two name-spaces in order to perform the serialization:

- **System.Runtime.Serialization**
- **System.Runtime.Serialization.Formatters.Binary**

The following code is for a test program that provides commands to save and load a collection of accounts. Some test accounts are created initially, and commands are provided to add and remove accounts, besides save and load.

```
// SerializeAccount.cs

using System;
using System.Collections;
using System.IO;
using System.Runtime.Serialization;
using System.Runtime.Serialization.Formatters.Binary;

public class SerializeAccount
{
   private static ArrayList accounts;
   public static void Main()
   {
      // Initialize accounts and show starting state
      accounts = new ArrayList();
      AddAccount(100, "Bob", 1);
      AddAccount(200, "Mary", 2);
      AddAccount(300, "Charlie", 3);
      ShowAccounts(accounts);
      // Command processing loop
      InputWrapper iw = new InputWrapper();
      string cmd;
      Console.WriteLine("Enter command, quit to exit");
      cmd = iw.getString("> ");
      while (! cmd.Equals("quit"))
      {
         try
         {
            if (cmd.Equals("show"))
               ShowAccounts(accounts);
            else if (cmd.Equals("remove"))
            {
               int id = iw.getInt("id: ");
               RemoveAccount(id);
            }
            else if (cmd.Equals("add"))
            {
               decimal balance = iw.getDecimal("balance: ");
               string owner = iw.getString("owner: ");
               int id = iw.getInt("id: ");
```

```
        AddAccount(balance, owner, id);
    }
    else if (cmd.Equals("save"))
    {
        FileInfo f = new FileInfo("accounts.bin");
        Stream s = f.Open(FileMode.Create);
        BinaryFormatter b = new BinaryFormatter();
        b.Serialize(s, accounts);
        s.Close();
    }
    else if (cmd.Equals("load"))
    {
        FileInfo f = new FileInfo ("accounts.bin");
        Stream s = f.Open(FileMode.Open);
        BinaryFormatter b = new BinaryFormatter();
        accounts = (ArrayList) b.Deserialize(s);
        s.Close();
    }
    else
        help();
}
...
```

Here are two consecutive sample runs of the program. In the first run, we add two accounts and remove one. We save. In the second run, we load and verify that we have gotten back the modified collection of accounts.

```
1    Bob         $100.00
2    Mary        $200.00
3    Charlie     $300.00
Enter command, quit to exit
> add
balance: 400
owner: David
id: 4
> add
balance: 500
owner: Ellen
id: 5
> remove
id: 3
> save
> quit
---- Second run ----
1    Bob         $100.00
2    Mary        $200.00
3    Charlie     $300.00
Enter command, quit to exit
> load
> show
1    Bob         $100.00
```

```
2   Mary        $200.00
4   David       $400.00
5   Ellen       $500.00
```

CUSTOM ATTRIBUTES

We have seen two examples, synchronization and serialization, of useful attributes provided by the system. The .NET Framework makes the attribute mechanism entirely extensible, allowing you to define custom attributes, which will cause information to be written to the metadata. Using *reflection,* you can then extract this information from the metadata at runtime, and modify the behavior of your program appropriately. In order to simplify the use of the custom attribute, you may declare a base class to do the work of invoking the reflection API to obtain the attribute information stored in the metadata. We will illustrate getting custom attribute information using reflection in this section, and in the following discussion we will discuss reflection in more generality.

We illustrate this whole process of defining and using custom attributes with a simple example, **AttributeDemo**, which uses the custom attribute **InitialDirectory** to control the initial current directory when the program is run. As we saw in the first section of this chapter, by default the current directory is the directory containing the program's executable. In the case of a Visual Studio C# project, built in Debug mode, this directory is **bin\Debug**, relative to the project source code directory.

Using a Custom Attribute

First, let's see an example of using the **InitialDirectory** custom attribute. We will then see how to define and implement it. To be able to control the initial directory for a class, we derive the class from the base class **DirectoryContext**. We may then apply to the class the attribute **InitialDirectory**, which takes a **string** parameter giving a path to what the initial directory should be. The property **DirectoryPath** extracts the path from the metadata. If our class does not have the attribute applied, this path will be the default. Here is the code for our test program:

```
// AttributeDemo.cs

using System;
using System.IO;

class Normal : DirectoryContext
{
}
```

```
[InitialDirectory(@"c:\OI\CSharp\Chap20")]
class Special : DirectoryContext
{
}

public class AttributeDemo
{
   public static void Main()
   {
      Normal objNormal = new Normal();
      Console.WriteLine("path = {0}",
                        objNormal.DirectoryPath);
      ShowDirectoryContents(objNormal.DirectoryPath);
      Special objSpecial = new Special();
      Console.WriteLine("path = {0}",
                        objSpecial.DirectoryPath);
      ShowDirectoryContents(objSpecial.DirectoryPath);
   }
   private static void ShowDirectoryContents(string path)
   {
      DirectoryInfo dir = new DirectoryInfo(path);
      FileInfo[] files = dir.GetFiles();
      Console.WriteLine("Files:");
      foreach (FileInfo f in files)
         Console.WriteLine("   {0}", f.Name);
      DirectoryInfo[] dirs = dir.GetDirectories();
      Console.WriteLine("Directories:");
      foreach (DirectoryInfo d in dirs)
         Console.WriteLine("   {0}", d.Name);   }
}
```

Here is the output:

```
path = C:\OI\CSharp\Chap20\AttributeDemo\bin\Debug
Files:
   AttributeDemo.exe
   AttributeDemo.pdb
Directories:
path = c:\OI\CSharp\Chap20
Files:
Directories:
   Assemblies
   AttributeDemo
   DirectoryDemo
   FileDemo
   ReflectionDemo
   SerializeAccount
   ThreadAccount
   ThreadDemo
   UnsafeAccount
```

```
UnsafeBlock
UnsafePointer
```

Defining an Attribute Class

To create a custom attribute, you must define an attribute class, derived from the base class **Attribute**. The convention is to give your class a name ending in "Attribute." The name of your class without the "Attribute" suffix will then be the name of the custom attribute. In our example, the name of our class is **InitialDirectoryAttribute**, and the name of the corresponding attribute is **InitialDirectory**.

You may provide one or more constructors for your attribute class. The constructors define how to pass positional parameters to the attribute (provide a parameter list, separated by commas). It is also possible to provide "named parameters" for a custom attribute, where the parameter information will be passed using syntax **name = value**.

You may also provide properties to read the parameter information. In our example, we have a property **Path**, which is initialized in the constructor.

```
// DirectoryAttribute.cs

using System;

public class InitialDirectoryAttribute : Attribute
{
    private string path;
    public InitialDirectoryAttribute(string path)
    {
        this.path = path;
    }
    public string Path
    {
        get
        {
            return path;
        }
    }
}
```

Defining a Base Class

The last step in working with custom attributes is to provide a means to extract the custom attribute information from the metadata. As we shall see in the next section, the .NET Framework provides an elaborate API, the Reflection API, for precisely this purpose. The root class for metadata information is **Type**, and you can obtain the **Type** of any object by calling the method **GetType**, which is provided in the root class **object**. To read custom attribute information, you need only one method, **Type.GetCustomAttributes**.

Although it would be quite feasible for the program using the custom attribute to perform this operation directly, normally you will want to make the coding of the client program as simple as possible. Hence it is useful to provide a base class to do the work of reading the custom attribute information from the metadata. In the previous section we saw an example of such a base class, **ContextBoundObject**, which was used when we wanted a class to be able to use the **Synchronization** attribute.

In our case, we provide a base class **DirectoryContext**, which is used by a class wishing to take advantage of the **InitialDirectory** attribute. This base class provides the property **DirectoryPath** to return the path information stored in the metadata. Here is the code for the base class:

```
// DirectoryContext.cs

using System;
using System.Reflection;
using System.IO;

public class DirectoryContext
{
    virtual public string DirectoryPath
    {
        get
        {
            Type t = this.GetType();
            foreach (Attribute a
                    in t.GetCustomAttributes(true))
            {
                InitialDirectoryAttribute da =
                a as InitialDirectoryAttribute;
                if (da != null)
                {
                    return da.Path;
                }
            }
            return Directory.GetCurrentDirectory();
        }
    }
}
```

We require the **System.Reflection** namespace. **GetType** returns the current **Type** object, and we can then use the **GetCustomAttributes** method to obtain a collection of **Attribute** objects from the metadata. This collection is heterogeneous, consisting of different types. We can use the C# **as**

operator to test if a given element in the collection is of type
InitialDirectoryAttribute. If we find such an element, we return the **Path**
property. Otherwise, we return the default current directory, obtained from
GetCurrentDirectory.

REFLECTION

At the heart of .NET is metadata, which stores very complete type information. The Reflection API permits you to query this information at runtime.
You can also dynamically invoke methods, and through the
System.Reflection.Emit namespace, you can even dynamically create and
execute MSIL code. In the previous section we saw an illustration of using
reflection to obtain custom attribute information. In this section we will provide a further example of dynamically obtaining a listing of all types defined
in an assembly. (A program's EXE file is an example of an assembly. We will
discuss assemblies in the next chapter, and see some further examples, such
as dynamic link libraries, or DLLs.) We are only scratching the surface of a
very large subject, but our example should help you get started.

As befits the name "reflection," our demo program **ReflectionDemo**
shows information about itself. The program contains two classes, **Dog** and
ReflectionDemo. The program calls the **Bark** method of Dog. It then calls
Assembly.GetExecutingAssembly to obtain its assembly. It shows all the
types in the assembly, and all the methods of each type.

```
// ReflectionDemo.cs

using System;
using System.Reflection;

public class Dog
{
    public static void Bark()
    {
        Console.WriteLine("woof, woof!!");
    }
}

public class ReflectionDemo
{
    public static void Main()
    {
        Dog.Bark();
        Assembly assem = Assembly.GetExecutingAssembly();
        ShowAssemblyName(assem);
        ShowAssemblyTypes(assem);
    }
```

```
public static void ShowAssemblyTypes(Assembly a)
{
    Type[] types = a.GetTypes();
    foreach (Type type in types)
    {
        Console.WriteLine(type);
        ShowMethods(type);
    }
}
public static void ShowAssemblyName(Assembly a)
{
    Console.WriteLine("assembly name = {0}", a.FullName);
}
public static void ShowMethods(Type t)
{
    MethodInfo[] methodInfo = t.GetMethods();
    foreach (MethodInfo m in methodInfo)
    {
        Console.WriteLine("   {0}", m.Name);
    }
}
}
```

Here is the output from running the program.

```
assembly name = TestBank, Ver=0.0.0.0, Loc=""
woof, woof!!
assembly name = ReflectionDemo, Version=0.0.0.0,
Culture=neutral, PublicKeyToken=null
Dog
    GetHashCode
    Equals
    ToString
    Bark
    GetType
ReflectionDemo
    GetHashCode
    Equals
    ToString
    Main
    ShowAssemblyTypes
    ShowAssemblyName
    ShowMethods
    GetType
```

You can examine information about any assembly by using the **ILDASM** utility. To run **ILDASM**, simply enter **ildasm** at a command prompt or use Start | Run. To examine a particular assembly, use the File | Open command. Figure 20–1 shows the types for **ReflectionDemo.exe**, which compares with the output from our **ReflectionDemo** program.

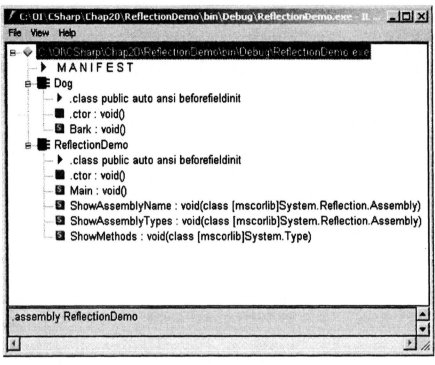

File View Help

C:\01\CSharp\Chap20\ReflectionDemo\bin\Debug\ReflectionDemo.exe

▶ M A N I F E S T

Dog
   ▶ .class public auto ansi beforefieldinit
   ■ .ctor : void()
   Bark : void()

ReflectionDemo
   ▶ .class public auto ansi beforefieldinit
   ■ .ctor : void()
   Main : void()
   ShowAssemblyName : void(class [mscorlib]System.Reflection.Assembly)
   ShowAssemblyTypes : void(class [mscorlib]System.Reflection.Assembly)
   ShowMethods : void(class [mscorlib]System.Type)

.assembly ReflectionDemo

Figure 20–1   *ILDASM top window shows the types in an assembly.*

UNSAFE CODE

The mainstream use of C# is to write *managed code,* which runs on the Common Language Runtime. As we shall see in the next chapter, it is quite possible for a C# program to call *unmanaged code,* such as a legacy COM component, which runs directly on the operating system. This facility is important, because a tremendous amount of legacy code exists, which is all unmanaged.

There is overhead in transitioning from a managed environment to an unmanaged one and back again. C# provides another facility, called *unsafe code,* which allows you to bypass the .NET memory management and get at memory directly, while still running on the CLR. In particular, in unsafe code you can work with *pointers,* which we will discuss later in this section.

Unsafe Blocks

The most circumspect use of unsafe code is within a block, which is specified using the C# keyword **unsafe**. The program **UnsafeBlock** illustrates using the **sizeof** operator to determine the size in bytes of various data types. You will get a compiler error if you try to use the **sizeof** operator outside of unsafe code.

```
// UnsafeBlock.cs

using System;

struct Account
{
   private int id;
   private decimal balance;
}

public class UnsafeBlock
{
   public static void Main()
   {
      unsafe
      {
         Console.WriteLine("size of int = {0}",
                        sizeof(int));
         Console.WriteLine("size of decimal = {0}",
                        sizeof(decimal));
         Console.WriteLine("size of Account = {0}",
                        sizeof(Account));
      }
   }
}
```

To compile this program at the command line, open up a DOS window and navigate to the directory **c:\OI\CSharp\Chap20\UnsafeBlock**. You can then enter the following command to compile using the **/unsafe** compiler option:

```
csc /unsafe UnsafeBlock.cs
```

(You may ignore the warning messages, as our program does not attempt to use fields of **Account**. It only applies the **sizeof** operator.) To run the program, type **unsafeblock** at the command line, obtaining the output shown below:

```
C:\OI\CSharp\Chap20\UnsafeBlock>unsafeblock
size of int = 4
size of decimal = 16
size of Account = 20
```

To set the unsafe option in Visual Studio, perform the following steps:

1.   Right-click over the project in the Solution Explorer, and choose Properties.

2.   In the Property Pages window that comes up, click on Configuration Properties and then on Build.

3.   In the dropdown for Allow unsafe code blocks, choose True. See Figure 20–2.

4.   Click OK. You can now compile your project in unsafe mode.

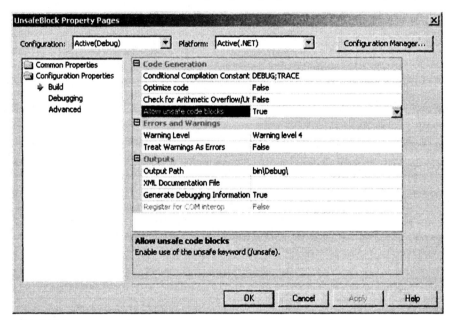

Figure 20–2   *Configuring a project for unsafe mode in Visual Studio.*

Pointers

In Chapter 9 we saw that C# has three kinds of data types:

* Value types, which directly contain their data
* Reference types, which refer to data contained somewhere else
* Pointer types

Pointer types can only be used in unsafe code. A pointer is an *address* of an actual memory location. A pointer variable is declared using an asterisk after the data type. To refer to the data a pointer is pointing to, use the *dereferencing* operator, which is an asterisk before the variable. To obtain a pointer from a memory location, apply the *address of* operator, which is an ampersand in front of the variable. Here are some examples.

```
int* p;              // p is a pointer to an int
int a = 5;           // a is an int, with 5 stored
p = &a;              // p now points to a
*p = 12;             // 12 is now stored in location pointed
                     // to by p. So a now has 12 stored
```

Pointers were widely used in the C programming language, because functions in C only pass data by value. Thus if you want a function to return data, you must pass a pointer rather than the data itself. The program **UnsafePointer** illustrates a **Swap** method, which is used to interchange two integer variables. Since the program is written in C#, we can pass data by reference. We illustrate with two overloaded versions of the **Swap** method, one using **ref** parameters and the other using pointers. Rather than using an **unsafe** block, this program uses **unsafe** methods, which are defined by including **unsafe** among the modifiers of the method. Both the **Main** method and the one **Swap** method are unsafe.

```
// UnsafePointer.cs

using System;

public class UnsafePointer
{
    public static unsafe void Main()
    {
        int x = 55;
        int y = 777;
        Show("Before swap", x, y);
        Swap(ref x, ref y);
        Show("After swap", x, y);
        Swap(&x, &y);
        Show("After unsafe swap", x, y);
    }
    private static void Show(string s, int x, int y)
    {
        Console.WriteLine("{0}: x = {1}, y = {2}", s, x, y);
    }
    private static void Swap(ref int x, ref int y)
    {
        int temp = x;
        x = y;
        y = temp;
    }
    private static unsafe void Swap(int* px, int* py)
    {
        int temp = *px;
        *px = *py;
        *py = temp;
```

```
      }
}
```

Again you should compile the program using the **unsafe** option, either at the command line or in the Visual Studio project. Here is the output. The first swap interchanges the values. The second swap brings the values back to their original state.

```
Before swap: x = 55, y = 777
After swap: x = 777, y = 55
After unsafe swap: x = 55, y = 777
```

Fixed Memory

When working with pointers, there is a pitfall. Suppose you have obtained a pointer to a region of memory that contains data you are working on. Since you have a pointer, you are accessing memory directly. But suppose the garbage collector collects garbage and moves data about in memory. Then your object may now reside at a different location, and your pointer may no longer be valid.

To deal with such a situation, C# provides the keyword **fixed**, which declares that the memory in question is "pinned" and cannot be moved by the garbage collector. Note that you should use **fixed** only for temporary, local variables, and you should keep the scope as circumscribed as possible. If too much memory is pinned, the CLR memory management system cannot manage memory efficiently.

The program **UnsafeAccount** illustrates working with **fixed** memory. This program declares an array of five **Account** objects, and then assigns them all the same value. The attempt to determine the size of this array is commented out, because you cannot apply the **sizeof** operator to a managed type such as **Account[]**.

It also illustrates the arrow operator for dereferencing a field in a struct, when you have a pointer to the struct. For example, if **p** is a pointer to an instance of the struct **Account** shown below, the following code will assign values to the account object pointed to by **p**.

```
p->id = 101;            // assign the id field
p->balance = 50.00m;    // assign the balance field
```

Here is the code:

```
// UnsafeAccount.cs

using System;

struct Account
{
```

```csharp
      public int id;
      public decimal balance;
      public Account(int id, decimal balance)
      {
         this.id = id;
         this.balance = balance;
      }
}

public class UnsafeAccount
{
   public static unsafe void Main()
   {
      int id = 101;
      decimal balance = 50.55m;
      Account acc = new Account(id, balance);
      ShowAccount(&acc);
      Account[] array = new Account[5];
      //Console.WriteLine("size of Account[] = {0}",
      //                  sizeof(Account[]));
      ShowArray(array);
      fixed (Account* pStart = array)
      {
         Account* pAcc = pStart;
         for (int i = 0; i< array.Length; i++)
            *pAcc++ = acc;
      }
      ShowArray(array);
   }
   private static unsafe void ShowAccount(Account* pAcc)
   {
      Console.WriteLine("id = {0}, balance = {1:C}",
                        pAcc->id, pAcc->balance);
   }
   private static void ShowAccount(Account acc)
   {
      Console.WriteLine("id = {0}, balance = {1:C}",
                        acc.id, acc.balance);
   }
   private static void ShowArray(Account[] array)
   {
      for (int i = 0; i < 5; i++)
      {
         ShowAccount(array[i]);
      }
   }
}
```

Here is the output:

```
id = 101, balance = $50.55
id = 0, balance = $0.00
id = 0, balance = $0.00
id = 0, balance = $0.00
id = 0, balance = $0.00
id = 0, balance = $0.00
id = 101, balance = $50.55
id = 101, balance = $50.55
id = 101, balance = $50.55
id = 101, balance = $50.55
id = 101, balance = $50.55
```

SUMMARY

This chapter examined a number of advanced features. We first looked at directories and files, which were used for examples later in the chapter. We examined multiple threading in detail. The .NET threading model is built on delegates. Synchronization can be accomplished through .NET Framework classes such as **Monitor** and through the C# **lock** statement. Attributes are a very powerful concept in .NET, making it possible to accomplish much without writing code. We looked at the built-in attributes **Synchronized** and **Serializable**, and we saw how to create a custom attribute. Custom attribute information can be read from metadata using the Reflection API. Finally, we looked at unsafe code.

Components and Assemblies

*U*p until now we have been building exclusively monolithic applications, consisting of a single executable file. Our applications have been logically modular, consisting of several classes, typically distributed among a number of files. But these files have all been compiled together, forming a single EXE. Modern large applications are rarely monolithic but instead are made up of a number of executable units. In the Windows environment an application will normally consist of an EXE and a number of DLLs. In this chapter we will see how to create class library DLLs, or components, which will expose classes and their methods to external programs. We begin by using command-line tools, and later in the chapter we will use Visual Studio.NET. We will also examine assemblies, which are the unit of deployment in .NET. An assembly can be a single EXE or DLL, or it can consist of several files, called modules. An assembly also contains a manifest, which describes how the elements of the assembly relate to each other and to external elements. An application in .NET can be composed of assemblies built using different languages, and you can even inherit across languages. As a somewhat larger example, we present a componentized version of our bank case study. We conclude the chapter by showing how to call a COM component from .NET.*

BUILDING COMPONENTS USING .NET SDK

Prior to .NET there was a big divide between using classes within an application and creating "software components" that implemented classes but could be called from independent executable units. With Microsoft software, the mechanism for creating such independent components was the Component Object Model, or COM. Implementing a COM component is nontrivial, as much "plumbing" code must be provided to facilitate proper operation across executable boundaries. Tools such as the Active Template Library in C++ were developed in individual languages to simplify the process. Visual Basic provided an easy way to create COM components, but this was specific to Visual Basic, and not all features of COM were supported.

.NET changes the picture completely. It is totally trivial to create a component from a class. You just need to build a different kind of project, a "class library." The .NET Framework takes care of the plumbing for you automatically. In this section we will see how to create a component using the command-line compiler.

Creating a Component: A Demonstration

Let's begin with a simple demonstration. Do your work in the **Demos** directory for this chapter. A completed version of the demonstration is available in **HelloSDK**.

CLASS LIBRARY

Using any text editor, create the file **HelloLib.cs**.

```
// HelloLib.cs

class Hello
{
   private string greeting = "Hello, I'm a DLL";
   public string Greeting
   {
      get
      {
         return greeting;
      }
      set
      {
         greeting = value;
      }
   }
}
```

Please type in this program exactly as shown, including the lack of any access specifier in front of **class Hello**. This class simply exposes the property **Greeting**. Notice that there is no **Main** method. This class is not intended to be used in an EXE file. To compile the file as a class library, enter the following at the command line:

```
csc /t:library HelloLib.cs
```

The command switch **/t**, or **/target**, specifies the kind of file to create. There are four options, as shown in Table 21–1.

Table 21–1	/target Output File Options
Option	**Meaning**
/target:exe	Console application EXE
/target:winexe	Windows application EXE
/target:library	Class library DLL
/target:module	Module (no manifest)

The default is **/target:exe**, or console application, which is what we have been building up until now. We will discuss Windows applications in Chapter 22, and we will discuss modules later in this chapter. We are now building a class library DLL. If you did not make any typing mistakes, you should get a clean compilation, and if you use the DOS **dir** command, you should see that the file **HelloLib.dll** has been created.

CLIENT PROGRAM

To exercise our class library we will need to create a client program. This could be either a console application or a Windows application. We will create a simple console application as a test program. Type in the following program and save in the file **TestHello.cs**.

```
// TestHello.cs

using System;

public class TestHello
{
   public static void Main()
   {
      Hello obj = new Hello();
      Console.WriteLine(obj.Greeting);
   }
}
```

Compile this program using the following command:

```
csc /r:HelloLib.dll TestHello.cs
```

The compiler option **/r**, or **/reference**, is used to import metadata from the specified class library. This makes any public classes in the class library available to the current compilation unit. You will get compiler error messages:

```
TestHello.cs(9,3): error CS0122: 'Hello' is inaccessible due to
its protection level
TestHello.cs(10,21): error CS0234: The type or namespace name
'obj' does not exist in the class or namespace ''
```

INTERNAL AND PUBLIC ACCESS

The problem comes from the fact that in the file **HelloLib.cs** we did not place any access modifier on the **Hello** class. The default access is **internal**, which means that the class can be accessed within the current assembly. We mentioned **internal** access in Chapter 13, but were not able to demonstrate its implications, because up until now, all our programs have consisted of only a single assembly. We will discuss assemblies in detail in the next section.

The fix is simply to make the **Hello** class **public**.

```
// HelloLib.cs

public class Hello
{
    ...
```

Make this change, and then recompile both files. Now you should get a clean compilation. You can then run the file **TestHello.exe** and obtain the expected output.

```
C:\OI\CSharp\Chap21\Demos>testhello
Hello, I'm a DLL
```

MONOLITHIC PROGRAM

The directory **MonolithicHello** contains a monolithic version of this program. There is a Visual Studio project consisting of the two files. The **Hello** class is left with no access modifier, so the default **internal** access is in place. This time there is no problem, because we are building only a single assembly.

ASSEMBLIES

In this section we will take a closer look at assemblies. We begin by examining the structure of assemblies in some detail, and then we will work through an example that illustrates creating and using different types of assemblies.

Assembly Structure

An assembly is a grouping of types and resources that work together as a logical unit. An assembly consists of one or more physical files, called *modules*, which may be code files or resources (such as bitmaps). An assembly forms the boundary for security, deployment, type resolution, and versioning.

Logically, an assembly holds three kinds of information:

* MSIL (Microsoft Intermediate Language) implementing one or more types
* Metadata
* A *manifest* describing how the elements in the assembly relate to each other and to external elements

The general structure of an assembly is shown in Figure 21–1.

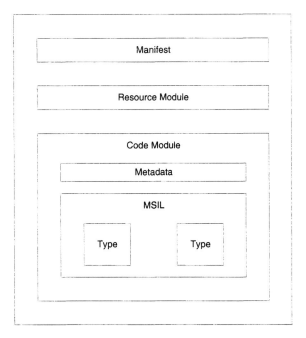

Figure 21–1   *Structure of an assembly.*

All of the information in an assembly could be stored in a single file, or it could be distributed among a number of files, called modules. All of the assemblies we have built so far, including the DLL we built in the preceding section, have been single-file assemblies. In a multiple-file assembly, the manifest could be a standalone file or it could be contained in one of the modules.

MANIFEST

The manifest contains comprehensive information about the contents of an assembly and facilitates other assemblies using the assembly. The manifest contains a number of elements:

- **Assembly identity**. The name of the assembly, version information (consisting of four parts for very fine-grained versioning), and culture (containing locale information suitable for globalization).
- **Files**. A list of files in the assembly.
- **Referenced assemblies**. A list of external assemblies that are referenced.
- **Types**. A list of all types in the assembly, a mapping to the modules containing the types, and visibility information about the types.
- **Security permissions**. Details needed by client programs that will determine whether or not they have rights to run the assembly.
- **Product information**. Information such as company, trademark, and copyright.
- **Custom attributes**. Special attribute information specific to this assembly. We touched on attributes in Chapter 20.
- **An (optional) shared name and hash**. This information facilitates running the assembly from a common location where multiple programs may access it. The hash protects client programs from running a corrupted version of the assembly.

Assembly Example

We will illustrate assemblies, including an assembly with multiple modules, with a version of our bank example. The general logic of this program should be very familiar by this point. Our example is intended to focus on different ways of packaging the units of the program. There are three assemblies in the example, as illustrated in Figure 21–2.

- **Account.dll** is an assembly consisting of two modules.
- **Bank.dll** is an assembly built from two source files.
- **TestBank.exe** is a test program.

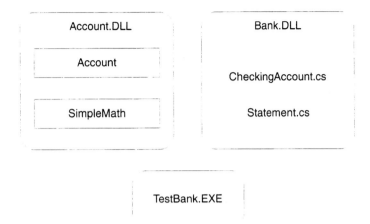

Figure 21–2   *Bank application consisting of three assemblies.*

MONOLITHIC VERSION

We begin with a monolithic version, consisting of a single assembly. A Visual Studio solution is provided in the directory **BankAssembly\Step1**. Since all the classes are in the same assembly, we can utilize **internal** accessibility. In the class **Account**, the field **numXact** has an **internal** access modifier. The **namespace** directive will be discussed shortly.

```
// Account.cs

namespace OI.NetCs.Examples
{
   using OI.NetCs.Examples;

   public class Account
   {
      protected int balance;
      private string owner;
      static private string bankName = "Fiduciary Bank";
      internal int numXact = 0;   // number of transactions
      ...
      public int Transactions
      {
         get
         {
            return numXact;
         }
      }
   }
}
```

This means that the **Statement** class can access this field directly, without going through the public **Transactions** property.

```
// Statement.cs

using OI.NetCs.Examples;

public class Statement
{
   public static string GetStatement(CheckingAccount acc)
   {
      string s = "Statement for " + acc.Owner + "\n" +
         acc.numXact + " transactions, balance = "
         + acc.Balance + ", fee = " + acc.Fee;
      return s;
   }
}
```

NAMESPACE

This example also illustrates the **namespace** directive. Look again at the **Account** class, which is enclosed in the namespace **OI.NetCs.Examples**.

```
// Account.cs

namespace OI.NetCs.Examples
{
...
```

The name of the class **Account** is rather generic, and if this code were part of a large system, with components acquired from many third-party vendors, we might well run into a name collision. By enclosing the class in a namespace, we can remove ambiguity. To refer to the **Account** class in another program, we would have to use the long, fully qualified name **OI.NetCs.Examples.Account**.

Such usage does indeed get around the possible name collision, but is also quite cumbersome. Hence, client programs can make use of the **using** directive, as illustrated in **Statement.cs**.

```
// Statement.cs

using OI.NetCs.Examples;

public class Statement
{
   public static string GetStatement(CheckingAccount acc)
   ...
```

Here we employ the short name **CheckingAccount** (the **CheckingAccount** class was also created in the namespace **OI.NetCs.Examples**).

This example of a namespace also illustrates a common sort of hierarchy:

* **OI** is a company/brand (Object Innovations).
* **NetCs** is an acronym for this book *(Introduction to C# Using .NET)*.
* **Examples** is for the example programs.

MULTIPLE ASSEMBLIES

BankAssembly\Step2 illustrates building multiple assemblies. You may compile at the command line. First, build **Account.dll**:

```
csc /t:module /out:SimpleMath.mod SimpleMath.cs
csc /t:library /addmodule:SimpleMath.mod Account.cs
```

The first line illustrates the **/t:module** option for compiling **SimpleMath.cs**. This will create a module without a manifest. We then could not obtain metadata in another compilation using the **/reference** option. To make clear that the output file is not an ordinary DLL, we use the **/out** option to explicitly allow us to name the output file. We make up a **.mod** extension (this is not standard; we are just using it to remind ourselves that we have created a module).

Since we cannot use the **/reference** switch to bring in metadata from **SimpleMath.mod**, we need another mechanism. The C# compiler provides the **/addmodule** option for this purpose. As the name suggests, this option will add a module to the current assembly that is being built. The target is a library, so the output file will be a DLL. We don't specify a name for the output file, so it will be **Account.dll**.

Next we will build **bank.dll** using the following command:

```
csc /t:library /r:Account.dll /out:Bank.dll
CheckingAccount.cs Statement.cs
```

Again we are building a class library, so we use the **/t:library** option. We need a reference to **Account.dll**. The source files are **CheckingAccount.cs** and **Statement.cs**. Finally, we specify the name of the output file **bank.dll**.

The last thing we build is **TestBank.exe**:

```
csc /t:exe /r:Bank.dll /r:Account.dll /out:TestBank.exe
TestBank.cs InputWrapper.cs
```

This time we need references to two DLLs, **Bank.dll** and **Account.dll**. The build is automated by the batch file **build.bat**. You can run this batch file at the command line simply by typing **build**. (In Windows Explorer you could run the batch file by double-clicking on **build.bat**.)

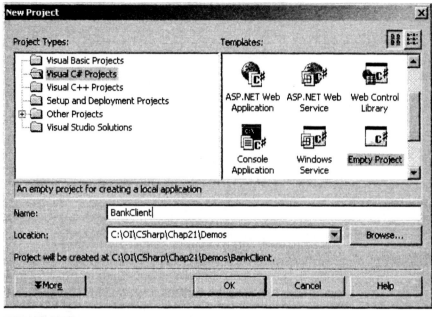

Figure 21-3   *Creating an empty C# project.*

ADDING THE SOURCE FILES

1. Using Windows Explorer, copy the files **BankClient.cs** and **Account.cs** from **BankMonolithic** into the current directory, **Demos\BankClient**.

2. In the Solution Explorer right-click over **BankClient**, and from the context menu choose Add | Add Existing Item.... In the dialog that comes up, select the two files **BankClient.cs** and **Account.cs** (you may use multiple selection by having the Control key pressed). Click Open.

3. Examine the code for the test program **BankClient.cs**. A new **Account** object is created, initialized with a starting balance of 100. A deposit is made, followed by a withdrawal. The balance is displayed at the beginning and after each transaction. (The prompt to read a string at the end will prevent a quick close of the application if you run it in the debugger.)

```
// BankClient.cs

using System;

public class BankClient
```

```
{
   static int Main(string[] args)
   {
      Account acc = new Account(100);
      Console.WriteLine("balance = {0}", acc.Balance);
      acc.Deposit(25);
      Console.WriteLine("balance = {0}", acc.Balance);
      acc.Withdraw(50);
      Console.WriteLine("balance = {0}", acc.Balance);
      Console.WriteLine("press Enter to exit");
      string s = Console.ReadLine();
      return 0;
   }
}
```

4. Examine the code for the **Account** class **Account.cs**. There is a constructor which initializes the starting balance and the methods **Deposit** and **Withdraw**. There is also a property **Balance**.

```
// Account.cs

public class Account
{
   private int balance;
   public Account(int balance)
   {
      this.balance = balance;
   }
   public void Deposit(int amount)
   {
      balance += amount;
   }
   public void Withdraw(int amount)
   {
      balance -= amount;
   }
   public int Balance
   {
      get
      {
         return balance;
      }
   }
}
```

CHANGING THE OUTPUT PATH

Up until now when we have built a project in Visual Studio, we have always excepted the default location for the executable. If we are building a Debug version of our project, the executable will be located in the **bin\Debug** directory. When we are working with an application that consists of several assemblies, it will be convenient for the our executable and component files to all reside in the same directory. At runtime our application can then easily find its components. We can achieve this goal by changing the output path of our executable to be the source directory. Later we will build our component to reside in the same directory.

1. In Solution Explorer, right-click on the **BankClient** project, and choose Properties.

2. In the Property Pages window that comes up, click on Configuration Properties and then on Build.

3. Click in the right side of the Output Path area, and then click on the three dots. Navigate to the **BankClient** directory. See Figure 21–4. Click OK.

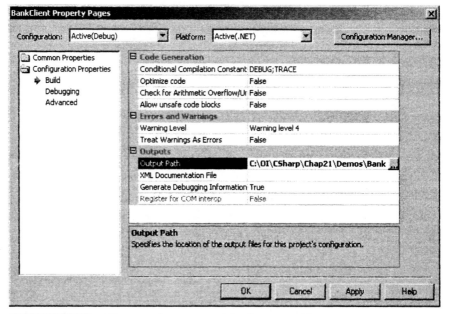

Figure 21–4   *Changing the output path for the executable*

4. Build and run. The executable **BankClient.exe** should be in the **BankClient** directory. You should see the following output:

```
balance = 100
balance = 125
balance = 75
press Enter to exit
```

ADDING A SECOND PROJECT

1. In Solution Explorer, right-click over the solution and choose Add | New Project. The Add New Project dialog comes up.

2. Choose "Visual C# Projects" as the Project Type and "Class Library" as the template. Click the Browse button and navigate to the **Demos\BankClient** directory. Click Open. Type **BankLib** as the name of the project. See Figure 21–5. Click OK. Observe that a subdirectory **BankLib** will be created underneath **BankClient**.

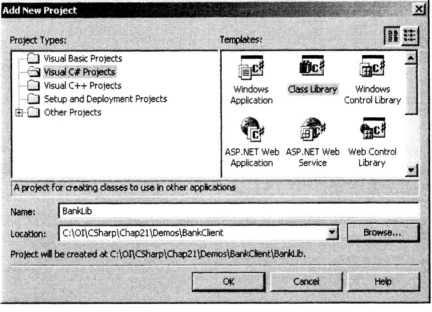

Figure 21–5   *Add New Project dialog.*

MOVE CODE TO THE SECOND PROJECT

1. The file **AssemblyInfo.cs** contains code that can be used to customize the manifest in the assembly. For simplicity, remove the two files **AssemblyInfo.cs** and **Class1.cs** from the new project (use Delete key or right-click on the project and choose Delete).

2. Move the file **Account.cs** from **BankClient** to **BankLib** (you can drag inside Solution Explorer).

3. Following the same procedure we used previously for the **BankClient** project, change the output path for **BankLib** to be the **BankClient**

source directory (so that **BankClient.exe** and **BankLib.dll** will wind up in the same directory).

4. Build the class library: Right-click on **BankLib** and choose Build.

5. Try to build the client test program: Right-click on **BankClient** and choose Build. You will get a number of error messages pertaining to **Account** not existing in the current namespace.

ADDING A REFERENCE

1. In Solution Explorer right-click on BankClient and choose Add Reference.

2. Click Browse and navigate to **BankLib.dll**. (It is in **BankClient**.) Click Open. See Figure 21–6.

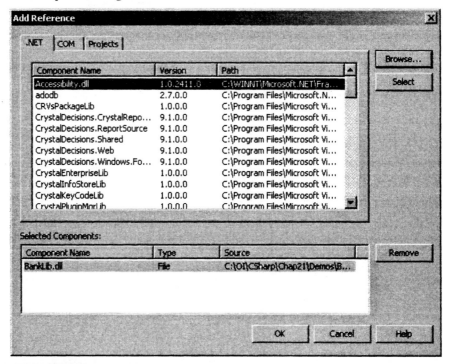

Figure 21–6   *Adding a reference.*

3. Click OK. You will now see a Reference in Solution Explorer. Note also the two projects in our solution.

4. Now build the client again. This time it should work! Run the client.

Solutions and Projects

We have now constructed a solution with two projects. Figure 21–7 shows Solution Explorer with this solution and its two projects.

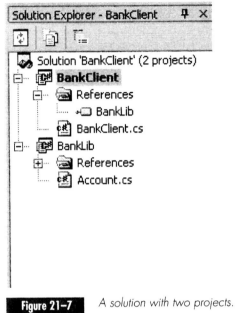

Figure 21–7   *A solution with two projects.*

BUILDING A SOLUTION

There are two build toolbar buttons: ▦ ▦ . The first button builds the currently selected project. You can select a project by clicking on it in Solution Explorer. The second button builds the entire solution.

PROJECT DEPENDENCIES

Continuing our demonstration, close the solution (menu File | Close Solution) and delete the **bin** and **obj** directories for both projects. (If you have trouble deleting the directories, close down Visual Studio.) Open up the solution again and build the entire solution. You will get build errors, because the client program is built first and the class library does not yet exist. To fix this problem, open up the Project Dependencies dialog from the menu Project | Project Dependencies. With the **BankClient** project selected from the Project dropdown, check **BankLib** in the Depends On list. See Figure 21–8. Click OK.

Figure 21–8 *Setting project dependencies.*

Now try building the solution again. This time the build should succeed, because the library will be built first.

Working with References

Working with a project that has references can sometimes be tricky. If you get into a situation where your client program does not build and you suspect the problem is that the reference to a dependent library is not found, try first removing the reference. Then add the reference again.

BANK CASE STUDY: COMPONENTIZED VERSION

We have built some small components. Now let's try something a little more elaborate. We will build a componentized version of our bank case study. The starting point is the Step 7 version from Chapter 18. We have a copy in the current chapter in **CaseStudy\Monolithic**. If you want to refresh yourself on the case study, you may build and exercise this monolithic version.

Our componentized version consists of three pieces:

* **Account.dll**. This class library is built from **AccountDefinitions.cs**, **Account.cs**, **CheckingAccount.cs**, and **SavingsAccount.cs**.
* **BankLib.dll**. This class library is built from **Bank.cs**, **Atm.cs**, and **InputWrapper.cs**. It contains a reference to **Account.dll**.
* **BankClient.exe**. This console application is built from **TestBank.cs** and **InputWrapper.cs**. It contains references to **Account.dll** and **BankLib.dll.**

Projects for these pieces are in the directories **CaseStudy\AccountLib**, **CaseStudy\BankLib**, and **CaseStudy\BankClient**. You may wish to examine these projects, build them, and exercise the client program. The **BankLib** directory contains a copy of **Account.dll**. The **BankClient** directory contains copies of **BankLib.dll** and **Account.dll**.

INTEROPERATING WITH COM

We have seen that .NET components can be built in different languages, such as C# and VB.NET, and interoperate with each. It is also possible for .NET components to interoperate with COM components.

* You can call a COM component from .NET.
* You can call a .NET component from COM.

The .NET Framework supports both of these kinds of interoperability, and tools are provided. We will illustrate the first scenario, which is the common one, of a .NET application calling a legacy COM component. We will use the **Type Library Importer** tool, which imports a type library for a COM component and generates a .NET proxy for calling a COM component from .NET. This tool is transparently invoked by Visual Studio when you add a reference to a COM component.

The subject of Microsoft's Component Object Model, or COM, is a large one, far beyond the scope of this book. For a discussion of COM and COM+ you can refer to the book *Understanding and Programming COM+*, by Robert J. Oberg. In Chapter 12 of that book you will find a discussion of the **Logger** component, which we use as an illustration in this section.

Calling a COM Component from .NET

We will demonstrate COM interoperability with a .NET application that calls a COM Logger component, which happens to be written in C++ using ATL, the Active Template Library. The sample program is in the directory **LoggerVc**. If you are curious about the code used to create a COM component, where the infrastructure code is in the component itself, you can examine the C++ code in **LoggerVc\Source**. It will probably give you a headache! It is *much* simpler to create components using .NET.

First we will run the sample program, and then we will switch to the **Demos** directory and create the test program ourselves.

RUNNING THE TEST PROGRAM

Open up the test program in **LoggerVc\TestLogger**. Try to build it. You will get an error message:

```
error CS0234: The type or namespace name 'LOGGERLib' does
not exist in the class or namespace ''
```

The reason for this error is that the COM component must be *registered* before it can be used. You can register the component by running the batch file **reg_logger.bat**. (In Windows Explorer you can double-click on this file to run it.) You will see a message box announcing that registration is successful. See Figure 21–9. (If by chance this component was already registered on your machine, you can try unregistering it by running the batch file **unreg_logger.bat**.)

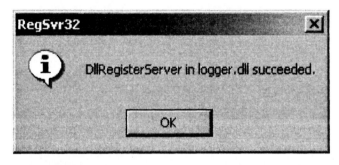

Figure 21–9   *Registering a COM component.*

Now you should succeed in building **TestLogger**. Running the program does not produce any output, because what the program does is write to a logfile, which for convenience we have located at the root of the **c:** drive. In any text editor (for example, Notepad), examine the file **c:\logfile.txt**. You should see the following test messages displayed:

```
first line
second line
```

CREATING THE TEST PROGRAM

Now let's create the test program. Do your work in the **Demos** directory.

1. Open up Visual Studio and create a new Empty C# project **TestLogger** in **Demos**.

2. Add a new empty C# file called **TestLogger.cs** to the project.

3. Type the following code into this file.

```
// TestLogger.cs

using LOGGERLib;

public class TestLogger
{
    public static void Main()
    {
        Log log = new Log();
        log.Write("first line");
        log.Write("second line");
    }
}
```

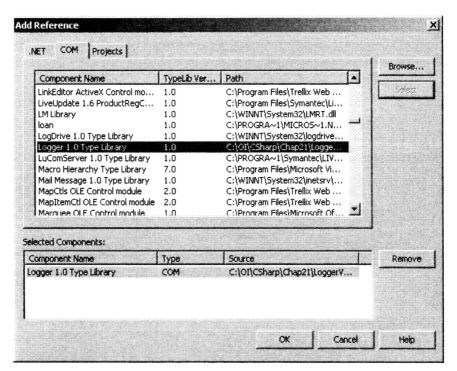

Figure 21–10 *Adding a reference to a COM object.*

4. In Solution Explorer right-click over References and choose Add References from the context menu. Click on the COM tab and click on "Logger 1.0 Type Library." Click Select. See Figure 21–10. Click OK.

5. A dialog will come up talking about a "primary interop assembly" and asking you if you would like to have a wrapper generated for you. See Figure 21–11. Click Yes. (The primary interop assembly is the DLL **Interop.LOGGERLib_1_0.dll**, which was in the **bin\Debug** directory of the **TestLogger** program that was provided for you.)

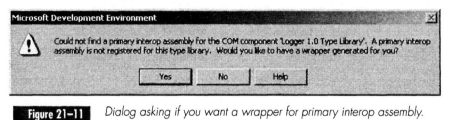

Figure 21–11   *Dialog asking if you want a wrapper for primary interop assembly.*

6. You should now be able to build and run the project. You should see two lines added to the log file **c:\logfile.txt**.

7. You can view the LOGGERLib library in the Object Browser, which you can bring up from the menu View | Other Windows | Object Browser. See Figure 21–12.

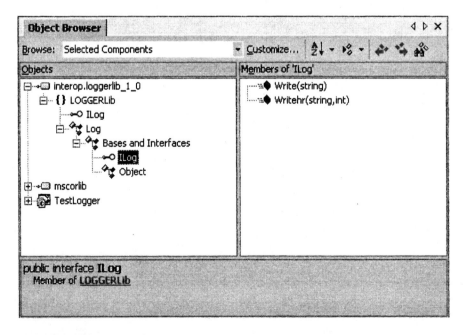

Figure 21–12   *Viewing a class library from a COM component using Object Browser.*

SUMMARY

Modern large applications are rarely monolithic but instead are made up of a number of executable units. In the Windows environment an application will normally consist of an EXE and a number of DLLs. In this chapter we saw how to create class library DLLs, or *components*, which expose classes and their methods to external programs. We began by using command-line tools, and later in the chapter we used Visual Studio.NET. We also examined *assemblies*, which are the unit of deployment in .NET. An assembly can be a single EXE or DLL, or it can consist of several files, called *modules*. An assembly also contains a *manifest*, which describes how the elements of the assembly relate to each other and to external elements. An application in .NET can be composed of assemblies built using different languages, and you can even inherit across languages. We presented a componentized version of our bank case study. We concluded the chapter by showing how you can call a COM component from .NET.

Introduction to Windows Forms

In this chapter we broaden our horizons to include implementing graphical user interfaces for our programs by using the Windows Forms classes in the .NET Framework. We begin by using Visual Studio.NET to implement a simple graphical user interface with Windows Forms and basic controls. We then explore the fundamentals by using the .NET Framework SDK to create simple Windows applications from scratch, without use of any special tools. We describe the fundamentals of drawing in Windows Forms, using a font and a brush. We explain the principles of event handling in Windows Forms and implement handlers for mouse events. We implement menus in Windows Forms and corresponding event handlers. We conclude with an illustration of a user interface for a simple customer management system.

WINDOWS FORMS

Windows Forms is that part of the .NET Framework that supports building traditional GUI applications on the Windows platform. Windows Forms provides a large set of classes that make it easy to create sophisticated user interfaces. These classes are available to all .NET languages.

Your application will typically have a main window implemented by deriving from the **Form** class. Figure 22-1 illustrates your class deriving from the Windows Forms hierarchy.

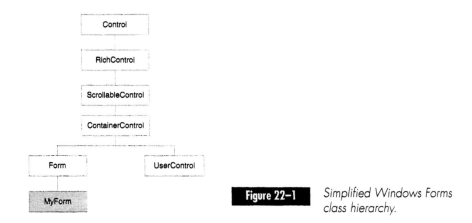

Figure 22–1   *Simplified Windows Forms class hierarchy.*

Windows Forms Demonstration

It is easy to create a Windows Forms application using the Forms Designer in Visual Studio.NET. This same Forms Designer is available to all .NET languages. Do all your work in the **Demos** directory for this chapter.

1. Create a new C# project **BankGui** of type Windows Application in the **Demos** folder. See Figure 22–2.

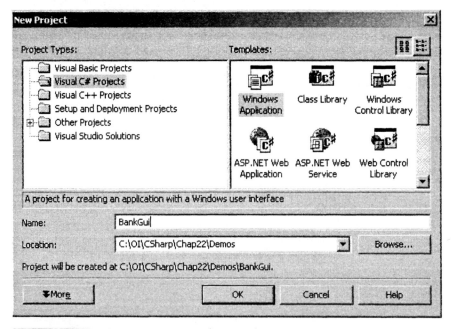

Figure 22–2   *Creating a new Windows Application project.*

2. Open up the Toolbox by dragging the mouse over the vertical Toolbox tab on the left side of the main Visual Studio window. If the Toolbox tab does not show, you can open it from the menu View | Toolbox. You can make the Toolbox stay open by clicking on the "push-pin" next to the X on the title bar of the Toolbox. (The little yellow box will say "Auto Hide" when you pause the mouse over the push-pin.)

3. From the Toolbox, drag two labels, two textboxes, and two buttons to the form. See Figure 22–3.

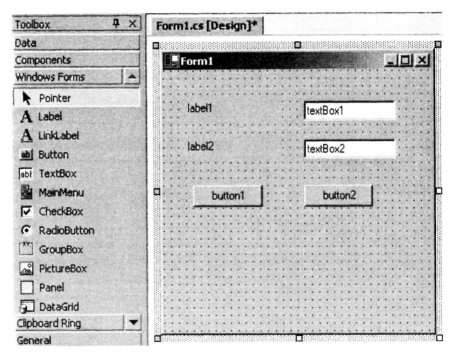

Figure 22–3   *Dragging controls from the Toolbox onto a form.*

4. Click on **label1** in the Forms Designer. This will select that control in the Properties window, just beneath the Solution Explorer. You can use the Properties window to make changes to properties of controls. Change the Text property to **Amount**. After you type the desired value, hit the carriage return. You will then see the new text shown on the form. Figure 22–4 shows the Properties window after you have changed the Text property of the first label.

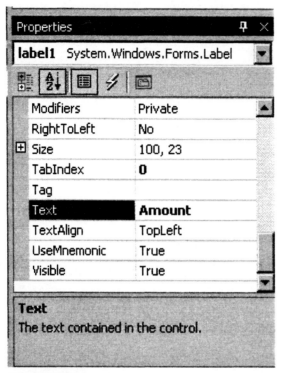

Figure 22–4   *Changing property values in the Properties window.*

5. Similarly, change the text of **label2** to **Balance**.

6. Enter property values for the textboxes and buttons, as shown in Table 22–1.

Table 22–1   *Property Values for Textboxes and Buttons*

Name	Text
txtAmount	(blank)
txtBalance	(blank)
cmdDeposit	Deposit
cmdWithdraw	Withdraw

1. Resize the form by dragging the sizing handles on the middle of each side. Reposition the controls as desired by dragging with the mouse, and resize the controls with the mouse, if you wish. When you are satisfied with the appearance of your form, save the project. Your form should now look similar to Figure 22–5.

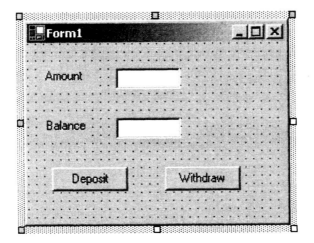

Figure 22-5 Form for BankGui application.

2. Add event handlers for the buttons by double-clicking on each button.

3. Add the following code:

```
public class Form1 : System.Windows.Forms.Form
{
  ...
   public Form1()
   {
      //
      // Required for Windows Form Designer support
      //
      InitializeComponent();

      //
      // TODO: Add any constructor code after
      // InitializeComponent call
      //
        txtAmount.Text = "25";
        txtBalance.Text = "100";
   }
   ...
   /// <summary>
   /// The main entry point for the application.
   /// </summary>
   [STAThread]
   static void Main()
   {
      Application.Run(new Form1());
   }
```

```
private void cmdDeposit_Click(object sender,
                             System.EventArgs e)
{
    int amount = Convert.ToInt32(txtAmount.Text);
    int balance = Convert.ToInt32(txtBalance.Text);
    balance += amount;
    txtBalance.Text = Convert.ToString(balance);
}

private void cmdWithdraw_Click(object sender,
                             System.EventArgs e)
{
    int amount = Convert.ToInt32(txtAmount.Text);
    int balance = Convert.ToInt32(txtBalance.Text);
    balance -= amount;
    txtBalance.Text = Convert.ToString(balance);
}
```

4. Build and run the application. It should behave like a standard Windows application. You should be able to make deposits and withdrawals.

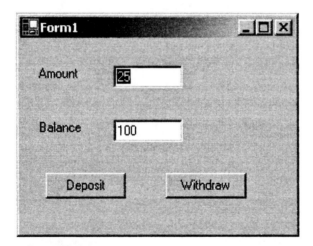

Figure 22–6   *The BankGui Windows application.*

SIMPLE FORMS USING .NET SDK

To gain insight into the fundamentals of Windows Forms it will be helpful to build a simple application using only the .NET Framework SDK. See the program **SimpleForm** with several progressive steps.

Step 0: A Simple Form

Step 0 demonstrates a simple form that displays a standard window. You can build it at the command line using the batch file **build.bat**. To run the batch file, open up a DOS window and navigate to the **SimpleForm\Step0** directory and type **build**. Remember that you must have the environment variables set up properly.

```
csc /target:winexe /r:System.dll /r:System.Drawing.dll
/r:System.Windows.Forms.dll SimpleForm.cs
```

The target is a Windows executable, and there are references to the required .NET libraries.

After you have built the application using the batch file, you can run it by typing **SimpleForm** at the command line. (Or in Windows Explorer you can double-click on the file **SimpleForm.exe**. Figure 22–7 shows this rather uninteresting application. (But there is already a tremendous amount of functionality implemented by the .NET Framework. You can drag the window around, resize it, etc.)

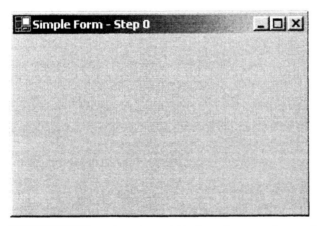

Figure 22–7   *A bare bones Windows Forms application (Step 0).*

CODE FOR A SIMPLE FORM

```
// SimpleForm.cs - Step 0
//
// This version relies only on the .NET SDK
//
// You need references to:
//     System
//     System.Drawing
//     System.Windows.Forms
```

```
using System;
using System.Windows.Forms;

public class Form1: Form
{
    public Form1()
    {
        Size = new System.Drawing.Size(300,200);
        Text = "Simple Form - Step 0";
    }
    public static void Main(string[] args)
    {
        Application.Run(new Form1());
    }
}
```

STRUCTURE OF A SIMPLE FORM

Our **Form1** class inherits from **System.Windows.Forms**. The class **System.Application** has static methods, such as **Run** and **Exit**, to control an application. The **Main** method instantiates a new form and runs it as the main window.

The constructor of the form does initializations: The **Size** field sets the size of the new form in pixels. The **Text** field specifies the caption to be shown in the title bar of the new form.

Step 1: Drawing Text on a Form

Step 1 illustrates drawing text on a form. Figure 22–8 shows a run of the application.

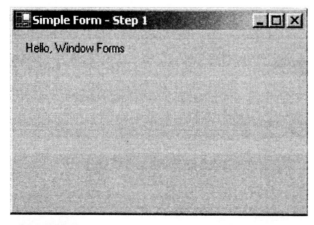

| Figure 22–8 | *Drawing text on a simple form (Step 1).* |

```
// SimpleForm.cs - Step 1

using System;
using System.Windows.Forms;
using System.Drawing;

public class Form1: Form
{
    private float x, y;
    private Brush stdBrush;
    public Form1()
    {
        Size = new System.Drawing.Size(300,200);
        Text = "Simple Form - Step 1";
        x = y = 10;
        stdBrush = new SolidBrush(Color.Black);
    }
      protected override void OnPaint(PaintEventArgs e)
    {
        e.Graphics.DrawString("Hello, Window Forms",
            Font, stdBrush, x, y);
    }
}
...
```

STRUCTURE OF DRAWING

To draw in Windows Forms, you must override the virtual method **OnPaint**. The class **PaintEventArgs** has a **Graphics** object as a read-only property. The **Graphics** class, part of the **System.Drawing** namespace, has methods for drawing.

The **DrawString** method has parameters for:

- The string to be drawn
- The font (**Font** is a property of **Form** that gives the default font for the form)
- The brush to be used
- The pixel coordinates (as **float** numbers)

A black **SolidBrush** is constructed as our standard brush.

Step 2: Handling a Mouse Event

In Step 2 a mouse click (any button) will reposition the location of the greeting string. Figure 22–9 shows the string relocated after we have clicked the mouse.

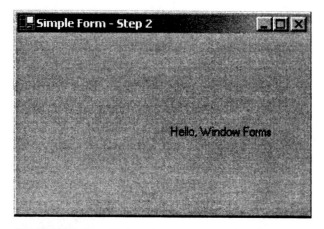

Figure 22-9	*Clicking the mouse repositions the text (Step 2).*

```csharp
// SimpleForm.cs - Step 2

using System;
using System.Windows.Forms;
using System.Drawing;

public class Form1: Form
{
    private void InitializeComponent()
    {
        this.MouseDown +=
            new MouseEventHandler (Form1_MouseDown);
    }

    private float x, y;
    private Brush stdBrush;
    public Form1()
    {
        InitializeComponent();
        Size = new System.Drawing.Size(300,200);
        Text = "Simple Form - Step 2";
        x = y = 10;
        stdBrush = new SolidBrush(Color.Black);
    }
    protected void Form1_MouseDown (object sender,
                                    MouseEventArgs e)
    {
        x = e.X;
        y = e.Y;
        Invalidate();
    }
    ...
```

WINDOWS FORMS EVENT HANDLING

GUI applications are event-driven: The application executes code in response to user events, such as clicking the mouse, choosing a menu item, and so on. Each form or control has a predefined set of events. For example, every form has a **MouseDown** event.

Windows Forms uses the .NET *event* model, which uses *delegates* to bind events to the methods that handle them. Windows Forms typically uses multicast delegates. A multicast delegate maintains a list of the methods it is bound to. When an event occurs in an application, the control raises the event by calling the delegate for that event. The delegate then calls all the methods it is bound to.

C# provides the overloaded += operator for adding a delegate to an event.

```
this.MouseDown +=
     new MouseEventHandler (Form1_MouseDown);
```

Events Documentation

You can find all the events associated with a class in the .NET Framework Reference. The screen shot in Figure 22–10 shows the predefined events associated with the **Form** class.

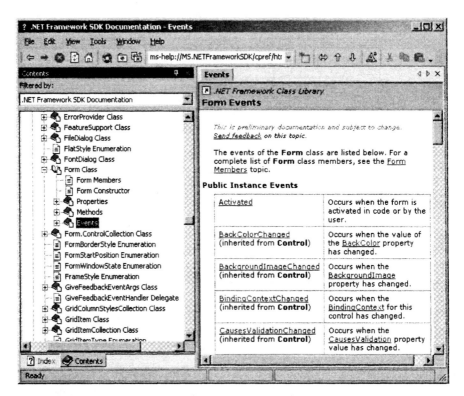

Figure 22-10 *Documentation of events in the **Form** class.*

MouseDown Event

One of the predefined events in the **Control** class, from which the **Form** class derives, is **MouseDown**.

```
public event MouseEventHandler MouseDown;
```

The event handler receives a **MouseEventArgs**, which has read-only properties to provide information specific to this event:

* **Button** specifies which button (left, right, etc.) was pressed.
* **Clicks** indicates how many times the button was pressed and released.
* **Delta** provides a count of rotations of a mouse wheel.
* **X** and **Y** provide the coordinates where the mouse button was pressed.

Step 3: Mouse Down and KeyPress events

Step 3 of our demonstration illustrates handling a number of additional events, including mouse down and key press.

HANDLING LEFT AND RIGHT BUTTONS

We can distinguish between left and right buttons by using the **Button** property of the **MouseEventArgs** parameter. Right button down is used for clearing the message string, which is now stored in a **StringBuilder** data member **str**.

```
protected void Form1_MouseDown (object sender,
                                MouseEventArgs e)
{
    if (e.Button == MouseButtons.Left)
    {
        x = e.X;
        y = e.Y;
    }
    else if (e.Button == MouseButtons.Right)
    {
        str = new StringBuilder();
    }
    Invalidate();
}
```

KEYPRESS EVENT

Step 3 also illustrates handling a **KeyPress** event. Every time the user presses a key, the corresponding character is appended to the greeting string. Note use of the **StringBuilder** class, which is more efficient to use in this context than **string**. **String** is immutable, and hence **string** objects would be continually created and destroyed while we append characters.

```
private StringBuilder str;
...
protected void Form1_KeyPress (object sender,
                               KeyPressEventArgs e)
{
    str.Append(e.KeyChar);
    Invalidate();
}
```

INVALIDATE

Note also the use of the **Invalidate** method both here and in the **MouseDown** event. **Invalidate** forces a paint event to be raised, so the greeting will be redrawn, reflecting the new information.

Figure 22–11 shows the Step 3 application after we have relocated the string by clicking the left mouse button, cleared the string by clicking the right mouse button, and then entered some text at the keyboard.

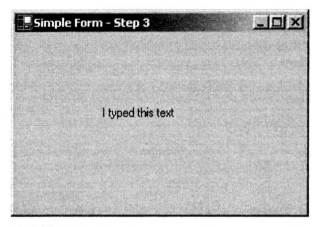

Figure 22–11   *Exercising mouse and key press events (Step 3).*

MENUS

In .NET menus are implemented in code. There is no separate resource file. Step 4 of our **SimpleForm** program illustrates adding a simple menu. File | Exit is used to exit the program. See Figure 22–12.

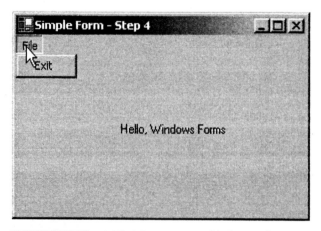

Figure 22–12   *A File | Exit menu is added to our form (Step 4).*

Menu Code

```
// SimpleForm.cs - Step 4
...
private MenuItem menuExit;
private MenuItem menuFile;
private MainMenu mainMenu1;
public Form1()
{
   InitializeComponent();
   Size = new System.Drawing.Size(300,200);
   Text = "Simple Form - Step 4";
   x = y = 10;
   stdBrush = new SolidBrush(Color.Black);
   str = new StringBuilder("Hello, Windows Forms");
}
private void InitializeComponent()
{
    this.mainMenu1 = new MainMenu ();
    this.menuFile = new MenuItem ();
    this.menuExit = new MenuItem ();
   // mainMenu1
    this.mainMenu1.MenuItems.AddRange
    (new MenuItem[] {this.menuFile});
   // menuFile
    this.menuFile.Index = 0;
    this.menuFile.MenuItems.AddRange
      (new MenuItem[] {this.menuExit});
    this.menuFile.Text = "File";
   // menuExit
    this.menuExit.Index = 0;
    this.menuExit.Text = "Exit";
    ...
    this.Menu = this.mainMenu1;
    ...
```

Menu Event Code

A delegate is hooked to the event, as with other Windows Forms events.

```
private void InitializeComponent()
{
  ...
    this.menuExit.Click +=
       new System.EventHandler(this.menuExit_Click);
  ...
}

private void menuExit_Click(object sender,
```

```
                        EventArgs e)
{
   Application.Exit();
}
...
```

We can exit the application by calling the static **Exit** method of the **Application** class.

NEXT STEPS IN WINDOWS FORMS AND .NET

We have made only the barest beginning in our investigation of Windows Forms. We worked with only the simplest controls:

* labels
* textboxes
* buttons

The next step is to investigate other controls, such as radio buttons, checkboxes, list boxes, and so on. Then you can investigate more advanced controls, such as list views and tree views. With the proper controls you can easily implement attractive user interfaces. And with simple program logic you can string forms together, so that, for example, pushing a button on one form will bring up a dialog box, which is another form. As an illustration of a just slightly more sophisticated user interface, you may like to study the code and build and run the program **AcmeCustomer** that implements a very simple customer management system for the Acme Travel Agency, where customers can register their name and email address. Figure 22–13 shows the main window, with a couple of preregistered customers.

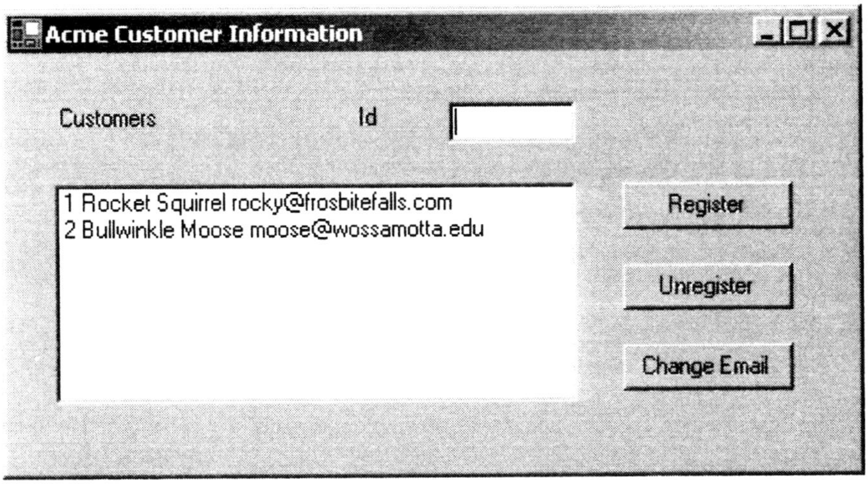

Figure 22–13 *Main window of a small customer management system.*

New customers register via the **Register** button, which will bring up a simple dialog for entering name and email address, as illustrated in Figure 22–14.

To unregister, click on the customer in the list box. This will select a customer, and show the customer Id of the selected customer. You may then click the **Unregister** button.

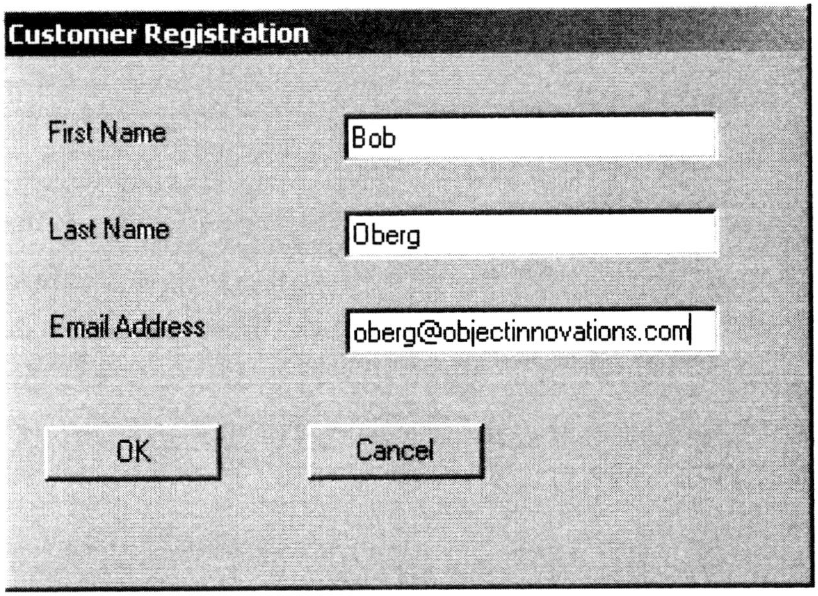

Figure 22–14 *Dialog for registering a new customer.*

To change the email address of a customer, select the customer in the list box, and then click the **Change Email** button. This will bring up a simple dialog that allows you to enter a new email address. See Figure 22–15.

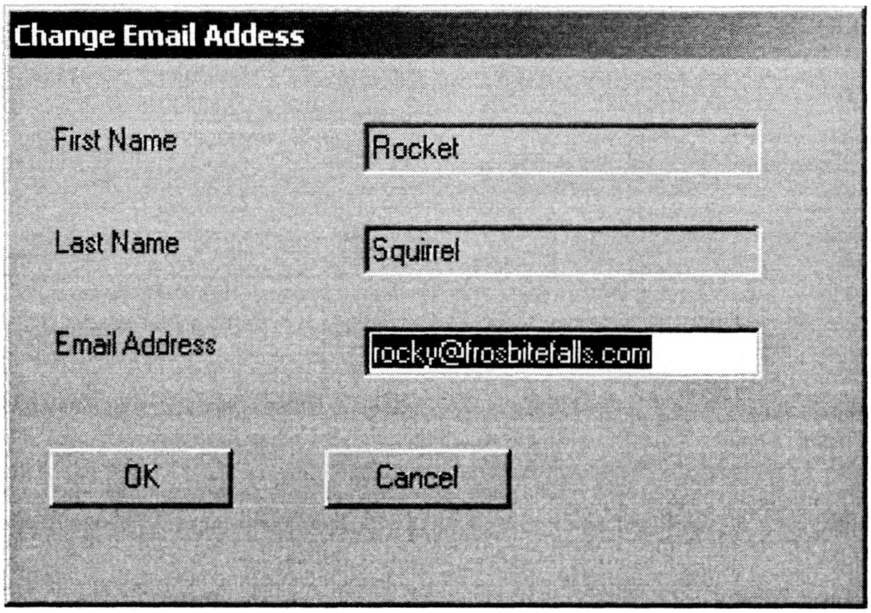

Change Email Addess

First Name | Rocket

Last Name | Squirrel

Email Address | rocky@frosbitefalls.com

OK | Cancel

Figure 22–15 *Dialog for changing the email address of a customer.*

We have come to the end of our journey in this introductory book on C#. The journey continues in our next book, *Application Development Using C# and .NET*. In that book the Acme Travel Agency will be elaborated to illustrate many features of programming the .NET Framework, including working with databases, web pages and web services. Bon voyage!

SUMMARY

Windows Forms is a set of .NET classes enabling the creation of GUI applications in many languages using the same forms model. With Visual Studio.NET you can implement a simple graphical user interface with Windows Forms and basic controls. The basic Windows Forms classes are easy to understand, and you can use the .NET Framework SDK to create simple Windows applications from scratch, without use of any special tools. Drawing in Windows Forms is done with the **Graphics** class in the **System.Drawing** namespace. You draw on a form by overriding the **OnPaint** function.

We concluded the chapter with an illustration of a slightly more complex user interface for the Acme Travel Agency.

Learning Resources

This book is an introduction to C# programming and .NET and thus is definitely not the last word. I have tried to make the book completely self-contained, so that the only thing you need in order to learn C#, besides this book, is the software and its documentation. One of the best ways to learn more is to try to do what you want to do in .NET and search the documentation when you get stuck. Random browsing in the documentation is probably not a good idea!

A good resource is the Microsoft Software Developers Network (MSDN). The quarterly library is now distributed on CD-ROM and DVD. It is quite extensive, currently requiring three CDs, containing much more information than you would like to download from the web.

Next comes the web. There are many websites with information about C# and .NET, but URLs change and new sites frequently appear. Hence rather than attempt a lengthy listing here, we give just two, which in turn will lead you much farther.

- http://msdn.microsoft.com/net/ is the official Microsoft website devoted to .NET.

- http://www.objectinnovations.com/dotnet.htm is the website for the Prentice Hall/Object Innovations .NET series. This site contains all the downloads for all the books in the series and much other information about .NET, including links to other websites, information about .NET training, and other useful information.

Next come periodicals. Although not as evanescent as websites, periodicals also come and go. Several long-time publications that contain good articles on programming languages include *MSDN Magazine, Dr. Dobb's Journal*, and *C/C++ Users Journal*. I expect to see increasing coverage of C# and .NET in these and other publications.

Finally, there are books in the field. .NET is very new, and many of the early books, although useful in helping you get started, may lack depth for long-time reading. Here are some suggestions, focused mainly on C#. There is also some mention of COM/COM+, which is an important predecessor technology to .NET and which will be important for interoperating with .NET for a long time. For other books on .NET technology, I suggest the other books in the Prentice Hall/Object Innovations .NET series, described on the overleaf of this book.

Archer, Tom, *Inside C#*, Microsoft Press, 2001.

Box, Don, *Essential COM*, Addison-Wesley, 1998.

Box, Don, et al., *Effective COM*, Addison-Wesley, 1999.

Gunnerson, Eric, *A Programmers Introduction to C#*, 2nd ed., Apress, 2001.

Microsoft, *C# Language Specification*, Microsoft Press, 2001.

Oberg, Robert J., *Understanding and Programming COM+*, Prentice Hall, 2000.

Stiefel, Michael, and Robert J. Oberg, *Application Development Using C# and .NET*, Prentice Hall, 2001.

Thui, Thuan L., *Learning DCOM*, O'Reilly, 1999.

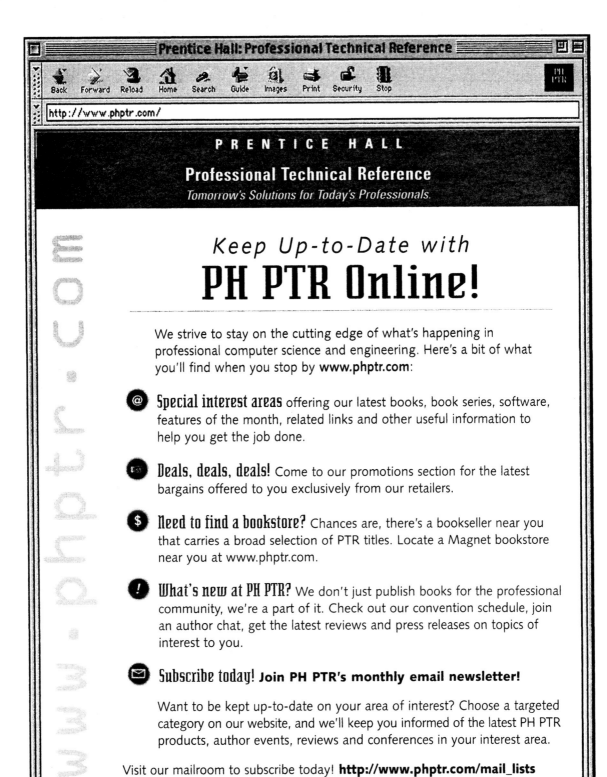

DEVELOPER TRAINING

OBJECT INNOVATIONS offers training course materials in fundamental software technologies used in developing applications in modern computing environments. We emphasize object-oriented techniques, with a focus on Microsoft® technologies, Java™, and Linux™. Our courses have been used by businesses, training companies, and universities throughout North America. End clients include IBM®, HP®, Dell®, Compaq®, FedEx®, UPS®, AOL®, U.S. Bank®, Mellon Bank®, and NASA. Our courses are frequently updated to reflect feedback from classroom use. We aggressively track new technologies and endeavor to keep our courseware up-to-date.

Founded in 1993, Object Innovations has a long record of firsts in courseware. Our Visual C++ course was released before Microsoft's, we introduced one of the first courses in JavaServer Pages, and our Linux Internals 2.4 kernel course came out several months before Red Hat's course. Now we are leading the development of comprehensive developer training in Microsoft's .NET technology.

.NET DEVELOPER TRAINING

Object Innovations is writing the premier book series on .NET for Prentice Hall PTR. These authoritative books are the foundation of our curriculum. Each book matches a corresponding course, and the student materials come bundled with the book, so students have comprehensive reference materials after the course. Each core course is five days in length and is very rich in content, containing well over five days worth of material. The courses are modularized, so background information or special topics not needed for a particular class can be cleanly omitted. On the other hand, the courses can be lengthened as required. Thus each course can be easily customized to meet the particular needs and interests of the students. We also have shorter courses.

The first group consists of shorter, overview courses:

    401   Introduction to .NET for Developers   (1 day)
    412   Programming C# and .NET   (3 days)
    422   Programming Visual Basic.NET   (3 days)
    452   Introduction to ASP.NET   (3 days)

The second group constitutes the full-length courses that correspond to the books in the Prentice Hall/Object Innovations book series:

    410   Introduction to C# Using .NET   (5 days)
    414   Application Development Using C# and .NET   (5 days)
    420   Introduction to Programming Visual Basic Using .NET   (5 days)
    424   Application Development Using Visual Basic.NET   (5 days)
    434   .NET Architecture and Programming Using Visual C++   (5 days)
    440   Programming Perl in the .NET Environment   (5 days)
    454   Fundamentals of Web Applications Using .NET and XML   (5 days)

MICROSOFT DEVELOPER TRAINING

Our Microsoft curriculum is very extensive, with introductory and advanced courses on Visual C++, MFC, COM/DCOM, OLE, COM+, and advanced topics in Visual Basic™. We also provide foundational courses in C++ programming. Selected courses include:

123   Programming COM and DCOM Using ATL   (5 days)
125   Programming COM and ActiveX Using ATL   (5 days)
127   Programming COM and OLE Using MFC   (5 days)
130   Programming COM and COM+ Using Visual C++   (5 days)
149   Distributed COM+ Programming   (5 days)
131   Programming COM and ActiveX Using Visual Basic   (3 days)
133   Distributed COM+ Programming Using Visual Basic   (5 days)
142   Visual C++ Windows Programming for C Programmers   (5 days)
145   MFC Windows Programming for C++ Programmers   (5 days)
146   Advanced Windows Programming Using Visual C++   (5 days)
153   C++ Programming for Non-C Programmers   (5 days)
156   C++ Programming for C Programmers   (5 days)
157   Advanced C++ Programming   (5 days

JAVA DEVELOPER TRAINING

Java training courses span the spectrum from beginning to advanced and provide extensive coverage of both client-side and server-side technologies. We emphasize distributed application development using Java. Selected courses include:

102   Introduction to Java for Non-C Programmers   (4 days)
103   Java Programming   (5 days)
105   Using and Developing JavaBeans   (4 days)
106   Advanced Java Programming   (5 days)
107   CORBA Architecture and Programming Using Java   (4 days)
109   Java Server Pages   (2 days)
110   Java Servlet Programming   (2 days)
111   Introduction to Java RMI   (1 day)
163   Enterprise JavaBeans   (4 days)
171   Developing Web-Based Software Using EJB and JSP   (5 days)
172   Java Foundation Classes   (5 days)

LINUX COURSES

Linux courses range from fundamentals and system administration to advanced courses in internals, device drivers and networking. Selected courses include:

135   Fundamentals of Linux   (4 days)
136   Linux System Administration   (4 days)
310   Linux Internals   (5 days)
314   Linux Network Drivers Development   (3 days)
320   Linux Network Administration   (5 days)

See our .NET website for complete course listings: www.objectinnovations.com/dotnet.htm

OBJECT INNOVATIONS' .NET TRAINING PARTNERS

For information about .NET training using OBJECT INNOVATIONS courseware,
please check with our .NET Training Partners.

ANEW TECHNOLOGY CORPORATION   www.Anew.net

Specializing in IT consulting, training, mentoring, and development, Anew Technology has been serving many satisfied clients. Our business mission is threefold: to stay at the forefront of IT technologies, to satisfy client needs by applying these technologies, and to provide the best service in our industry. Anew Technology is a business partner with Object Innovations in operations and courseware development.

COMPUTER HORIZONS   www.ComputerHorizons.com/Training

For over sixteen years Computer Horizons Education Division (CHED) has been providing on-site, instructor-led IT training and customized workshops for organizations nationwide. We have developed extensive curriculum offerings in Web Technologies, Relational Databases, Reporting Tools, Process Improvement, UNIX™ and LINUX™, Client/Server, Mainframe & Legacy Systems, Windows® 2000, and much more. CHED will design, develop and deliver a training solution tailored to each client's training requirements.

COMPUWORKS SYSTEMS, INC.   www.CompuWorks.com

CompuWorks Systems, Inc. is an IT solutions company whose aim is to provide our clients with customized training, support and development services. We are committed to building long term partnerships with our clients in an effort to meet their individual needs. Cutting-edge solutions are our specialty.

DB BASICS   www.DBBasics.com

DBBasics, founded in 1988 as a Microsoft® solution development company, has developed and delivered Microsoft technology training since its inception. DBBasics specializes in delivering database and developer technology training to corporate customers. Our vast development experience, coupled with the requirement for instructors to consistently provide hands-on consulting to our customers, enables DBBasics to provide best of breed instruction in the classroom. In addition to instructor-led training, DBBasics also develops customized eLearning solutions and provides database technology consulting.

DEVCOM   www.dev-cominc.com

Devcom Corporation offers a full line of courses and seminars for software developers and engineers. Currently Devcom provides technical courses and seminars around the country for Hewlett® Packard, Compaq® Computer, Informix® Software, Silicon Graphics®, Quantum/Maxtor® and Gateway® Inc. Our senior .NET/C# instructor is currently working in conjunction with Microsoft to provide .NET training to their internal technical staff.

ISRG   www.isrg.com

The I/S RESOURCE GROUP helps organizations to understand, plan for and implement emerging I/S technologies and methodologies. We closely watch the evolution of both business and technology. By combining education, training, briefings and consulting, we assist our clients to effectively apply I/S technologies to achieve business benefits. Our eBusiness Application Bootcamp' is an integrated set of courses that prepares learners to utilize XML. Object Oriented Analysis & Design, Java™, JSP, EJB, ASP, CORBA and .NET to build eBusiness applications. Our eBusiness Briefings pinpoint emerging technologies and methodologies- the building blocks that form the foundation of successful enterprise computing.

RELIABLE SOFTWARE   www.ReliableSoftware.com

Reliable Software, Inc. uses Microsoft technology to quickly develop cost-effective software solutions for the small to mid-size business or business unit. We use state-of-the-art techniques to allow business rules, database models and the user interface to evolve as your business needs evolve. We can provide design and implementation consulting, or training.

/TRAINING/ETC INC.   www.trainingetc.com

A training company dedicated to delivering quality technical training, courseware development, and consulting in a variety of subject matter areas, including Programming Languages and Design (including C, C++, OOAD/UML, Perl, and Java), a complete UNIX curriculum (from UNIX Fundamentals to System Administration), the Internet (including HTML/CGI, XML and JavaScript™ Programming) and RDBMS (including Oracle and Sybase).

WATERMARK LEARNING   www.WatermarkLearning.com

Watermark Learning provides a wide range of IT skill development training and mentoring services to a variety of industries, software/ consulting firms and government. We provide flexible options for delivery: onsite, consortium and public classes in three major areas: project management, requirements analysis and software development, including e-Commerce. Our instructors are seasoned, knowledgeable practitioners, who use their industry experience along with our highly-rated courseware to effectively build technical skills relevant to your business need.